JAN EHRENWALD, M.D., presently Consulting Psychiatrist to Roosevelt Hospital, New
York City, has taught at the Long Island College of Medicine and the State University of
New York. Among his many books are *Telepathy and Medical Psychology* (1948), *From
Medicine Man to Freud* (1956), *Psychotherapy:
Myth and Method* (1966), and *History of Psychotherapy: From Magic Healing to Encounter*
(1976).

The ESP Experience

Books by Jan Ehrenwald, M.D.

Telepathy and Medical Psychology
(1947)

New Dimensions of Deep Analysis
(1953, 1975)

From Medicine Man to Freud
(1956)

Neurosis in the Family and Patterns
of Psychosocial Defense
(1963)

Psychotherapy: Myth and Method
(1966)

The History of Psychotherapy: From Healing Magic
to Encounter
(1976)

THE

ESP Experience

A Psychiatric Validation

JAN EHRENWALD, M.D.

Basic Books, Inc., Publishers

NEW YORK

Library of Congress Cataloging in Publication Data

Ehrenwald, Jan, 1900–
  The ESP experience.

  References: p. 289
  Includes index.
  1. Psychical research. I. Title.
BF1031.E47   133.8   77-75242
ISBN: 0-465-02056-9

For Anny

CONTENTS

vii

Contents

PREFACE

TELEPATHY and related psychic or psi phenomena are the subject matter of the new science of parapsychology. Critics have rightly pointed to its dubious origin from magic and witchcraft and are still inclined to relegate it to the lunatic fringe of our culture. Yet since its acceptance as a legitimate subject for scientific study, in 1969, by the American Association for the Advancement of Science, parapsychology has gained academic recognition and has by now grown into a formidable research effort sponsored by government agencies, university centers, foundations, and a number of professional organizations both in this country and abroad.

Paradoxically, clinical psychiatry has been slow in taking cognizance of the new findings. My own contributions to the field have largely passed unnoticed. So have Freud's and Jung's first pioneering forays into the realm of the "occult." So has the subsequent work of some of my psychiatric and psychoanalytic confreres. The fact is that psi-related incidents in the mother-child relationship, in mental and neurotic patients, or in diverse attempts at unorthodox healing have opened up a vast new frontier of psychiatry. It can, for convenience, be described as parapsychiatry: the clinical counterpart of parapsychology or physical research. The term "metapsychiatry," proposed by Stanley R. Dean (1975), addresses itself to the same issue but with a different philosophical slant.

Parapsychiatry, as it is conceived here, is the study of psi phenomena that are involved in both familiar and not so familiar psychiatric conditions, including clinical pictures that merely show a close affinity to psi phenomena or mimic their characteristic features. They encompass hysterical conversion symptoms and mental dissociation in trance states, motor and sensory automatisms, so-called spiritualistic psychoses, certain schizophrenic reactions, purported spirit possession, out-of-the-body experiences, and alleged poltergeist disturbances.

Inevitably, such a discussion has to be preceded by a review of the major findings of modern parapsychology, its correlations with magic mentality, the psychodynamics of psi phenomena, and pertinent observations in the psychoanalytic situation. In effect, parapsychology is to parapsychiatry as physiology is to internal medicine and neuropathology. In turn, we shall see that the study of miscarried, pathological aspects of psi can throw new light on some hitherto mysterious or poorly understood "normal" aspects of telepathy and related phenomena. They are significant aspects of the "ESP experience."

Indeed, as in other fields of medical research, pathology is apt to throw the modus operandi of the healthy individual into sharper perspective. The chapters that follow will show that myth, magic, and the latter-day magic of psi phenomena do not stand apart from the rest of human experience. They are part and parcel of the same overarching psychosomatic continuum ranging from the mindless stirrings of the instinct to samadhi or satori, from metabolism to gut feelings, from transcendental meditation to artistic creation. Yet I will also try to show that once we are ready to make the necessary revisions and adjustments in our traditional concept of a tightly closed, walled-in personality structure, of Euclidian, Newtonian, pre-Einsteinian, or Freudian paradigms and habits of thinking, psi phenomena do fall into place and are subject to the same laws that govern Einsteinian physics, quantum theory, and post-Freudian psychodynamics.

It is true that psi presents us with a vision of the world—or psychic reality—in which space seems to be expanding and contracting like a rubber balloon, in which time's arrow may come to a standstill in midflight or may be seen to reverse its course, and in which matter may appear to dissolve and liquefy as in a surrealist nightmare. In the extreme case, such a vision may culminate in the collapse of the ego and its merging with the nonego. But it may also be conducive to novel, ecstatic forms of experience, to a mode of existence wholly incompatible with the accumulated wisdom and time-tested know-how handed down to us from our evolutionary past.

Still, we shall see in Part Four of this book that the theory proposed here is in no need of introducing a new deus ex machina, some novel physical, biological, bioplasmic, or other mysterious form of energy into our equation. The mystery of "ordinary" human awareness and volition is big enough to accommodate psi. Paraphrasing a famous passage from Hippocrates, *On the Sacred Disease*, it could be stated: "It is thus with regard to the manifestations called occult: they appear to me to be nowise more divine nor more occult than other mental manifestations, but have natural causes from which they originate . . . ."

J. E.

ACKNOWLEDGMENTS

EARLY VERSIONS of some chapters of this book are based on articles that appeared before in several technical journals. I am greatly indebted to the following for permission to quote from:

"Mother-Child Symbiosis: Cradle of ESP," *Psychoanalytic Review*, vol. 58, no. 3 (1971): 455–66.

"The Telepathy Hypothesis and Schizophrenia," *Journal of the American Academy of Psychoanalysis*, vol. 2, no. 2 (1974): 159–69.

"Possession and Exorcism: Delusion Shared and Compounded," *Journal of the American Academy of Psychoanalysis*, vol. 3, no. 1 (1975): 105–19.

"Out-of-the-Body Experiences and the Denial of Death," *Journal of Nervous and Mental Disease*, vol. 159, no. 4 (1974): 227-33.

"Hitler: Shaman, Schizophrenic, Medium?" *Parapsychology Review*, vol. 6, no. 2 (March-April 1975): 3–9.

"Psi Phenomena and the Seven Dragons," paper read to the Symposium of the American Society for Psychical Research, on Parapsychology: Today's Implications, Tomorrow's Applications, May 18, 1974.

"The Psi Syndrome and Cerebral Localization," *Journal of Nervous and Mental Disease*, vol. 161, no. 6 (1975): 393-398.

"Placebo, Ploy, Psi Effect, Research Tool, or Psychoactive Agent?" *Parapsychology Review*, vol. 5, no. 5 (Sept.-Oct. 1974): 1–4.

"Psi Phenomena and the Existential Shift," *Journal of the American Society for Psychical Research*, vol. 65, no. 2 (April 1971): 162–72.

"Precognition, Prophecy, and Self-fulfillment in Greco-Roman, Hebrew and Aztec Antiquity," *International Journal of Parapsychology*, vol. 9, no. 4 (Winter 1967): 227-33.

Line drawings made by Uri Geller for tests by R. Targ and H. E. Puthoff, in "Information Transmission under Conditions of Sensory Shielding," *Nature* 252, Oct. 1974.

Illustration from *Mind to Mind* by René Warcollier, p. 8, New York: Creative Age Press, 1948.

Illustration from *The Working Brain* by A. R. Luria, p. 119, New York: Basic Books, 1973.

Acknowledgments

I am grateful to the Parapsychology Foundation and the late Mrs. Eileen Garrett for a grant toward research into out-of-the-body experiences, possession, and exorcism. I also wish to express my thanks to Dr. Gardner Murphy and Dr. J. B. Rhine for their critical comments on early versions of this book, as well as to Mrs. Laura Dale for her editorial assistance.

J. E.

Part One

ORIGINS

1

Parapsychology:

From Magic to Science

PARAPSYCHOLOGY is usually described as a systematic inquiry into such out-of-the-ordinary occurrences as telepathy, clairvoyance, psychokinesis, and precognition which, until recently, have largely remained outside the pale of science. Parapsychology, therefore, is supposed to represent a new frontier of psychology, seeking to advance man's knowledge of himself into unknown territory.

Yet parapsychology does not break entirely new ground; it rather advances its exploration to greater depth, using up-to-date methods of eliciting, sampling, and evaluating findings. It is in effect a radically revised, refined, and expurgated version of magic. It shows close structural similarity with the magic system of thought, yet differs from magic in one major respect: it does not merely believe in the possibility of "magic"—it seeks to subject it to experimental and clinical tests.

Nevertheless, its historical ties with the magic tradition are apt to put students of parapsychology on the defensive. They feel that they must at all costs avoid the appearance of falling back on long-discredited fallacies and superstitions. They must expressly dissociate themselves from such frankly untenable beliefs as actions at a distance, "mind over matter," or the omnipotence of thought; all these are characteristic of preliterate man, of the child, of the neurotic, and indeed of the paranoid schizophrenic. It is partly to cover up the traces of such doubtful ancestry that parapsychology felt constrained to devise a new, nonprejudicial language of its own and introduce such more or less neutral terms as extrasensory

3

perception (ESP) and psychokinesis (PK), as well as the Greek letter psi (for "psychic phenomena") as the overall designation of its subject matter.

There can be no doubt as to the necessity of such a new vocabulary. Chemistry and astronomy, rising from the ashes of ancient alchemy and astrology, had to go through a similar process of purification and self-renewal in the past two or three centuries. But parapsychologists find themselves confronted with difficulties of a different order from those which their confreres in the natural sciences face: they have to contend with modern man's ingrained resistance to the very exploration of the phenomena under review. They come face to face with a striking tendency to "explain away," to deny their reality—indeed the possibility of their occurrence. This is an attitude clearly absent in relation to the hard facts brought to light by other scientific disciplines. It is apparently in the hope that such difficulties might be overcome by a verbal repudiation of ties with a dubious past that parapsychologists try to present to their contemporaries a latter-day, thoroughly expurgated and denatured—if not altogether emasculated—version of their ancient heritage.

Yet the continued exclusion of the new data from our overall body of knowledge shows that nomenclature is not enough to bring about a change in this state of affairs. Obviously, psi phenomena are incompatible with modern man's habits of thinking, with his whole outlook on the world. The German poet Christian Morgenstern put it succinctly:

> For, he argues pointedly:
> That which cannot, must not be.

However, three recent developments call for a revision of this intransigent posture. One is the accumulation, in scores of university centers and research laboratories, of a mass of experimental findings which can no longer be explained away as artifacts, statistical errors, or the results of a bizarre international conspiracy of fraud and collusion. The second is a growing number of observations involving ostensible telepathic incidents in the psychotherapeutic situation. The third is the changing attitude of modern theoretical physics and philosophy of science toward the classical concepts of time and space and the supposedly immutable laws of cause and effect. The fact is that relativistic physics and quantum theory have brought about a radical change in our traditional concepts of Aristotelian logic, Euclidian geometry, and Newtonian mechanics. I submit that the data of parapsychology are leading to a similar development in the field of psychology: they force on us a radically revised concept of human personality which is no longer impervious to psi phenomena and therefore is compatible with the occurrence of such phenomena both in the laboratory and under spontaneous conditions.

The story of the new experimental approach to psi phenomena begins with the founding, in 1882, of the (English) Society for Psychical Research by Henry Sidgwick, F. W. H. Myers, and other distinguished thinkers of that era. The goals of the society were the collection of well-authenticated spontaneous psi occurrences (aided by a "census of hallucinations"), the study of hypnotic phenomena, and the observation of trance mediums and trance manifestations. Yet psychical research, conducted along these lines, remained largely an observational rather than an experimental science, comparable to geology or to astronomy—at least prior to the advent of space exploration. Informal experiments in "thought transference" such as those carried out by Gilbert Murray and his family (1952) are more in the nature of parlor games than of methodical experimentation. More ambitious were attempts at the telepathic transmission of drawings by René Warcollier (1921) in France and Upton Sinclair and his wife (1930) in the United States. They were followed by the well-controlled drawing experiments of Whately Carington (1947) in England, which took both experimenter and subjects by surprise when, in addition to a number of striking telepathic responses, they also produced some apparently precognitive results. In the much-quoted Brugmans–Van Dam experiments (1922) at the University of Groningen in Holland, an agent succeeded in guiding telepathetically the hand of the percipient to a randomly determined "target" square on a "checkerboard" consisting of 48 squares.

But it was J. B. Rhine's methodical ESP experiments, beginning in the 1930s at Duke University, which raised psychical research to the level of a quantitative science and marked the real beginning of experimental parapsychology (1937, 1947, and Pratt, Rhine and their associates, 1966). Rhine, like Charles Richet (1884) in France before him, was not satisfied with trying to catch a casual glimpse of psi phenomena in their native habitat. He sought to "breed" them in the laboratory and to study their behavior and characteristics under controlled experimental conditions. To do this he used a population of five geometrical symbols on cards (Rhine's Zener cards), randomized in such a way that the probability of guessing any one of them correctly was five in twenty-five, or one in five. The experiments varied between telepathic conditions, when the target was known to the agent or experimenter, and clairvoyant conditions, when it was unknown to either.

Rhine and his followers on both sides of the Atlantic have accumulated a staggering amount of data during the past three or four decades. They found that specially gifted subjects are capable of scoring far in excess of chance expectation, their results giving astronomical odds against chance coincidence. S. G. Soal and F. Bateman (1954) in England as well as the physicist Helmut Schmidt (1969, 1974) and others in this country produced striking evidence of precognition under laboratory conditions. Helmut Schmidt in particular developed ingenious techniques of generating random numbers for target selection and automatic data processing. Recording the data directly on punch cards, he was able to eliminate most intermediate steps of human intervention with its attending sources of error. The odds against Schmidt's results under either precognitive or PK conditions amounted to more than 10 million to one.

Psychokinesis, or PK, is another important discovery of J. B. Rhine and his co-workers (1947, Cox 1965, and others). It is based on a subject's apparent ability to influence by his volition the fall of dice thrown by hand or by a mechanical tossing device. A recent review of the field was made by E. Girden (Girden et al. 1964).

Popular accounts like to emphasize the astronomical extrachance figures compiled in these tests. Despite the dissenting voices of a number of informed—or not so well informed—critics, some of the experimental series published by Rhine, Pratt (1964), Ryzl and Pratt (1963), Schmidt (1969), and others have sufficient safeguards built into their designs to exclude faulty observation, clerical or statistical errors, or fraud on the part of experimenter and/or subject.

A major contribution is the work of Gertrude R. Schmeidler and R. A. McConnell (1958) with students at Harvard and later at the City College of New York. On separating the ESP scores of "believers" in the possibility of ESP from the "disbelievers," they found that the believers, or "sheep," scored in excess of chance expectation, whereas the scores of disbelievers, or "goats," fell within chance limits or below. A series of group-administered classroom experiments with 1,157 subjects gave a "sheep-goat" scoring difference significant at the probability level of 0.00003.

Another important series of tests was carried out by J. G. van Busschbach in Holland and later in the United States (1953). In these experiments the subjects were fifth- and sixth-grade school children, their teachers serving as agents or experimenters. Results under these conditions were highly significant. "Classroom" experiments of this order were repeated by Margaret Anderson and Rhea White (1956). Working under clairvoyant conditions, they found that scores obtained by pupils "liking" their respective teachers were significantly higher than those obtained from pupils expressing negative attitudes toward them. In turn, the teacher's positive attitude toward his pupil had a favorable effect upon ESP scores. Yet replication of results by other workers was only partly successful.

There is another built-in difficulty in the classical experimental design of the ESP type. This is the very nature of the tests themselves, involving as they do trivial, artificially restricted, and, as it were, dehydrated target materials. Such a "forced choice" technique is an important prerequisite of a quantitative procedure. It enables the experimenter to work with well-defined variables, to ask unequivocal questions, and to obtain equally unequivocal answers from his subjects. We have seen that such an approach has indeed paid ample dividends in terms of a staggering amount of raw, statistically significant data. Schmeidler has summarized this aspect of ESP research by stating that "the most important basic finding about ESP is that it occurs" (1969).

Yet the new technique has done more than merely establish the reality of ESP. It has shown that the subject's performance tends to decline in the course of an experimental session (Rhine 1947). It has uncovered what Ryzl and Pratt (1963) and Pratt (1964) have described as a "focusing effect" upon certain target materials. It has demonstrated the dependence of test results on changing moods, expectations, interests, and various physiological conditions of agent or percipient. It suggests that congenial people—for example, married or engaged couples, identical twins, or mother and child pairs—work better together under telepathic conditions than strangers or psychologically incompatible agents and percipients. The techniques has made it possible, at least to the satisfaction of some experimenters, to separate ESP under telepathic (or so-called GESP, or general ESP) versus precognitive conditions. It has adduced, furthermore, J. B. Rhine's (1952) observations of psi-missing, that is, of ESP responses suggesting that a negativistic subject is capable of *avoiding* specific ESP targets at a rate in excess of chance expectations, though despite his apparent resistance to psi, he must have had a way of identifying the target prior to its rejection.

Veridical or premonitory dreams have attracted the interest of priests, prophets, and sages since the dawn of recorded history. The psychoanalytical situation has been a rich source of observations along these lines. There has been a spate of articles on telepathic dreams, including their presumable predisposing and conditioning factors.

Recent experiments by Montague Ullman, Stanley Krippner, and their associates at Maimonides Medical Center (Ullman, Krippner, and

Vaughan 1973) have opened up a new "nocturnal" dimension of testable psi phenomena specifically in telepathic dreams. By utilizing the rapid eye movement (REM) technique, applied to a sleeping subject, they have succeeded in "programming" the relationship between an agent looking at a target picture and a percipient sleeping in a properly isolated dream laboratory. Using all conceivable safeguards, they found that the sleeper was capable of incorporating details of the unknown target into the fabric of the dreams he had during that night. The technique lends itself to determining the degree of correspondence between the target picture and the dream protocol. Using a matching procedure carried out by two or more independent judges, the results obtained can be objectively evaluated and subjected to mathematical treatment.

Another significant contribution along the same lines are experiments with subjects in the waking state, carried out by Thelma Moss and J. A. Gengerelli of the University of California (1967). As telepathic targets they used highly charged emotional stimuli presented to agents by means of photographic slides and sound tracks. They depicted such episodes as President Kennedy's assassination or a song entitled "The Stripper," showing partially undraped or nude girls. The percipients were instructed to describe their impressions and give their free associations. The safeguards used and the methods of matching and judging apparent correspondences were similar to those developed by the Maimonides group. Here, too, results were statistically evaluated and proved to be highly significant.

Confining attention to work done in the United States, however, would fall short of telling the whole story. Extensive studies done abroad that are on a par with the best work done in American and British centers include those carried out by Professor W. H. C. Tenhaeff at the Parapsychology Institute in the Univeristy of Utrecht; by Professor H. Bender at the Institut für Grenzgebiete der Psychologie und Psycho-hygiene in Freiburg; by Professor L. L. Vasiliev and his successor, P. I. Gulyaev, in the department of physiology of the University of Leningrad; and by E. K. Naumov in Moscow. For obvious reasons, it cannot be given justice in this condensed report. The titles listed in a 1965 review of modern Russian parapsychological literature alone extends to over six pages. S. Ostrander and L. Schroeder's book *Psychic Discoveries behind the Iron Curtain* (1970) contains a comprehensive survey of parapsychology in the U.S.S.R., Czechosolvakia, and Bulgaria.

One of the recent major parapsychological discoveries in Russia is that of the Leningrad housewife Nina Kulagina, whose exploits in psychokinesis attracted the attention of such prominent scientists as L. L.

Vasiliev, E. Naumov, G. Sergeiev, and others. She is capable, by sheer "will power," of moving in broad daylight such objects as the top of a fountain pen, a wineglass, or a box of matches, pulling them towards herself or pushing them in the opposite direction. Her performance was also witnessed by several qualified Western observers including J. Keil, an Australian psychologist, B. Herbert from England, M. Ullman, and J. G. Pratt (1976) from the United States. Films brought to this country likewise tend to bear out the genuineness of Mrs. Kulagina's PK performances.

Another much quoted Russian discovery is a technique of photography in high-frequency electrical fields, producing luminescent, aura-like effects around living tissues or the whole organism. These "Kirlian" effects are attributed to the presence of a "bioplasmic" body surrounding living organisms, which is also supposed to be responsible for various parapsychological phenomena.

Yet it may well be that the only link of Kirlian photography to our issue is its appeal to the imagination of advocates of a physiological or physical theory of psi phenomena. It may be more closely related to the electrophysiological or chemical changes involved in the familiar psychogalvanic reflex than to a mysterious human aura or to a technicolor picture of the human soul.

A recent Israeli counterpart of Mrs. Kulagina is Uri Geller with his controversial exploits in psychokinesis. His reported feats of bending keys or other metallic objects by PK are truly "mind-bending." So are reports of similar exploits in children—and some adults—who were watching Geller's television appearances. The cases of Uri Geller and Matthew Manning, another PK progidy, will be discussed in Chapter 17.

Of considerable interest are recent experimental studies by Joe Kamiya and his associates (1969), Charles Tart in California (1969), Charles Honorton in New York (1969), Rex and B. E. Stanford in Virginia (1969), and others. They are concerned with the electroencephalographic monitoring of brain waves of subjects in altered states of consciousness thought to be conducive to psi phenomena. Apart from the REM stage of sleep, these states include hypnosis, trance states, out-of-the-body experiences, and transcendental and Zen meditation.

Another intriguing experiment—without the benefit of EEG—was recently carried out by Dr. Gertrude R. Schmeidler at the City College of New York (1970). She obtained the ESP scores of six college students under "ordinary" conditions. The scores were well within the range of chance expectation. Immediately following this pretest, an Indian swami addressed the group and invited them to join him in meditation and breathing exercises. After twenty minutes Dr. Schmeidler retested the same students, using the same procedure as before. This time the results were significant ($P = 0.01$).

Reports of supposedly occult phenomena in hypnotic or somnambulistic states go back to Mesmer and the eighteenth century Mesmerists. Some were replicated and confirmed by Janet (1894), Richet (1884), and others in France; Edmund Gurney and Frank Podmore in England; and many others. E. J. Dingwall (1968) collected data from the nineteenth century in a series of four volumes.

Important new contributions to hypnosis and telepathic suggestion at a distance were made by Professor L. L. Vasiliev (1963) and his associates in Leningrad. Recent surveys of the field have been published by Honorton and Krippner (1969) and R. L. Van de Castle (1964). Van de Castle, summarizing the findings of J. Fahler, R. Rao, C. Honorton, M. Ryzl, and others, found overwhelming evidence for "facilitation" of ESP in hypnotic states as compared with the waking scores of the same subjects.

One of the most successful experiments in this area was carried out by the Czech parapsychologist M. Ryzl (1962), now in the United States. His findings were confirmed by a long series of experiments conducted by J. G. Pratt and his associates (1964). Ryzl prepared his subject, Pavel Stepanek, in a series of hypnotic sessions, training him to develop vivid visual hallucinations and so on. He attributes the sustained high scoring obtained in variations of the familiar ESP and clairvoyance tests to this procedure. Together with S. G. Soal's subjects, Basil Shackleton and Mrs. Gloria Stewart, or W. Roll's Lalsingh Harribance, and, more recently, Ingo Swann, Mr. Stepanek ranks among the best sensitives in the history of parapsychology.

The latest chapter in experimental parapsychology is even more promising. Following up on their EEG investigations, Charles Tart, Joe Kamiya, and their associates have designed ESP experiments in which the subject is informed by a suitable signal each time he scores a hit. This electronic feedback technique reinforces the inner attitudes and subliminal internal cues which accompany successful ESP responses and should help the subject to improve his scores. The "Espatester" devised by Tart is in fact a new version of a Skinnerian teaching machine (Tart 1966).

Another striking observation along these lines is that a properly trained subject is capable of controlling the electrical activity of his brain at will. He can produce an increase in alpha wave activity in his EEG tracings. The alpha state is, in turn, closely correlated with trance and meditation—and thereby supposedly with higher scores in ESP tests (Honorton 1969). A no less promising new departure is Honorton's experiments under conditions of partial sensory deprivation (Honorton and Harper 1974). He exposes his subject to a homogenous visual field (*Ganzfeld*) and "white noise" to increase the yield of extrachance responses in ESP tests.

Douglas Dean's experiments (1962) approach the problem from another angle. He uses the fluctuations in a subject's blood supply to a finger as measured with the plethysmograph as indicators of telepathic responses to emotionally charged stimulus words. Experiments of this kind, which bypass the subject's psi-related verbal or perceptual responses, have yielded highly significant results.

There can be no doubt that all these findings take psychical research far beyond a mere collecting of anecdotal observations: they have raised parapsychology to the level of a scientific discipline in its own right. But the question is, to what extent can the experimental evidence be regarded as a duplication in the laboratory of psi phenomena as they are encountered spontaneously, "in the raw," under conditions of ordinary life—for example, in situations of crisis or of emotionally charged interpersonal relationships, during psychotherapy, psychoanalysis, or in a clinical-psychiatric setting? The question is whether parapsychology, having succeeded in "breeding" a new, properly refined, domesticated, and mathematically treatable species of forced-choice psi phenomena, is not apt to lose sight of their original prototype, a more elusive but culturally and biologically more significant one. We have to ask whether Rhine's ritualized question and answer game, cultivating the "small fry" that can be observed in the ESP laboratory, does not run the risk of losing sight of the "big game" of major psi occurrences of the type which have struck man's mind with wonder and awe from the dawn of history? It may be that by opening our door by little more than a tiny crack, we bar the entrance into our purview of all but a few flattened out, microscopic slices of a lost psychic reality.

Goethe, in the early nineteenth century, raised his voice against excessive reliance on the microscope as an instrument of scientific fact finding. He demanded a broader, more comprehensive, indeed global approach to nature and to human experience in general. The early workers in psychical research paid almost exclusive attention to this broader aspect of psi. More recently, L. E. Rhine (1961); L. A. Dale, R. White, and G. Murphy (1962); and Ian Stevenson (1970) have made significant contributions to this field in their studies of spontaneous cases. A similar approach, though from a different angle, will be proposed in the chapters that follow.

It is an approach that takes us back to the clinical and observational stage of parapsychology. But it is a matter of historical record that psychology itself has passed through a similar stage. No scientific discipline can afford to skip such a holistic stage. For centuries past it was man observed with the naked eye who has been "the proper study of man." This was followed in due course by the painstaking studies in Wundt's or Titchener's psychophysiological laboratories, by Pavlov's or Skinner's experiments on conditioned reflexes or operant conditioning, and by more recent quantitative studies in perception, learning theory, cognitive control, and the like.

Still, all the minutiae of laboratory investigations cannot do justice to the totality of man in his social and interpersonal aspects, to his relationship with his fellow man and the universe at large, to his world of value— artistic, religious, or otherwise—to his "ultimate concerns." The same is true of the new—or old—vistas of psychic reality opened up by the validation of psi phenomena. Confining our attention to experimental subjects capable of piling up unusually high ESP or PK scores in the parapsychological laboratory would severely restrict our view of human potentiality.

Indeed, at the risk of rocking the still somewhat wobbly boat of experimental parapsychology by shifting the emphasis from lab to life, from computer printouts to plain clinical observation, it may be well to realize that the vast body of statistical findings amassed in the past four decades provides only a fragmented view of the real thing. ESP, PK, and flashes of apparent precognition are responses in a question-and-answer game played according to arbitrary, man-made rules. The rules dictate compliance with such conventional measures as statistical significance, levels of confidence, and tables of random numbers; they demand strictly defined experimental procedures, endless repetition of tests, and replication of positive results if possible.

But we had better face the fact that the yield of all this Herculean effort has been rather disappointing. Charles Tart of the University of California (1976) has rightly pointed out that the standard experimental approach of the card-calling or dice-throwing type is apt to extinguish rather than to encourage the emergence of psi incidents. It would perhaps be unfair to describe such incidents as little more than freakish laboratory artifacts (Brown 1957); they rather amount to fitful bursts of subliminal behavioral responses, leaving tracks written in invisible ink behind them that can only be made visible in the flickering light of the statistical method. They may be "ESP," but they do not amount to an ESP *experience*. Indeed, we shall see in Part Three of this book that psi phenomena of the statistical type are largely due to occasional flaws in our mental organization permitting the random intrusion into our consciousness of ESP or PK incidents or behavior that have no psychological significance or tangible survival advantage. They will be described as *flaw-determined*.

We shall also see that, by contrast, there is a world of nonsensory, extrasensory, transpersonal, psychic reality which is difficult to catch in the entomologist's butterfly net, to break down into well-defined statistical variables, but which—perhaps for this very reason—is nevertheless possessed of marked psychological signficance and a powerful emotional charge. Incidents of this type are apt to meet deep-seated emotional needs in those involved in the experiences. They will be described as *need-determined*.

Need-determined, psychologically—though not statistically—significant psi phenomena are in effect the principal topic of the chapters that follow. They call for an essentially clinical, psychodynamic approach. Their proving ground is not the experimental laboratory; it is life in the raw: the parent-child relationship, the family situation, clinic and consulting room, and human affairs in general. In effect, some of the parapsychologists mentioned above have gone far to bridge the gap between spontaneous and experimental phenomena. There is the work of T. Moss; of the Maimonides group, including C. Honorton; of C. Tart, and especially of Rex Stanford (1974), to say nothing of L. LeShan (1973), or Inge Strauch (1977).

Thus, with all these qualifications and mental reservations, it is only fair to say that the psychiatrist or parapsychiatrist deriving his facts from people rather than from figures has reaped ample benefits from the labor of those distilling them chiefly from figures. In case of doubt, he can still turn to the experimenter for support and reassurance. If necessary, he can even put part of the blame on him for his failure to convince the skeptic. The point is vividly illustrated by a passage from a letter Professor Albert Einstein wrote to me in 1946: "Very interesting, and actually of greater significance to me, are the tests with the nine-year old retarded girl (Ilga K., see p. 18 herein). . . . Also, the experiments with drawings. (Upton Sinclair) seem to me to be of greater weight than the large-scale statistical tests in which the discovery of a minute systematic error may upset everything." Perhaps the reader will note that Professor Einstein's remarks had a seminal influence upon the argument presented in this book.

2

Parent-Child Symbiosis:

Cradle of ESP

ALL ATTEMPTS at arriving at a reasonable understanding of psi phenomena must come to grips with the question of their origin. Where do they come from and at what point do they emerge in the course of individual development? To answer these questions, we must turn our attention to the infancy of the human child and to the early stages of the mother-child relationship.

There are five major sources from which we can draw for such a study. The first is observations made by perceptive parents themselves. The second is the adult's recollections of early childhood memories. The third is direct observations by child psychologists and psychiatrists studying the behavior and the interactions of parent and child in the family setting, the clinic, or the consulting room. The fourth is attempts at reconstructing a patient's early infantile past in the psychoanalytic situation. The fifth source is experimental studies of the ESP type combined, if possible, with modern electronic monitoring devices which record the EEG, various autonomic indices, and the like.

The following is an early observation of my own, suggestive of telepathy between my wife and my daughter, aged four at that time. The incident happened in 1940, during my wartime exile in England. My wife had just received a letter from her cousin Clarence in the United States. She had spent a happy time with his family a few years before we got married, and Clarence, too, had married in the meantime. There was a photograph of Clarence's wife, Matilda, attached to his letter, showing her in the company of two more ladies. My wife, engaged in housework, was pondering the letter and photograph, while Barbara was absorbed in play by her side. At that very moment the child, for no apparent reason, uttered the name "Matilda." I may add that this name in its English version had been quite unfamiliar to the child. When asked on the next day whether she remembered the name, she replied, "Yes, I was having a game with Mummy."

My wife produced the following chain of associations: "No, I do not know Matilda . . . I was wondering which one she was on the picture. I only know they had married about the same time as we did and that they have a child about Barbara's age . . . and Clarence now writes that they are going to have another baby. These lucky Americans . . . they can afford such a luxury."

My wife's associations speak for themselves. They show that there was a marked emotional charge to her thinking of Matilda. She was evidently identifying with Clarence's wife and it was this attitude which may have been responsible for the apparent telepathic transmission of the name.

Mrs. Louisa Rhine published a number of similar observations (1961). A woman was pondering the name of a man whose telephone number she was reluctant to call. At that moment, her two-year-old daughter said his name: Arno Kraus. In another of Mrs. Rhine's cases, a child, aged four, echoed her mother's thoughts when she asked, "Are we having spaghetti for dinner?" Dr. Rhine's own daughter, aged four, did the same thing when she piped up: "Mamma are you fatter now than you have been?" Her mother was at that moment struggling with the temptation to eat just one more piece of buttered toast.

Dr. Berthold Schwarz, a psychiatrist, has assembled a unique collection of similar observations in his daughter Lisa and his younger son Eric when they were between one-and-a-half and fourteen years old. He describes early incidents with Lisa in which he or his wife played the role of the telepathic agent. The following example may illustrate the point: "I walked into the kitchen feeling quite exuberant and thought I would clown by showing Lisa a Nijinsky-like kick and do a little dance. However, before I could demonstrate, she started to kick and do a little dance. She had never done this before. In this way perhaps, she acted out, in motor fashion, my happy behavior that was about to emerge from its silent incubation" (1971, p. 24). Similar observations involved telepathy between Eric and his parents.

The overall impression gained from Dr. Schwarz's 1,520 (!) "possible" incidents suggests that there were three major predisposing or conditioning factors involved in the occurrences. First, the close emotional ties or the symbiotic aspects of the child-parent relationship. Second, the child's tendency to what I described as doctrinal compliance, that is, the tendency to provide evidence confirming her father's emotionally charged expectations regarding his pet scientific hypothesis concerning ESP. (We shall see in Chapter 6 that this is a striking counterpart to doctrinal compliance in the therapeutic situation, psychoanalytic or otherwise.) A third factor seems to have been Lisa's own psychological needs, and especially her mood of contentment.

A reliable informant, Mrs. R. P., has recorded a number of observations along similar lines. The incidents occurred with her daughter Lisbeth, aged two years and nine months at the time of the first incident and three years and four months at the time of the last incident. I may add that on a few subsequent occasions it was Mrs. P. who had acted as a percipient, usually in response to anxiety-laden situations connected with the child.

In the following two examples Lisbeth functioned as the percipient. "I was standing folding Lisbeth's diapers on the counter in the bathroom when I thought idly that it would be fun for us to go away somewhere over Labor Day and wondered if this would be practical, and if so, where we would go. At this precise instant Lisbeth ran in from her bedroom where she had been playing quietly for some time and asked, 'Pat, we going on a trip?' Absolutely nothing had been mentioned on this subject; the thought had just struck me at that moment."

Another incident harks back to a very early phase of the mother-child relationship. "Lisbeth rested her hand on my breast as I was changing her for bed on her counter. I can't recall her doing this since she was an infant. As I looked down at her, I wondered if she could possibly remember nursing, when both her hands would be on my breasts. I had only been able to nurse her the first five weeks of her life. I didn't say a word but Lisbeth suddenly looked up and said, 'I eat your skin all up,' and laughed. I asked, 'Where?' She said, 'Your chest,' pointing to my breast. She had never before given utterance to any words or line of thought even remotely resembling the above."

This incident is of particular interest in the present context. It focuses on the early symbiotic stage, when mother and child are tied together by the intimacy of nursing and being nursed, of holding and being held, of caring and being cared for. In short, it goes back to the very biological matrix of human existence rooted in love and social cooperation.

Another group of direct observations throws light on another side of the picture. They are cases described by Johnson and Szurek (1952),

Melitta Sperling (1954), and other psychoanalysts. It involves neurotic children who tend to act out their parents' repressed antisocial impulses. In some instances such acting out may lead to delinquency or other behavioral disturbances. Erik Erikson (1950) referred to the same principle when he remarked that children tend to live out their parents' secret dreams.

Here is an example of my own. Little Dick C., aged four, acted out his mother's hostile-destructive impulses toward Mr. C., twenty years his wife's senior. He attacked him with a knife, threw mother's jewelry (a gift from Mr. C.) out of the window, and so on. Dick was the issue of one of his mother's extramarital affairs. Although this had, for obvious reasons, remained a closely guarded secret, the boy drove his mother to desperation by his repetitive compulsive questioning: "Is daddy my real daddy? Yes, he is my daddy, but is he my real daddy?" In this instance, Dick's hostile-destructive behavior toward Mr. C. is amenable to interpretation along "orthodox" psychiatric lines. But his compulsive questioning is not. It contains reference to a specific point of information which could not have reached him through the usual channels of communication and which he was unlikely to have arrived at by rational inference. At the same time it was conspicuously tagged by what can be described as telepathic "tracer elements," that is, bits of information which point more specifically to their telepathic or "heteropsychic" origin than do such ill-defined patterns of behavior as aggression or destructiveness. The specificity of this line of questioning is open to debate, but Joan Fitzherbert (1960) in England has reported similar cases of apparent ESP in adopted children.

Child psychiatrists and psychoanalysts have described many observations along similar lines. They have, however, skirted the telepathy hypothesis to account for their modus operandi. Instead we are offered such explanations as unconscious expressive movements, empathy, instinct, or mutual "cuing" between mother and child. Or else we are told that "one unconscious" should be able to communicate directly with "another unconscious"—whatever this is supposed to mean.

A notable exception is Jung and his followers. According to Jung, Aniela Jaffé (1971), and other Jungians, the mother-child relationship represents "an archetypal situation par excellence" in which telepathy and other incidents suggestive of synchronicity are apt to occur. Another significant contribution is by Dorothy Burlingham, a Freudian analyst who reported three apparently telepathic incidents, one involving her ten-year-old son (1935). It was concerned with gold coins in a apparent response to a similar story mentioned by one of Dr. Burlingham's patients undergoing psychoanalysis at that time. In another case, a mother had just gotten the idea of giving her child a bicycle for Christmas. The child, in another room, called out, "I know what you are going to give me for Christmas: a bicycle." In a third case, the child "guessed" that the mother was pregnant before it was known to her.

Another group of observations is of an altogether different order. They feature an abnormally prolonged symbiotic relationship between mentally defective or otherwise handicapped children and their mothers. The first case is that of Ilga K., published by Ferdinand von Neureiter, a professor of forensic medicine in Germany (1935). Ilga, aged nine, was suffering from a severe reading disability. She was, however, able to "read" any text if and when her mother was perusing it at that same time. Experiments revealed that she could do so even when the mother was sitting behind a curtain or in another room.

Five years later Dr. Hans Bender, the noted German parapsychologist, reported on the findings of a commission which was delegated to repeat the Neureiter investigations. In giving details of his experimental setup, Bender makes an observation which is of significance in the present context. He explains that when he was trying to duplicate the original Neureiter tests, Ilga's mother, Mrs. K., could not be restrained from constantly prodding the child in exclamations such as: "Ilga, think! Say it right!" He describes how the child recited words read by the mother in syllables in a monotonous tone of voice often impatiently, while "the lips of the woman who was an unusually excitable motor type and difficult to manage were often moving simultaneously with the child's utterances" (1940).

Such observations point to a striking simultaneity between Mrs. K.'s attempt to function vicariously in behalf of her mentally defective child and Ilga's apparent telepathic response to this attitude. Far from detracting from the merits of the case, as far as telepathy is concerned, it throws its symbiotic aspect into sharper perspective.

A similar case, that of little Bo, a retarded boy, aged eleven, was described by R. M. Drake of Wesleyan College, Macon, Georgia (1938). He too seemed capable of "reading" only when his mother, a tense and overanxious woman, was present, functioning vicariously in his behalf, as it were. Originally Bo was thought to be a "lightning calculator" because he was able to do complicated sums or multiplications despite his intellectual limitations. It soon transpired that this too he could do only when his mother was doing the calculations in her head.

A third case, in which the subject is known only as the Cambridge Boy, was recently published by Recordon, Stratton, and Peters in England (1968). The boy was suffering from spastic diplegia and congenital cataracts in both eyes. Yet his ophthalmologist was puzzled by his striking ability to "read" the visual acuity charts when the boy's mother was hovering over him. He too was unable to do so in her absence. A telepathic factor was suspected to account for this unexpected performance, and a series of long-distance experiments between him and his mother indeed seemed to confirm the telepathy hypothesis.

To sum up, the last three illustrative cases have four things in common. First, all involve a handicapped child or adolescent. Second, their respective mothers had a strong, sometimes frantic, motivation to help their offspring to overcome their disability. Third, there was *prima facie* evidence of a telepathic factor—of clear-cut telepathic "tracer elements" —involved in the youngsters' performances. Last, in all three the telepathy hypothesis had specifically been put to the test by the observers.

The cases differ, however, from those discussed before in that they occurred in individuals long past the early symbiotic phase and also in that the ostensible telepathic communication involved highly specific material such as numerals, letters of the alphabet, or printed sentences. Last, the performance of the telepathic twosome served an eminantly utilitarian purpose: it was triggered and sustained by the respective mothers' powerful motivation to compensate, through their own efforts, for their offsprings' disabilities: They tried to function vicariously in their behalf. Thus it appears that in these examples it is the existing psychological emergency combined with unmet societal demands which is responsible for the prolongation of specific features of the symbiotic phase. In recent years the emphasis has increasingly shifted to experimental data. ESP and PK studies involving children of school and preschool age published in the parapsychological literature have by now come close to 150 entries.*

The following observation takes us to a spontaneous incident a long way past the symbiotic stage and turns the table upon the two partners involved: a grown-up daughter assumes the maternal role toward her aged mother and responds to the mother's mortal crisis in terms of what can be described as telepathic acting out.

Lottie is a married woman of forty. A native of Prague, she and her husband came to this country in 1938. Owing to circumstances beyond her

---

* A promising contribution along these lines is by E. Spinelli (1976) in England, who surveyed a population of some 1000 subjects and found higher ESP scores in the youngest age group (three and four years), and a gradual lowering of scores in the young adult and adult group.

control she was forced to leave her widowed mother, aged fifty-eight, behind in the country threatened by Nazi occupation. Lottie was torn with remorse for having done so, and she continued to do all in her power to obtain a visa for the old lady and to bring her over to the United States. On April 12, 1939, between 10 and 10:30 A.M., Lottie was suddenly overcome by a feeling of anxiety and restlessness. She had a sense of some impending disaster and went into an uncontrollable crying fit. This happened in her apartment in New York. Helen, her maid, tried her best to calm her down and to find out the reason for Lottie's anxiety. But all Lottie could tell her was that she felt something terrible had happened to her mother, or maybe to her mother-in-law. Helen's consolation that she would not have to cry so bitterly if something had happened to her mother-in-law did not help matters. Lottie rushed to the phone and tried to put through a transatlantic telephone call to her mother. Owing to technical difficulties this was of no avail. She shared her anxiety with her husband and the next morning Lottie went to her safe deposit vault to parcel out what family heirlooms she had brought from the old country so that her mother, on her arrival here, would have an equal share of the jewels with her daughter—provided she would ever arrive. On her return from the bank Lottie's husband broke the news to her that in the night from April 11 to April 12, her mother had suddenly passed away. The cable, sent by a relative, mentioned a carbuncle for which she had an operation. But Lottie learned a month or so later that her mother's death had been a suicide. On the critical night she had opened the gas jets in her apartment. Making allowance for the six hours' time difference between New York and Prague, Lottie's anxiety attack may have occurred after a latency period of twelve-to-sixteen hours following her mother's death. As in many cases of this kind, however, there is no information available as to the exact time she had succumbed to the gas poisoning.

Lottie's case is wholly in the tradition of older reports found in the literature of psychical research. But owing to the circumstances in which it came to my notice, it provides some added insight into the nature of the relationship which may—or may not—be conducive to an occasional telepathic incident. In Lottie's case the relationship between mother and daughter had always been very close. An only child, she had lost her father at the age of three and had thus become the only source of joy and emotional security to her widowed mother. In fact, throughout her life she had been conditioned to cater to her mother's emotional needs: to become her friend and companion rather than her child. Gradually her mother developed a paradoxical dependence on her daughter, reversing, in a way, the usual pattern. Lottie married late, at the age of twenty-nine.

Even at that time she felt rather guilty over what to her appeared as a desertion of her mother. Her guilt was further enhanced by her emigration to the United States about a year after her marriage. Her mother, on the other hand, had quite obviously fostered Lottie's sense of guilt. Although she had resigned herself to the inevitable and accepted Lottie and her son-in-law's emigration without open remonstrations, Lottie had rightly sensed all along that her mother had never really let go of her and never acquiesced in the final separation from her daughter. The telepathic incident between the two shows in effect Lottie's reaction to her mother's death.

She responded with a spasm of guilt and anxiety—although she was unable to tell exactly why she felt compelled to rush to the phone to put in the long distance call and to establish some sort of connection with her mother. Neither was she fully aware of the deeper reasons for her actions —or acting out—on the following day. Yet these can well be understood along psychoanalytic lines. We must surmise that her parceling out of the family heirlooms was a symbolic gesture designed to expiate her sins, while at the same time it served as a denial of her mother's death, of which she had learned in a telepathic way.

What, then, do we learn from the clinical and experimental observations reviewed so far? They indicate that under certain well-defined psychological conditions, a telepathic factor may indeed be involved in the early—or even later—child-parent relationship. They suggest, furthermore, that at the early symbiotic stage, telepathy is more than an incidental feature of the symbiotic twosome.

Symbiosis has been defined as a physiologically reciprocal dependent relationship between two different organisms, beneficial for both. In man, symbiosis involves both physiological and psychological aspects of their concerted functioning and is certainly more than a mere figure of speech. In any case, there is general consensus among child psychiatrists and psychoanalysts, Freudian, Jungian, and otherwise, that in the early postpartum phase, the mother's and the neonate's ego boundaries have not as yet been delineated. Their respective egos or "selves" are merged into one. The baby is a direct extension of his mother's body image. She does "the doing" for him. She feeds him when he is hungry; she gives him warmth when he is cold. She lifts his covers when he is warm. She diapers him when he is wet. She monitors his physical and social environment on his behalf. She is the omnipotent, omniscient, bountiful mother figure. Psychoanalytic reconstruction suggests that the baby in turn partakes of her purported omnipotence. Mother or mother's breast, as well as the universe at large, are there at his beck and call. Indeed from his point of view it is he who exercises virtual control over his mother's behavior. His signals of distress, his whimper or cry, his kicking and flailing, send her scurrying to his aid. This is what Freud's early disciple Sandor Ferenczi has called the omnipotence of movements (1950), or what Masud Khan has termed symbiotic omnipotence, as reflected in the psychoanalytic situation (1969).

Dovetailing or interlocking behavioral attitudes of this order are evidently a direct continuation of the embryo's and the maternal organism's flawless biological cooperation. Indeed, symbiosis has been described as extrauterine gestation, as the continued functional unity of the mother-child dual, or "basic unit."

How, then, despite the physical separation of parent and offspring, is this biological unity and reciprocity being maintained? What is responsible for their perfect "fit," for their delicately balanced homeostasis and functioning in concert? The neonate, though highly vocal, is nonverbal. His expressive movements can barely indicate more than distress or comfort, hunger or satiation. He lacks fully functional afferent or efferent neural pathways. The myelinization or wiring of his nerve sheaths is delayed up to the fourth or fifth month of extrauterine life. Still, the efficacy of interaction between mother and baby seems to exceed the limited repertoire of whatever conventional signaling code joins them together as one functioning whole. In short, how does mother know if baby cannot tell? How does baby respond when he doesn't understand?

I hinted that it is at this point that the telepathy hypothesis comes to our aid. Telepathy, to the extent that it is taken for granted by the general public, is usually considered as a mere psychological curiosity, as a freakish and ambiguous means of communication, without an apparent goal or discernible purpose. Yet we have seen that the early symbiotic phase confronts us with a relative communication gap in the mother-child dual without a tangible means to bridge it. The fact is that in the preverbal or nonverbal phase signals are exchanged and "mutual cuing" occurs in a way which runs far ahead of the infant's capacity to make himself understood. At the same time mother seems to "understand" in a way which is difficult to account for in terms of the "ordinary" means of communication.

It is true that recent audio-visual studies monitoring mother-infant interaction suggest that more nonverbal communication is going on between them than meets the unaided eye. But this does not obviate the need for an added psi factor helping to choreograph their movements by remote control, as it were. There is reason to believe that it is in effect PK from the mother that triggers off her baby's supposedly imitative smile (and other motor responses), even in the absence of fully functional neural pathways. We have seen on an earlier page that similar considerations apply to the mothers of retarded children trying to function vicariously in their behalf. Far from detracting from the validity of our argument, this is rather apt to lend it added support. The presumed modus operandi of two separate "brain regions" acting in concert will be discussed in Part Four of this book.

Thus, introducing the telepathy hypothesis into the symbiotic model of the child-parent relationship helps to fill the gap in our understanding of its functioning. But it does more than that: it assigns an important physiological function to an otherwise seemingly superfluous vehicle of communication, telepathy. It accounts for the modus operandi of the exchange of an infinite variety of preconceptual messages or "proto messages," preverbal instructions, and do's and don'ts between mother and child. At the same time, it suggests that telepathy is in effect the embryological matrix of communication or information transfer which is later destined to be superceded by speech.

We have to realize, however, that protomessages of this order do not convey as yet clear-cut "bits" of information or well-defined cognitive content. They convey distress calls or messages of comfort, endearment, or elementary reassurance. They are geared to influencing behavior. They may impart information of sorts. But if so, it is on an elementary, preconceptual level, comparable to the complex patterns of instruction carried by the genetic code imbedded in the DNA of the cell nucleus. More often than not, the messages are so vague and unobtrusive that they altogether escape the attention of the outsider—at least by presently available means of observation.

Nevertheless, the concerted evidence of the cases reviewed here, in conjunction with a vast body of related experimental evidence, goes far to show that telepathy is in all likelihood a significant feature of the early child-parent relationship. This is forcefully impressed on us by observations under pathological conditions, and we may well extrapolate from there to less conspicuous "normal" situations, when clear-cut, unequivocal evidence is hard to come by. If this is true, telepathy, at the symbiotic stage, is indeed a vitally important means of communication serving the smooth functioning of the mother-child unit and, thereby, its very survival as a viable entity.

Data culled from the field of comparative biology give added support for such a thesis. We know that man, as compared with other animals, is a late bloomer. The human neonate is completely dependent and helpless at birth, certainly more so than any other primate. In a similar vein, the human infant's sensori-motor skills and perceptual functions lag far behind those of other animals. Even the myelinization of his neural pathways is incomplete up to the age of four or five months. This state of affairs has given rise to the theory of *fetalization* or *neoteny* proposed by biolgists. The terms refer to the extension of the fetal or embryological stage of development from the intrauterine period to the period of prolonged help-lessness or extrauterine gestation after birth.

Thus, fetalization is a specifically human attainment. But at the same time, it is a specifically human handicap, conducive to a major develop-mental crisis in the life of every human child. It leaves him, among all other animals, the most dependent on his parents or parent substitutes. This, in turn, makes the maintenance of proper lines of communication and interaction with his social environment (and especially with his mother) a vital necessity for his survival. In the absence of speech, and with the stunting of such other means of communication as a highly de-veloped sense of smell or social hormones available to the newborn of other species, the human neonate's lines of communication with his mother are rudimentary. Indeed, he is the only animal which can be said to find itself in something like a communications blackout in the early symbiotic phase.

According to the hypothesis proposed here, the psychological gap is bridged by telepathic communication, though this may be conceivably aided by sensory cues. To be more precise, owing to the continued fusion of the maternal with the neonatal ego, there is no psychological gap between the two; telepathy follows the patterns of intrapsychic communication within one single, psychologically as yet undifferentiated personality structure.

However, with the gradual maturation of the child's nervous system and with the passing of the symbiotic stage, the child emerges from the period of partial communication blackout. His babbling and cooing is gradually supplanted by speech. His ego boundaries, until now fused with those of his mother, become more sharply delineated. He sets up a barrier between his mother's mental processes and his own. He is no longer part and parcel of her personality. He establishes himself as an indi-vidual in his own right. Taking a cue from the diagrammatic picture of cell division, this process can be described as "psychomitosis"; it has been conceptualized by Jung as individuation, and more recently it was de-scribed by Margaret Mahler as the phase of separation-individuation (1968).

As this comes to pass, the direct sharing of psychic processes between mother and child is no longer necessary, nor indeed possible. The child can monitor his own environment. He can ward off excessive environmental stimuli from outside. He can direct his actions toward external objects. He can express his needs in words. At the same time, the earlier telepathic patterns of communication become rudimentary. In fact, he erects increasingly effective barriers against their intrusion into the confines of his personality. With increasing vehemence he protects himself against continued telepathic encroachment from outside: he wants to "do his own thing," however nebulous that may be. He becomes allergic to telepathic—or "heteropsychic"—influences, much the same way as his organism as a whole is allergic to foreign protein. Indeed, we shall see in Chapter 11 that if he fails to insulate himself from influences of this order, he may head for a psychotic breakdown: he may turn into a schizophrenic child of the symbiotic or autistic type as described by child psychiatrists.

It should also be noted at this point that there is a striking similarity between the screening out of heteropsychic influences and the repression of Freud's primary process functioning in the course of the child's individual development. The process is reinforced by what amounts to a mechanism of cultural repression directed against the return of ESP.

The fact is that both Western man and his culture are programmed in such a way that the return of primitive mentality, as well as of telepathy and related phenomena, is prevented and, if necessary, penalized by all means of social disapproval and ostracism practiced by the group. The rejection and repudiation of the telepathic factor by the growing child's ego has become mandatory in our culture.

Still, the gradually evolving negative attitude toward ESP does not spell the end of occasional flashes of telepathic interaction between person and person in later life. It is true that telepathy, like the fetal circulation, ceases to be operational as a viable means of communication once the umbilical cord is cut. Yet, by contrast to anatomical structures, telepathy does not become altogether atrophic and defunct. Under special circumstances the abandoned track can be reopened and traffic on them reactivated again. A fleeting telepathic incident of the spontaneous type may make its appearance, though if it does, the reactivated function still tends to exhibit telltale signs of its embryological origin: it shows all the characteristics of Freud's primary process functioning, of symbolic representation, of prelogical thinking, or of Piaget's "preoperational" reasoning. They are characteristics which carry the imprint of the particular time in the individual's life cycle at which they first made their appearance. This accounts for their regressive quality, for their resemblance to magic or to what Lévi-Strauss described as the "concrete logic" of the savage mind. This also is the reason for the stigma of irrationality attached to them, as well as for our tendency to their repudiation, denial, and cultural repression.

Still, the vast body of data amassed in close to a hundred years of psychical research testifies to the stubborn survival of psi elements in interpersonal relationships. Ian Stevenson has made a careful survey of both old and new cases of telepathic impressions under spontaneous conditions (1970). His survey shows that 33.8 percent of his cases within the family involved parent and child relationships, 15 percent siblings, and 13.7 percent husbands and wives. Members of the extended family were involved at a decreasing rate of frequency. Findings of this order once more impress on us the relevance of our symbiotic model, although Stevenson rightly emphasizes that emotional ties seem to be more important for the origin of the phenomena than biological relationships.

This is how we arrive at a concept of a *symbiotic gradient,* ranging from the early symbiotic phase to psi functions operating in the doctor-patient or teacher-pupil relationship and in society at large. Such a scheme indeed throws developmental aspects of psi phenomena into sharper perspective. Yet we must realize that the symbiotic gradient, as it is conceived here, is a purely descriptive term. It helps to assemble a welter of observations in a comprehensive, overarching system but glosses over the differences between spontaneous, need-determined, *macro*psychological incidents, and the minor, *micro*psychological ESP responses of the card-calling type.

Even more problematic is the implied linear extension of the gradient to such clairvoyantly perceived inanimate objects as geometrical figures, letters sealed in an envelope, or Rhine's Zener cards; to telekinetically activated dice rolling from a cup; or to stones thrown about in the presence a poltergeist child. In the last analysis, such a scheme embraces the whole congeries of atoms, protons, and electrons from which both animate and inanimate nature has sprung: We arrive at a symbiotic gradient trailing off from the *here* and *now* to the outermost reaches of time and space and the universe at large.

Such a proposition admittedly harks back to ancient Far Eastern philosophies or to Gnostic and medieval Christian mysticism. Yet at the same time, it is in good keeping with the world picture of modern theoretical physics and quantum mechanics (LeShan, 1973). More than that. The major, *macro*psychological events of the spontaneous type, obeying as they do familiar psychodynamic principles, can well be compared with ordinary, *macro*physical, causally determined events. Incidentally, this may have been one of the reasons why the case of Ilga K. or the Upton Sinclair tests mentioned earlier, seemed to be the "lesser evil" to Professor Einstein. By contrast, Rhine's *micro*psychological ESP experiments of the card-calling type show a close affinity to the randomness and indeterminacy of quantum physical events on the subatomic scale which ran counter to Einstein's faith in a harmonious, well-ordered universe. This may have been an added reason for his suspicion of Dr. Rhine's results. Rhine may well have made his mark by playing with Zener cards. But God, in Einstein's view, did not play with dice.

We shall return to this intriguing issue in Part Four of this book. In the chapter that follows we will turn our attention to the origins and vicissitudes of psi phenomena in the historic perspective.

3

The Decline of Magic and

the Metamorphosis of Witches

PSI PHENOMENA can be described as refined and expurgated derivatives of magic handed down to us from a past age. In the preceding chapter we traced back their origin in the individual to the mother-child relationship at the early symbiotic stage. But what is the origin of magic and magic mentality in the broader historical perspective? The usual answer is that they were essential features of the human mind at the dawn of consciousness. Yet with man emerging from a primitive, pre-literate, prelogical phase, magic mentality, including witchcraft and sorcery, were doomed to decline and ultimate extinction, like the appendix in the evolution of our digestive tract. It was discredited, repudiated, and disowned by a more rationalistic age. Together with psi phenomena and the pagan gods of antiquity, it was relegated to the netherworld of the human mind.

If this is true, the abominations of the medieval or Renaissance witch craze were in effect due to Western man's miscarried reaction and overreaction to his discredited archaic heritage. Indeed, to the extent that psi phenomena were embedded in these atavistic survivals, they too were subjected to the relentless forces of cultural—as opposed to individual—repression. In the end, organized religion, followed by rationalistic science, proceeded to empty the baby out with the bath water. In this respect individual development seems to repeat the vicissitudes of magic and psi phenomena in the course of cultural development at large.

Yet the forces of cultural and individual repression notwithstanding, the past is still alive in the present. On reviewing the annals of history, witchcraft and demonology appear like the scenario of modern psychical research reflected in a distorting mirror or seen through the swirling mists of a nightmare. The ingredients are all there: mental phenomena like telepathy, clairvoyance, precognition and such physical manifestations as psychokinesis, levitation, or out-of-the-body experiences. Witches read the witch finder's mind. They foretell the future. They can raise tempests or cause destruction to crops, impotence in men, sterility in cattle. They ride on phallic brooms to the witches' Sabbath, cohabitate with the devil, and cannibalize little children. Indeed, the misogynic monks of the Middle Ages and the supposedly more enlightened witchhunters of the Reformation projected the whole repertoire of Krafft-Ebing's *psychopathia sexualis* upon their innocent victims. This tendency was in turn reinforced by ideological factors: by the dictates of cultural repression superimposed on the defenses against the return of the Freudian or personally repressed.

On trying to follow the vicissitudes of magic mentality in the course of Western civilization and to track the path of destruction left in the wake of the witch craze on both sides of the Atlantic, we must not be misled by changes of nomenclature. Few observers would pause to acknowledge the historic continuity of magic with the present-day realities of psi phenomena. Still, I have noted that the term psi itself is an antiseptic, expurgated, or sanitized version of magic. It is aimed at dissociating modern parapsychology from its doubtful ancestry, at removing the old stigma attached to it. Psi phenomena are in effect derivatives of magic that have been dehydrated, deboned, and filleted to make them disgestible for scientific consumption. Such physical manifestation as psychokinesis, levitations, or poltergeists are more or less antiseptic equivalents for sorcery; out-of-the-body experiences or "traveling" clairvoyance, for flights of the shaman or for bilocation of Christian saints. I have hinted that precognition as the forward displacement of ESP scores in the laboratory is a modern counterpart of divination, while references to telepathy, clairvoyance, or "general ESP" are intended to erase the last vestiges of the occult from so-called mental manifestations.

By the same token, the image of the witch has changed nearly beyond recognition in the past centuries. Yet no sooner had the last ecclesiastic courts of inquiry into witchcraft adjourned sine die than we could observe Dr. Mesmer's patients congregating around the magnetized water in his "baquet" to seek relief from their afflictions—and adding to them, presumably in compliance with the good doctor's scenario, some more hysterical convulsions to fit the occasion.

The family resemblance of these productions with those of the devils of Loudun or of the afflicted children of Salem is unmistakable. The new departure in Mesmer's scenario is that his patients no longer trafficked with the devil. Instead of volunteering bizarre confessions about cohabitating with incubi and succubi, they produce all the "mesmeric" phenomena the imaginative Viennese doctor could have wished for in order to bear out his theories of animal magnetism. It is a graphic illustration of what I describe as doctrinal compliance (see Chapter 6).

In the decades that followed, the somnambulists—or hypnotized subjects—of Count Maxíme de Puységur or of the Portuguese Abbé Faria came one faltering step closer to the ancient prototype. They too went into trances, or what Faria called the "lucid sleep," and exhibited a variety of telepathic, clairvoyant, and precognition phenomena. Janet and Gilbert's subject, Léonie, caused a stir in the late 1880s in Paris by her striking clairvoyant exploits. Léonie also had the ability to go into trance when hynotized from a distance of 500 meters or more. The Janet-Gilbert experiments were subsequently repeated and confirmed by Charles Richet and others.

However, the French investigators' interest in the matter soon faltered. By the end of the nineteenth century, the hysteric patients demonstrated by Jean-Martin Charcot were stripped of the last vestiges of the lucid sleep, clairvoyance, precognition, and other paranormal phenomena. Instead, they produced in the hypnotic state all the symptoms that supported Charcot's own pet scientific hypotheses. There were the diverse types of conversion hysteria, including the *attitudes passionelles,* the *arc de cercle,* the *grande hystérie.* There were the convulsions, the paralyses, and the anesthetic spots, or *tâches du diable,* duplicated in the trance. Needless to say, they too may have been largely due to doctrinal compliance.

In the meantime a strange new psychological epidemic made its appearance on the other side of the Atlantic. It all started with the Fox sisters in Hydesville, Wayne County, New York, in 1848. The sisters were reportedly disturbed by mysterious "spirit rappings" in their home. Belief in the extramundane origin of these occurrences soon spread in ever-widening circles throughout the United States, until, in 1854, some 2 million adherents were claimed by the new spiritualistic creed. Its spread was not halted by the self-exposure of one of the Fox sisters. Ultimately the cult was transplanted to Europe by several visiting American mediums, leaving a spate of controversy and reams of pro- and anti-spiritualistic literature in its wake.

It was partly in response to the uncritical, fanciful claims of the spiritualists that F. W. H. Myers, Henry Sidgwick, Edmund Gurney, and other distinguished English scholars joined together to found the (English) Society for Psychical Research (SPR). As already noted, one of the early objectives of the SPR was a more critical approach to trance mediums and trance phenomena in the séance room. The accounts of their investigations in this field fill many volumes of the *Proceedings* published by the SPR since 1882.

What, then, is the connecting link between the witches of a past age and trance mediums of the nineteenth and twentieth centuries? In order to find the connection we have to view the two prototypes within a sufficiently broad, transcultural frame of reference. We know today that the original image of the witch was made up of three ingredients: (1) her personality makeup and individual psychopathology; (2) the motivation, expectations, and personal psychopathology of the inquisitors; and (3) the prevailing precepts of the culture in which they were immersed.

Similar considerations apply to today's trance mediums and their surrounding circumstances. We know that, given a certain degree of neuroticism and a tendency to mental dissociation, the trance state may become a veritable breeding ground for the development of so-called secondary personalities (Prince 1906). It is usually followed by amnesia. In addition, the trance state enables the medium to act out in dramatic fashion her own repressed unconscious tendencies. When permitted to write her own scenario, as it were, a romantically inclined young lady may produce the figure of a chivalrous knight as a secondary personality. This, for instance, was the case with a medium studied by Jung in his doctoral dissertation (1902).

Viewed from the psychoanalytic angle, it is readily understood that the creation by a female medium of a male secondary personality is apt to meet the needs of her own unconscious or "repressed" masculine tendencies. This may be the reason for the frequent appearance of male characters among the dramatis personae of most female trance mediums. Other personality needs that may be met in the trance are latent exhibitionistic or masochistic tendencies, the desire for magic omniscience and omnipotence, the wish for mystic union with the nonself, or, on a more conscious level, doctrinal compliance and the wish to meet the sitter's need for solace and consolation in the case of bereavement. More recently, the psychoanalyst Emilio Servadio (1976) has pointed out that such a purely psychiatric evaluation of the trance state fails to do justice to its broader parapsychological aspects. He stresses the emergence in the trance medium of a "kind of thinking" totally different from her ordinary state of mind. Metaphorically speaking, it amounts to a descent into a "universal, nonconscious, fearless, spaceless thought," with the abandonment of her conscious individualized awareness.

It is needless to say, however, that without closer analytic inquiry, the reasons for the choice of specific trance personalities or controls is difficult to assess. Mrs. Eileen Garrett (Progoff 1964), one of the great mediums of the twentieth century, lost both her parents shortly after her birth. In her case, it may well be the need to conjure up a belated symbiotic relationship with a parent figure that is involved in the development of her psychic powers; Uvani and Abdul Latif, her habitual "spirit controls," may have taken the place of her lost father, a man of Spanish extraction and therefore of a slightly exotic cast. It is interesting to note that female controls are indeed conspicuously absent in Mrs. Garrett's trance repertoire. A certain degree of deprivation of parental affection has also been noted by Mrs. Rosalind Heywood and other gifted sensitives. Gerard Croiset, the Dutch psychic, spent his early childhood years in an orphanage and in a succession of six foster homes.

By contrast, Nina Kulagina, the Russian psychical medium, had undergone all the hardships of the postrevolutionary period in her childhood years and suffered prolonged periods of starvation during the Leningrad siege. The possible part played by early traumatic experiences in Uri Geller and Matthew Manning will be discussed in Chapter 17.

Who plays the part of the inquisitioners in the scenario of modern trance states? Their role has been taken over by the sitters or experimenters in the séance room. It is true that on the face of it, they are barely recognizable in their nineteenth century reincarnation. Their fanatical purpose is forgotten and defunct; the psychic investigators' goals bear no resemblance to those of their spiritual forebears. Their techniques have been harnessed to prove a point worlds apart from the witch burners' fanatical or frankly sadistic motivations. Nevertheless, the sitters too are anxious to prove a point. They want to prove survival after death, immortality of the soul, reincarnation, or some other esoteric doctrine. They use no means of psychological or physical torture, but they too have an axe to grind. They wish and expect that the medium, by her verbal productions and by the whole stagecraft of her behavioral repertoire, will corroborate their beliefs. It is this highly charged complex of wishes and expectations to which the medium responds in terms of doctrinal compliance or the "demand characteristics" of the trance state. The witches of Salem or Loudun incriminated themselves with their confessions because it was confessions which their tormentors wished to obtain. In a similar vein, though fortunately at a safe distance from the torture chambers of the Middle Ages, the spiritualistic medium tries to provide proof positive of the survival of discarnate entities, spirit communicators, or whatnot because this is what the experimenter or sitter wants to obtain. This point is illustrated by the trance manifestations of Mrs. Osborne Leonard in the sessions with the physicist Sir Oliver Lodge (1917), who felt sure that it was his son Raymond, killed in World War I, who communicated with him though Mrs. Leonard's vocal apparatus.

The recent case of Bishop James Pike (1967) is in some respects a rerun of Sir Oliver Lodge's experiences in the séance room. Pike was satisfied that during his sessions with Arthur Ford and other mediums the discarnate spirit of his son Jim, who had committed suicide, had made his appearance. The bereaved father must certainly have obtained some consolation when his departed son, through the voice of the mediums, gave him "loving affirmation" of loyalty from beyond the grave. In both Sir Oliver's and the bishop's case the part played by emotionally charged doctrinal compliance is unmistakable.

On the whole, the sitters recruited from the members of the SPR tried more or less successfully to emancipate themselves from the preconceptions of their spiritualistic predecessors. Yet inevitably their approach was influenced by the cultural artifacts they set out to explore, and their language was inspired by the vocabulary of spiritualism, if not of even older, more primitive traditions. They may not have gone along with the theory that the subject of their study acted as a "medium" for communications from the "spirit world"; they may have questioned the actual production of "discarnate" entities, or direct-voice communications, and the like in the medium's performance; but the very language they were committed to use had a persuasive quality which was difficult to escape.

It was due to the concerted efforts of such distinguished researchers as F. W. H. Myers and G. W. Balfour in England, and William James, James H. Hyslop, and Walter Franklin Prince in this country, working with such celebrated mediums as Mrs. Piper, Mrs. Willett, and Mrs. Leonard, that a solid body of observational data emerged. There is little doubt that over and above the symptoms of mental dissociation and doctrinal compliance, some of the information supplied by these mediums could not have been derived from their own knowledge or "mental content" alone, that is, from their own conscious or unconscious mental residues. A vast amount of time, money, and painstaking research has gone into establishing these facts. They led to the hypothesis of telepathy, clairvoyance, precognition, or retrocognition as the most probable sources of such veridical material. In short, the trance state indeed proved to be a rich breeding ground for psi phenomena. Like a deep mountain lake, it is stocked with several fascinating species of fish: diverse modalities of ESP.

Still, a distinguished minority of investigators was not satisfied with a telepathic explanation. They claimed they could identify the voluminous data supplied by a few trance mediums as bits of information which would not have been derived from any living source. In a complicated jigsaw puzzle of so-called cross-correspondences, in which several sensitives worked independently, the patterns characteristic of one or another deceased person, of his personality profile, seemed to emerge. This, for example, was the case with Frederic Myers supposedly acting as a "communicator" following his death in 1910. Those familiar with the details of his family history, his personal interests, his idiosyncracies, and, above all, his published work and style of writing, were struck with the lifelike quality of the Myers personality which emerged from these investigations. Some were indeed satisfied that the material included clues which could have originated only from a surviving part of Myers' personality. More about this will be found in Chapter 18.

At this point it may suffice to note that there is no compelling need for interpreting the cross-correspondence material in terms of survival. Rather, the material suggests once more the part played by the third ingredient of the trance manifestation reviewed here. The third ingredient is the culture or subculture from which the phenomena originate. The mediums, the sitters, and the circle of friends clustering around them form a closely knit network of communication, verbal and non-verbal, telepathic or otherwise. Their enthusiasm, their expectations, their convictions and interest are sustained by a circular pattern of feedback in which one of the threesome tends to reinforce the operation of the others. As a result, the evidence provided by the three contributing sources—the mediums, the sitters, and their friends—has all the hallmarks of truth. At the same time, those contributing to the common pool of information and experience share the conviction that they, and they alone, are in a position to judge the authenticity of the material. Anthropologists have pointed out that a similar, virtually foolproof system of consensually validated beliefs held by a tribal group is responsible for the status of the shaman or medicine man in their respective societies. Lévi-Strauss (1966) went so far as to ascribe some of the therapeutic results of psychoanalysis and other schools of psychotherapy to the concatenation of similar factors.

Formal characteristics of this order are not, however, the only link between the witch and the trance medium. The most obvious feature common to the two is the diverse manifestations of trance and mental dissociation: the production of secondary personalities and states of apparent possession, of specific symptoms of conversion hysteria, of what Renaissance physicians called melancholia or what the witch hunters of Salem dubbed the suffocating mother.

Thus, viewed in the perspective of modern clinical psychiatry, there is an unbroken line of continuity from the fits and convulsions of the nuns of Loudun or Louviers, the witches of Salem, Mesmer's somnambulists, and Charcot's hysterics to some of the more dramatic manifestations of the mediumistic trance.

The trance itself has been a recurrent feature in the vast literature of witchcraft and sorcery all over the world and in all historical periods. It is found in Egypt and the Far East, as well as in the Sibyls and Pythias of Greco-Roman antiquity; it was among the well-nigh obligatory credentials of the Hebrew prophets from Amos and Hosea to Jeremiah and Isaiah. It is part of the folklore of most preliterate peoples from the voodoo priests and priestesses of Haiti and other witch societies of the West Indies to the medicine men and shamans of South America, Siberia, and Central Africa. The religious raptures and ecstacies or some other altered states of consciousness, sometimes amounting to trance, are among the characteristics of many Catholic mystics and saints. Some of them, including St. Theresa of Avila and Joan of Arc, seem often to have teetered on the borderline between witchcraft and saintliness.

In clinical parlance, such trance manifestations have been described in terms of a regression to primitive ego states, with an attending loss of identity and a tendency to a merging of the self with the nonself, at times amounting to a sense of a symbiotic unity with the divinity or the universe at large. We shall see in Part Three that possession by devils, demons, or poltergeists is part of the same continuum. It merges imperceptibly with Plato's divine madness and with the picture of schizophrenic reactions on the frankly pathological side of the continuum.

All these variations on the ancient prototype of the witch bring us once more to the question: What is the part played by psi phenomena on both the normal and the pathological end of the scale? More specifically: What is the evidence of such incidents supposedly embedded in the trance manifestations? I have noted that in the witches of a past era the reality of psi phenomena is no longer amenable to verification. But I also stated that in their latter-day reincarnations the evidence can no longer be dismissed. Such high-class mediums as Mrs. Piper, Mrs. Osborn Leonard, Mrs. Willet, or Mrs. Eileen Garrett produced a wealth of veridical manifestations. They were studied by such distinguished sitters as Sir Oliver Lodge, the earl of Balfour, William James, Franklin M. Prince, William MacDougall, J. B. Rhine, and many others. Owing to their social position, their personal integrity, and the academic standing of their sponsors, they have been described as the aristocracy among the mediums of the late nineteenth and mid-twentieth century. Their club may be joined by such noted sensitives as Rosalind Heywood, Joan Grant or Douglas Johnson in England, or Ingo Swann in this country. At the same time most (though not all) of them show a conspicuous absence of overt psychopathology and readiness to subject themselves to the rigors of scientific investigation. This is certainly a far cry—or agonized scream—from the downtrodden and tortured women dragged before the ecclesiastical courts of the Middle Ages and the Renaissance—from the crazed nuns of Loudun, the hysterical children of Salem, or even the gypsy fortune tellers or itinerant soothsayers of the nineteenth century.

Yet the links with a redoubtable past are still discernible in Eusapia Palladino, the Italian peasant woman whose hysterical antics, combined with cheating and occasionally striking exploits as a physical medium, have stirred considerable controversy (Carrington 1909), or in the Schneider brothers from Braunau (the birthplace of Adolf Hitler, their contemporary and fellow "sensitive"). Their record of mediumistic performances was likewise marred by stories of cheating and exposure of fraud.

The perplexing story of Ted Serios and his exploits in "psychic" photography is still sub judice. He too has a history of marked personal pathology and emotional instability. Yet Jule Eisenbud's extensive investigations (1967), coupled with the grudging endorsement by a number of well-qualified witnesses, make his *"thoughtography"* one of the major cases of physical phenomena in our time.

The Russian housewife Nina Kulagina is yet another variation on the ancient theme. Her performances as a physical medium are among the best in the history of psychical research. But she too was accused of fraud by Soviet authorities. The charge was subsequently changed into one of trivial black market activities. She was later exonerated on both counts but still left with the stigma of a witch, taken right out of a Russian fairy tale. Similar considerations apply to Uri Geller, her Israeli counterpart.

On the other end of the scale are the countless small-time mediums, amateur and professional, with doubtful credentials. Many are psychiatric borderline cases, holding strong personal convictions or clinging to pathetic delusions of grandeur. They belong to the lunatic fringe of our society. Their ranks include assorted cranks, eccentrics, and self-styled witches and warlocks, claiming supernatural powers, embroidered upon by gleanings from the occult lore of their own backgrounds or loaned from diverse foreign cultures and historic periods with which they happen to be acquainted. Some may merely strike a bizarre pose in order to call attention to alleged gifts of divination or unorthodox healing. Others are harmless camp-followers of a recent version of the medieval children's crusade: the hippies, flower children, or street people on their tracks to rock and roll festivals at Haight-Ashbury or Woodstock. Others are full-fledged schizophrenics, aided by the use of diverse psychedelic drugs. A small minority like the Manson "tribe" are given to frankly destructive, antisocial behavior. In another age they were the ones most likely to be charged with witchcraft and earmarked for death at the stake. Pathetic cases of this order are perhaps little more than cultural throwbacks, atavistic remnants left over from the heydays of the ancient or medieval witch craze.

Others, again, merely engage in uninhibited acting out, reminiscent of the tarantula dancers or of the epidemics of *chorea lasciva* described by Paracelsus in the Renaissance. Another variant in our time, the "gangbang," wife swapping, and organized group sex, emulates the witches' Sabbath or the furtive ceremonials of the Black Mass, suitably adapted, sublimated and transferred from the Brocken in the Harz Mountains to the Big Sur in California or to the *dolce vita* in the drawing rooms of Rome, Peyton Place—or Great Neck, Long Island.

Here, again, the combination of the loosening of social inhibitions and the growing preoccupation with the occult does not seem to be coincidental. It is a corollary of what amounts to recurrent crises in the self-regulation of Western society which seeks to keep the lid down on the pressures arising from repression of the sexually as well as the culturally repressed: from both the Dionysian and the demoniacal *Perils of the Soul*. The much-discussed "occult explosion" of our time is in effect nothing but a massive breakthrough of the culturally repressed into modern man's conscious awareness or overt behavior in a period of severe social stress.

There is one more version of the ancient prototype of the witch: the much-maligned "schizophrenogenic" mother of our time. We shall see that charging her with the sole responsibility for the mental disorder of her offspring is, except on rare occasions, grossly unfair and unjustified. But so were the charges leveled against her medieval forerunners. Nevertheless, the old suspicions and misgivings linger on. In the chapter that follows, we shall examine her case under the less prejudicial heading of the neurotic mother.

4

The Neurotic Mother:

Witch of Our Time?

Freudian psychoanalysis has not been gentle in its scrutiny of the human family. It has cast doubt on the angelic innocence of the child; it has made sibling rivalry a household word in the English language; it has pointed an accusing finger on the tightly controlled hostile impulses of the stalwart Victorian paterfamilias and of the male species in general. In the past decades, it has even proceeded to tarnish the picture of the hitherto untouchable idealized mother.

Recent psychoanalytic literature is replete with references to the bad, frustrating mother figure, charging her with bossiness, possessiveness, and a wholly nondenominational version of Momism, long before Portnoy's agonized "Complaints" about the Jewish mother. The image of the Madonna versus the prostitute has become a literary cliché since Weininger's *Sex and Character* (1903); and a recent headline in a New York newspaper asking "Is Motherhood Holy?" comes to the conclusion "Not any more."

This is certainly quite a change from the image of the bountiful, life-sustaining, omnipotent mother of the symbiotic stage. But the fact is that there are built-in limitations even to the best mother's capacity of ministering to her baby's needs. She seems to vanish in thin air when he needs her most. She may withhold his bottle or her breast when he is frantic from hunger. She may be insensitive to his desire for warmth, for body contact—or she may offer it to him when he wants no part of it.

This is how the picture of the "bad" versus the "good" mother was added to psychoanalytic nomenclature. A variation on the Freudian theme is Jung's splitting of the mother figure into two contrasting or complementary archetypes of the great, all-knowing, nurturing mother and her terrible, devouring counterpart, the witch. Another variation was offered by Melanie Klein (1948). She called attention to mother's breast as the source of sweet, nurturing milk as well as of bitter, poisonous milk, striking terror and engendering rage, depression, or ideas of persecution in the infant's mind. Anna Freud has considerably toned down such extreme formulations, but she too found that all the love and devotion a mother can bestow on her infant does not prevent him from experiencing her at times as a bad, rejecting, or frustrating parent (1966). Many child psychiatrists—and perhaps some babies as well—tend to agree with this position.

However, the "Bad Mother" does not exist merely in the infant's psychoanalytically reconstructed imagination. The potentially destructive impact of a mentally disturbed parent on the child's personality development has been recorded in countless psychiatric case histories. Children who tend to act out their respective mothers' repressed hostile, aggressive, or otherwise antisocial impulses were mentioned in an earlier chapter. More often than not, they may thus be groomed for the career of delinquency. On the other hand, an overly controlling, possessive mother may seek to act vicariously on behalf of her offspring. In so doing, she may stifle his initiative and his ability to take action and stunt his personality growth. There is a general consensus that a mother may be overprotective in order to cover up her own unconscious resentment, for example, against an unwanted offspring. Her opposite number is the openly destructive, "castrating" mother who stifles the masculinity of her son and may steer him toward an homosexual outcome. In other cases, the mother's inconsistent, "double binding" behavior—aggravated by a weak, ineffectual father—may be conducive to serious mental illness in the child. This is what psychoanalysts have described as the "schizophrenogenic mother."

John Rosen expressed such views in even sharper terms: "A schizophrenic is always one who is reared by a woman who suffers from perversion of the maternal instinct" (1962). Concurring with the idea of Melanie Klein, he equates the bad mother with the poisonous breast and adds: " . . . poisoning comes from the mother who is not gifted with the divine attunement that makes her understand what the baby is crying for."

More recently the psychoanalyst J. C. Rheingold argued that a wide variety of psychotic reactions, including nightmares and the fear of death, are due to the impact of "maternal destructiveness" upon the child (1967,

p. 106). The infant, he stated, has an "astonishing ability to detect maternal attitudes affecting its survival." It is an ability, apparently provided by instinct, which "seems to be of maximal efficiency during infancy and then undergoes progressive extinction, either naturally or as the result of repression."

The child's sensitivity to its mother's unconscious or repressed mental content is illustrated by many observations in the psychotherapeutic situation. In one of my cases, Sarah, age seven, the daughter of an obsessive-compulsive patient, had the following dream: "Mother was a bear. She came in through the window and wanted to kill me." The fact is that the patient harbored a great deal of repressed hostility against her daughter. It was camouflaged by her show of excessive concern and overprotectiveness toward her.

A dream reported to Jung by a psychotic woman who had kept her children tied to her "with unusual devotion" deals with the same theme: "The dreamer saw herself in her dreams as an animal, especially a wolf or a pig, and acted accordingly. This is how she became a symbol of the devouring mother" (1959).

In one of Rheingold's (1967) cases, it was observed that the newborn child of a young mother reacted differently to her than to a practical nurse. "Whenever the latter handled the baby, it showed no signs of distress, but whenever the mother picked her up, it immediately stiffened, held its breath and then cried." The mother returned three weeks postpartum from the hospital and reported the following dream: "I see a beautiful girl of sixteen standing in the sunlight. The girl is my daughter. I am lurking in the shadow. Suddenly I change into a wild beast and leap at the girl's throat and tear it open with my teeth."

The patient had recurrent dreams featuring similar atrocities. Still, except for her dreams, she would have been completely unaware of her sadistic impulses. Nevertheless, "the threat was communicated to the infant, who reacted to it with terror" (1967, p. 107).

Dreams featuring corresponding fears and phobias are a familiar motif in the case histories of patients, both male and female, reared by schizophrenic mothers. From early childhood they are plagued by nightmares in which they are threatened, pursued, and eaten up by wild beasts which can easily be recognized as the evil, devouring mother figure. It is only fair to note, however, that the evil, poisonous mother is not the only source of the child's lingering fears of a destructive parent. This observation is borne out by the recurrent accounts of ogres, bogeymen, and man-eaters in dreams and fairy tales, in virtually all cultures and all ages.

Nevertheless, a census of nightmares and anxiety dreams in both children and adults is likely to point to the bad, threatening "witch-mother" as the principal culprit.

The same is true for myths which have rightly been described as products of the collective daydreams of peoples. There is Kali, the Black One, the cannibal goddess of Hindu mythology, who lives on the blood of her children. There is the Egyptian goddess Isis, the One with the Myriad Names, the protector of her son Horus, but also known as the One Who "Washes in Your Blood, Bathes in Your Gore." There is Lilith, the queen of demons, the consort of Satan-Samael who tried to kill all newborn children, the symbol of sexual lust and sexual temptation. There is Aisha Qadisha, the she-demon of northern Morocco, who causes illness and possession in her victims, and there is Lamia, the female vampire of Greek antiquity, the kidnapper and killer of newborn babes.

All these mythological figures can easily be recognized as the counterparts of the medieval and Renaissance witch or the Hansel and Gretel witch of contemporary fairly tales—if not of the allegedly "schizophrenogenic" mother of modern clinical psychiatry.

Who is the adult counterpart of the omnipotent and omniscient mother of the early infantile stage, or for that matter, the clinical successor of the evil, maleficent witch-mothers of the adolescent girls of Salem? She appeared in my office in person after making a telephone call for an appointment under an assumed name. Mrs. G. was a short, stocky, red-faced woman, tense and controlling during our one-sided interview, giving me little chance to put in a word edgewise. She did not come to see me as a patient, she stated. She came to see me about her son, Allen, age twenty-nine. When going over the contents of his pockets she found my bill indicating that he had been under my care for several months. She was greatly concerned about this discovery. He had always been a sickly child and it was she who nursed him back to health. There was nothing wrong with him mentally. She was dead-set against psychiatric treatment. It would leave a stigma on him for the rest of his life, jeopardizing his career and his chances to find a decent wife. In fact, the only trouble with him was that he refused to go out with any nice girl she tried to introduce to him. She ended with a tearful plea to release Allen from my clutches and with the promise that she would do everything in her power for her only child. She also asked me not to mention to him that she had come to see me about him.

Allen's description of his mother fit the picture presented in our interview. He described her as a driving, compulsive woman of fifty-two, domineering and emasculating with her husband, oversolicitous and over-protective with her son. Allen had been suffering from allergies and bronchial asthma from the age of five. She wheeled him around in a wheel-chair until the age of eight. She kept him away from the company of other children lest he be hurt by bigger boys. She took him on a round of vari-ous hospitals and child specialists to do something about his asthma; she saw to it that his tonsils were taken out and that he was fitted with braces and eyeglasses. She kept him on special diets and constantly watched his bowel movements and weight. Until he was sixteen she personally super-vised his bathing, soaping and massaging him in the shower.

Allen described his father as a "nonentity." Once, when Mr. G. was taken ill, his mother cautioned Allen: "Don't show him any sympathy—he'll only be the worse for it!" It was the mother who up to his college years gave Allen his weekly allowance, who made him visit his maternal grandparents, uncles, and aunts, and who kept him away from relatives on his father's side. When Allen started to go out on dates, his mother warned him of the danger of venereal disease or of getting "hooked" by a girl friend if he showed too much interest in her. At the age of twenty-one, Allen became halfheartedly involved with a college girl of his own age. To his dismay he found that he was impotent. After two more un-successful attempts with younger girls, he finally started an affair with a woman ten years his senior who seemingly liked to play the role of the aggressor and did not mind his sexual inadequacies.

His analysis revealed that he had never been able to accept the mascu-line role. His sexual fantasies involved women lying on top of him. He would be prostrate, with legs spread apart; the woman would insert a syringe or an enema tube in his rectum, the way his mother used to do in his childhood. On most of these occasions he would be helpless, tied up with ropes or strapped to a bed while phallic objects would be passed along on a conveyor belt and inserted in his body openings, masturbating him in a mechanical manner. In all these fantasies the patient himself played the feminine role or was watching a woman undergoing such tortures while he put himself in her place. Masturbatory acts connected with such fantasies were usually of an anal nature and often involved the use of a variety of bizarre bodily postures and mechanical contrivances.

He remembered that his mother made no secret to him of her wish that he had been a girl. He was also aware of her consistent attempts to tie him as closely as possible to her person and to remove him from what-ever influence his father might try to exert on him. Allen, in turn, re-mained dependent on his mother up to his college years. Daily exchanges of letters and frequent telephone calls saw to it that his temporary absence from home did not sever the symbiotic bonds between mother and son. This was a pattern which continued until the beginning of his treatment.

Allen's decision to seek therapy was the first major step he had ever taken without consulting his mother. It was forced on him by his growing uneasiness and anxiety in relation to a "certain type" of man. One of them was Mr. X, a colleague in his office who insisted on "making friends" with him, inviting him for a drink in a bar or in his apartment. Also, Mr. X liked to pat him on the back, to put his arm around him, or to stare at him in a provocative manner. It was gradually dawning on Allen that Mr. X was in effect a homosexual whose apparent friendly interest in him was due to ulterior motives. Yet despite Allen's studied reserve, he was unable to shake off the persistent Mr. X. His colleague, he said, "was mother all over again." Finally Allen had to change his job in order to escape Mr. X's attentions.

Mr. X was not, however, the only person whose presence had become increasingly threatening to the patient. Occasional acquaintances, men traveling with him in the subway or bus, gave him the same anxiety. Nor were his pursuers confined to the male sex. He complained that "middle-aged ladies" frequently accosted him in bars, drew him into conversation, tried to get him to dance with them, or openly propositioned him. Or else he felt that they were watching his movements wherever he was, whatever he was doing. He remembered that as a child his mother had given him the same feeling. He believed a camera operated by her was trained on him, although he knew quite well that this could not have been possible. His attitude toward me was beset by similar fears. He wondered whether the therapeutic sessions were being recorded by concealed cameras or tape recorders; he was afraid that he might be drawn into a relationship of dependence and control similar to that which had existed between him and his mother.

Allen's fear of women was expressed in many of his dreams. In one dream he had to jump from a high precipice into a big sprawling factory building with a shaft in the middle. He woke up in terror. Another dream showed clearly his feminine identification. He found himself traveling in the subway with a girl about his own age and stature. There were explosions all around him. He took the girl by the hand and tried to escape with her. His chief concern was the safety of the girl—representing his own feminine self.

What, then, is the relevance of Allen's case history to our issue? Viewed in the light of the preceding discussion it shows that, even long past the symbiotic stage, the supposedly omnipotent and omniscient mother does not necessarily lose her grip over her offspring. In Allen's case, there is indeed a direct linear connection between his early conditioning by Mrs. G. and the development of his delusional trend in which he felt threatened and pursued by sexually aggressive women—or by a man who, in Allan's words, appeared to be "like mother all over again."

It is this all-powerful, all-knowing, "phallic" woman, the wielder of the enema tube—or of the broomstick of a bygone age—who is the latter-day reincarnation of the medieval or Renaissance witch. It is she who literally invaded his personality, who established herself in his ego as a "maternal introject," who robbed him of his manhood, his spontaneity, and his sexual identity. This is why she became the central figure of his paranoid projections, the originator of his delusional trend. Yet her live performance in my office indicates that Allen's picture of his overpowering symbiotic mother was not quite unrealistic after all. It was based upon his actual, though delusionally distorted, perception of a slice of psychic reality conveyed to him on several levels of experience—conceivably including the psi level. It was the psychic reality of the archetypal witch-mother and her continued stranglehold over him. More about that will have to be said in Chapter 11.

The following clinical vignettes throw light upon yet another facet of a warped mother-child relationship. They are closely related to the examples of youngsters acting out their respective parents' repressed anti-social neurotic tendencies discussed in Chapter 2.

One of the cases is little Dick C. whose compulsive questioning, "Is my daddy my real daddy?" has spelled out the closely guarded secret of his illegitimate birth (see Chapter 2). Caught in the crossfire of his parents' marital conflict, Dick acted out his mother's destructive impulses toward her husband. Yet analysis showed that he did more than that. Mrs. C., frustrated in her marriage, tried to groom him to become a miniature husband and substitute lover to her. Analytically speaking, she encouraged the development of a full-fledged Oedipal complex. Dick had been toilet trained at twelve to fifteen months. Yet at age three and a half he started to wet his bed again.

Needless to say, bedwetting, like most neurotic symptoms, is over-determined. But in the present context it is tempting to conjecture that Dick's bedwetting developed in response to the telepathic promptings of Mrs. C., demanding a level of performance years ahead of his biological stage of development. Dick did his best to oblige—and wet the bed. Tactful interpretation to Mrs. C. of this state of affairs had a palliative effect on Dick's enuresis.

Mrs. M.'s marital problem and her relationship to her son Oliver, two years younger than his sister Doris, was much the same as Mrs. C.'s. Oliver was *her* boy, the apple of her eye, while Doris had always been closer to her father. Mr. M. was a passive, obsessive-compulsive type of personality who had failed to live up to his wife's expectations, sexual and otherwise. Here, too, little Oliver tried to meet his mother's needs on a level of performance which was far beyond his reach. Unable to function as yet on the genital level, he wet the bed. Like little Dick, he did so till he reached puberty.

Mrs. J.'s and her son Danny's problem is another case in point. Mrs. J. had recently divorced her husband. He was a playboy, a latent homosexual, "sponging" on his wife, and at best an absentee father. Mrs. J. lavished all her love and devotion on Danny, aged four. He slept in her bed, watched her dress and undress, shared her bathrom and shower. In turn, he soon developed marked sexual interest in his mother. Visibly intrigued, she reported that he had erections when she was handling him.

Danny had been toilet trained at one and a half years. But like his colleagues Dick and Oliver, he too became hopelessly enuretic by night and a spiteful wetter of his pants by day.

The sexual origin of Danny's enuresis is even more marked than in the two preceding cases. He seems to respond to maternal seduction with the closest approximation of genital acting out available to a child his age. Indeed, Mrs. J.'s sexual frustrations and her seductiveness are so obvious that invoking a psi factor in the clinical picture is perhaps unnecessary. But it is the concerted evidence of cases of this order which is suggestive of such involvement. They are in good keeping with the observations of Johnson and Szurek (1952) and others in which children were acting out parental complexes of a different order.

This is not the place to go into the broader analytic and therapeutic implications of these examples. Nor is it possible to attribute a more than hypothetical role to the psi factor in their psychodynamics. The findings of similar family constellations would presumably lend added support to such an assumption. Beyond that, the clinical vignettes reviewed here are apt to add to the long list of grievances society has been in the habit of placing at the doorstep of the neurotic (or purportedly schizophrenogenic) mother. We know today that a variety of neurotic as well as psychotic disorders are due to a wide range of intrapsychic, interpersonal, and environmental influences. In schizophrenic reactions in particular, genetic as well as biochemical factors play an important part.

Still, the image of the bad mother, raised to the status of a witch, has always been a convenient scapegoat to hold responsible for all the ills that beset the disenchanted or alienated youths—and grown-ups—in troubled times. We shall see that smoldering filial resentment has been one of the major contributing factors to some of the more bizarre features of the Salem trials. We have also seen how, viewed in the historic perspective, the witch-mother gradually receded into the background, to be replaced by Mesmer's or de Puységur's somnambulists and then by the trance mediums of the nineteenth and twentieth centuries.

Table 1 shows how in the process she lost the nefarious, magical qualities of the original prototype. Stripped of the aura of both malignancy and martyrdom, her latest reincarnation is barely recognizable for what it stands for. Nothing is left of her erstwhile diabolic aspects and

TABLE 1
Metamorphosis of Witches

Types	Witches	Trance Mediums	"Schizophreno-genic" mothers and fathers
Era	Antiquity, Middle Ages, Renaissance, up to 18th century	18th–20th century	Contemporary
Sex	Female:male approx. 10:1	Female:male approx. 10:1	Female:male approx. 10:1
Frequency distribution, Epidemiology	Major epidemics or endemics	Clustering in certain periods	Isolated or clusters of clinical observations
Psychodynamics and clinical aspects	Hysteric or psychotic acting out, projection, doctrinal compliance	Mental dissociation, conversion symptoms, doctrinal compliance	Obsessive-compulsive, phobic personality, schizophrenic, character disorders
Trance	Occasional	Usual	No trance
Customary value judgment	Evil, except "white" witch: Sibyls and Pythias	Neutral or idealized	Evil or sick
Psi factor involved	Suggestive	Strongly suggestive or confirmed	Suggestive but controversial

only residues of social disapprobation or blame for untoward influences upon her offspring or spouse linger on.

Yet whatever be the clinical label attached to her, she can still be seen sitting wearily in the waiting rooms of today's child-guidance clinics, anxious to hear the verdict which would pronounce her guilty or innocent in the eyes of the world—and before her own conscience.

Part Two

PSYCHODYNAMICS

> If the phenomenon of telepathy is only an activity of the unconscious mind, then no fresh problem lies before us. The laws of unconscious mental life may then be taken for granted as applying to telepathy.
>
> Freud, 1922

5

Telepathy in the Psychoanalytic

Situation: Variations on

the Symbiotic Theme

THE doctor-patient relationship, and in particular the psychotherapeutic situation, is in many ways a faithful replica of the early symbiotic relationship between parent and child. This is a point on which most schools of psychotherapy tend to agree. The biological facts of life and cultural exigencies cast both therapist and patient into such a derivative role, whether they are aware of it or not. Virtually all forms of therapeutic intervention, from faith healing and acupuncture to surgery or X-ray therapy, from counseling to psychoanalysis, conform to this pattern. Even the novelty of the existential encounter cannot ignore the legacy of its early infantile prototype.

Under such circumstances the occurrence of telepathy and related phenomena can only be expected. This is borne out by a vast number of observations recorded in the psychoanalytic literature in the past decades and need not be reviewed in the present context (see Devereux 1953; Ehrenwald 1948, 1954; Eisenbud, 1946-1970*a*; N. Fodor 1947; and Servadio 1953 in: Devereux; also Ullman 1975).

But while at the early symbiotic stage telepathy is usually confined to the apparent transmission of vague, ill-defined protomessages with a paucity of cognitive content, incidents at a later stage—for example, in the psychoanalytic situation—are more sharply defined and of a more complex nature. In the ideal case, they are "tagged" with what I have described as specific tracer elements; they carry specific "bits" of information which are amenable to analytic scrutiny and verification.

Adequate documentation and verification of the data has in fact long been the primary concern of early psychoanalytic contributions to the problem—including my own (1954). They focused on occasional "striking" cases such as a telepathic dream containing a unique item in its manifest content whose correspondence with a similar, usually emotionally charged item in the therapist's mind could not reasonably be attributed to chance alone. In most instances, however, it was the combination of specific distinctive features contained in both dream and reality upon which the claim of a telepathic correspondence could be based.

The following is a typical example which was published elsewhere in more detail (1954). Ruth, an unattached patient of mine, aged thirty-eight, produced a drawing of her "dream house," which bore a striking resemblance to the layout of a new apartment into which I and my family had just moved. The resemblance was borne out by comparing her sketch with an architect's blueprint of the layout of my new home. The telepathic interpretation of her dream was based on this well-documented correspondence. At the same time analysis indicated that the dreamer wished to move with the therapist into his apartment and to be accepted as a member of his family. Thus, in this dream, the reenactment and duplication in the transference relationship of the early symbiotic model is unmistakable.

The next observation is another variation on the symbiotic theme. Mrs. D., age thirty, is a professional woman with an obsessive-compulsive trend and a marked ambivalent attachment to her domineering father. In her third year of analysis she had made considerable progress and was ready for termination. On September 29, 1972, she reported the following dream: "I was back at school and had to recite a poem. But I had lost the page—or I could not remember it. Also, the poem was not finished; I tried to figure out the last verse." Preceding this dream fragment, she saw herself on a vacation trip with her boss who had, in the past, been the object of her guilt-laden Oedipal fantasies, but with whom she had since developed a more realistic working relationship.

There was nothing in her associations to account for the second fragment. She felt it was quite uncongenial to her since she never had a knack for poetry. Where, then, did the reading of poetry in the dream come from?

As it happened, it had originated from me. On September 28, 1972, that is on the night her dream occurred, I attended the annual dinner meeting of the Schilder Society in New York. The members were invited to report some highlights of their travel experiences during the summer. I chose instead to treat my colleagues to my translation of a humorous poem by the German poet Christian Morgenstern. I had translated its first two verses a few years before, had lost the draft, and tried hard to reconstruct it from memory. Worse still, the lost verse had never come off to my satisfaction and I spent half the night preceding the banquet trying to finish the poem.

On Thursday night it was ready for my recital and it was well received by my colleagues for its brevity, if not for other reasons. Comparing Mrs. D.'s dream with what happened on my side of the picture, the correspondence of five features in reality and dream is unmistakable:

1. The dreamer is reciting a poem—as I did.
2. She is at a loss to find the text—as I was.
3. The last part or verse of the poem is somehow missing—as was the case with my own script.
4. She manages to produce the missing lines—and so did I.
5. There is a clear temporal coincidence between dream and real event.

There are thus five distinctive features supporting the telepathic interpretation of the dream. The "mandatory" recital of the dream constitutes what I described as a specific telepathic tracer effect. It comes close to the criterion of *uniqueness* which can be found in the manifest content of a few "striking" dreams reported in the psychoanalytic literature. The multiplicity of distinctive features common to both dream and reality can be described as the second criterion. The third criterion upon which the telepathic reading of such observations can be based is less apparent. It can be described as the criterion of *psychological,* as opposed to *statistical,* significance, used in the natural sciences and in experimental parapsychology. It is based on the meaningful nature of the telepathic reading of the dream fragment under review.

Clearly, its telepathic interpretation indicates that in this case the dreamer tries to take the analyst's place. She reaches out for the missing part of the poem, and her ultimate success in retrieving it dramatizes her identification with the therapist as the once hated—and secretly beloved —father figure. At the same time it lifts her positive transference on her therapist—that is, her identification with him—to the level of artistic sublimation, stripped of the more sensuous aspects of her earlier neurotic fantasies.

Another fringe benefit of the telepathic interpretation derives from the fact that it is wholly consistent with the thinly veiled Oedipal significance of the first dream fragment in which she allows herself to go on a trip with another father surrogate. It is through introducing the telepathic interpretation that we can fill a gap in the dynamic understanding of the dream. Like the missing piece of a jigsaw puzzle, it suddenly falls into place: it is "psychologically significant." To this we may add the gain in our clinical understanding of the progress made by the dreamer in the course of the preceding years of analytic treatment. It shows her readiness to be on her own, while at the same time emulating some of her therapist's personal interests, values, and preoccupations.

I submit that in the end it is the criterion of *psychological significance* which tips the scale in favor of a telepathic reading of cases of this order. It should be noted, however, that as a general rule, one criterion alone does not suffice to carry conviction. This is true even for forced-choice experiments of the ESP type. Despite their attending criterion of statistical significance—or what amounts to clear-cut "tracer effects"—they do not seem to "make sense." They are not, in themselves, psychologically significant. On the other hand, the criterion of psychological significance alone may likewise be misleading. In the extreme case its "meaningful" nature may turn out to be a rationalization of ideas of reference or a delusion in disguise.

What is the therapist's contribution to such incidents? I noticed that one of the ingredients is an emotionally charged belief in, or preoccupation with, telepathy itself. Another contributing factor is the presence of thoughts, preoccupations, or conflicts, complementary to or dovetailing and interlacing with those of the patient. It may be aided by the activation or reactivation of the therapist's parental impulses, of his motivations to help, meeting halfway, as it were, the patient's corresponding hopes and expectations to be helped by a benevolent parent figure.

Such attitudes may lead to what has been described as the therapist's regression in the service of treatment, matching the patient's corresponding tendency to regression to the symbiotic stage. In other cases, it is the therapist's repressed or ill-concealed anxieties, resentments, or other manifestations of countertransference which may be picked up by the patient in a telepathic way. If so, it is needless to say that they may have an adverse effect upon the outcome of the treatment.

There is another aspect of the therapist's potential telepathic involvement in the treatment situation which should be mentioned in this context: his own sensitivity to occasional extrasensory clues emanating from the patient. The case histories in my files are studded with a number of observations of this kind recorded in recent years. Unfortunately, even a sketchy account of a single, seemingly trivial incident requires a lengthy account of the patient's history, of the transference relationship and its surrounding circumstances, and of some personal details on my side of the picture.

The following is an observation in which telepathy between myself and a patient was suggested by a clear-cut tracer effect. Mr. H. is a bachelor of forty-three, a college graduate who was referred to me for consultation on the advice of Dr. Gardner Murphy, then president of the American Society for Psychical Research. The patient presented the picture of a full-fledged paranoid schizophrenia. He complained that he was under the influence of evil spirits, that he was persecuted by German barons and dukes; he was hearing voices and had developed an elaborate system of delusions which he interpreted in terms of ESP. In the course of our first interview (the only one I had with the patient) I tried to point out to him the delusional nature of his experiences. "Your German barons and dukes, and even your Barbara Hutton," I stated, "are just split-off parts of your own personality." The patient was visibly taken aback by my remark: "How do you know that Barbara Hutton is among them? Did she tell you?" The fact is that he had not, in the preceding half hour, mentioned the heiress's name to me. Nor was she referred to in a covering letter sent to me by his previous psychiatrist. Thus, my mentioning her name was either "sheer coincidence"—or it was determined by the fact that Barbara happened to be my daughter's name. Or else, one may argue, my empathy with Mr. H. went so far as to reflect—or even try to improve upon—his delusional ideas: "Yes, it is possible to pick up telepathically another person's thoughts—even *I* can do it for you." It should also be noted that it was Dr. Murphy who had suggested that Mr. H. should be referred to me in the first place. The possibility of a genuine element of ESP being involved in his case may therefore well have entered my mind at the beginning of the interview.

The following incident lacks comparable criteria of specificity or uniqueness, but its psychodynamics is more meaningful and transparent. Fred L., a married man of forty-nine, was involved in a "telepathic triangle" with another of my patients during a first period of treatment in 1952. The incident is described in some detail in my book *New Dimensions of Deep Analysis* (1954) under the heading "When the Therapist Has a Dream." In 1968, Fred returned for a second period of treatment. He was now working as a furrier in his aunt's firm. In one of his sessions he talked at great length about his aunt reproving him for having caused some minor damage to sable skins he had prepared for a customer. Fred did not bring to an end his guilt-laden recital of the incident that day, and I opened the next session by noting that he obviously felt unduly guilty about mis-treating the skins because they actually stood for women and "women's skins"; they symbolized his sadistic-destructive impulses against them. "You feel guilty about the sable skins because deep down it is a woman's skin which you want to hurt." Thereupon the patient, visibly taken aback by my remark, reported the following dream he had the night before: "I hit Selma [the firm's telephone operator]. She complained of headaches. She said I have damaged her scalp [*sic!*]. Her hair was falling out at places. I got scared she'll sue me. Her scalp will look like a [damaged] genital area."

So much for the dream. Fred said that in reality he had gotten angry with Selma for "messing up" his telephone messages. "Women are messy," he added by way of an afterthought.

The deeper analytic implications of this dream need not be discussed here. The crucial point is that my opening remarks in the last session had *preceded* his account of the dream and in fact anticipated its analytic interpretation.

The following incident illustrates the same point. Mrs. S., age forty-two, is a stabilized schizophrenic who hoards fantastic amounts of rubbish such as old newspapers, cardboard boxes, handbags, and bedroom slip-pers. Unable to part with them, they clutter up her apartment and en-croach on her and her husband's living space. Analysis revealed that they were fetish objects, serving as collective representations of her symbiotic mother who had died two years earlier. In one of our sessions, talking in a jocular vein, I suggested a compromise: "Get your thirty pairs of bed-room slippers, the newspapers, handbags, etc., into a few big cartons, rent space in a warehouse and have them 'buried' there. It is like putting them in a coffin and paying for a cemetery lot." Thereupon the patient reported the following dream: "Mother is dead, but she is still around. Then all of a sudden, she makes a final speech; tells me she is irretrievably dead. Her voice breaks telling me that, and I get terribly upset."

To be sure, in the absence of unequivocal tracer elements, the tele-pathic nature of most incidents of this order is debatable. It may also be argued that in view of the therapist's close familiarity with his patients and their problems, he might well have been able to predict their dreams anyway. It may be stated, furthermore, that the patients' doctrinal compli-ance made them prone to produce just the type of dreams their therapist had been expecting at that particular juncture. Another alternative is that the incidents are in effect evidence of the therapist's doctrinal compliance with his patient—that is, of the familiar process operating from patient to therapist instead of the other way around. In either case it is not a presumed unidirectional telepathic incident which is relevant in the present context, but the pattern of circular feedback between therapist and patient, telepathic or otherwise. In this respect, the incidents described are nearly perfect duplications in the treatment situation of a similar circular pattern operating between mother and child in the early symbiotic stage.

In summary, the evidence derived from both situations suggests that in the symbiotic phase as well as in the therapeutic setting several levels of communication come into play. They range from subliminal sensory clues, empathy, and "enkinesis" (Ehrenwald 1954), to something like a telepathic feedback loop operating in two directions. It may be facilitated by the child's identification with his parent and his ready response to parental promptings, by the patient's doctrinal compliance with his therapist, and by the therapists's "intuitive" appraisal of his patient's personality and of the total dynamic situation at the time the incident occurs.

In the last analysis, it is the therapist's idiosyncratic use of "hunches" and "intuitions"—or of his telepathic sensitiveness—which may be responsible for his personal style as well as for his success or failure as a therapist.

These sketchy remarks about the psychodynamics of telepathy in the analytic situation cannot possibly do justice to the mass of pertinent observations and to the growing literature in the field. The present discussion is mainly concerned with throwing into sharper perspective the close correlation between the symbiotic model of ESP and the reenactment of its original prototype in the doctor-patient relationship.

The inclusion of a larger number of clinical observations—perhaps of more "striking" and more elaborately documented cases—might conceivably carry greater weight with the skeptic. But the amassing of more and more repetitive case histories is not likely to change the conclusions drawn from the limited sample reviewed here. We may take a leaf from the botanist's, the zoologist's, or the entomologist's book. He is confident that the careful study of even a few rare specimens of flowers, birds, or butterflies provides all the needed information about their anatomy or physiological functions. The same is true for psi phenomena observed in the psychoanalytic situation. They can serve as paradigms for the study of the anatomy and physiology of psi incidents under spontaneous conditions and, with certain qualifications, even in the parapsychological laboratory.

6

The Four Faces of Psi

in Psychotherapy

In EARLIER chapters we were mainly concerned with two closely related problems. I tried to present reasonably convincing evidence of psi phenomena in the parent-child and the therapist-patient relationship and to throw light on their underlying psychodynamics. In the pages that follow I propose to examine some of the wider implications of these findings. Yet in doing so we have to realize that excessive eagerness to convince the skeptic and to place our argument on a solid factual basis is apt to put us on the wrong track. We may pay undue attention to "striking" incidents which wave a red flag at the observer, as it were. We may focus on telepathic tracer effects—on the criterion of specificity or uniqueness—in order to prove the telepathic nature of a given case. But we may do so at the price of disregarding less conspicuous, less obtrusive but nonetheless more significant manifestations of psi in our material. In short, we may fall victim to sampling errors which every statistics textbook cautions against.

The risk is very real indeed in the psychoanalytic situation. Excessive preoccupation with conspicuously labeled tracer effects may be misleading in two ways. It may give us a biased picture of the nature of psi phenomena and at the same time contaminate with extraneous material the analyst-patient relationship itself. This may be one of the reasons why many experienced analysts still hesitate in coming to grips with the available observations of psi in psychotherapy. Michael Balint (1955), the noted English analyst, while readily accepting the occurrence of telepathy, put his finger on the point when he cautioned that if and when psi incidents occur in the treatment situation, they are usually due to error in analytic technique and therefore are nothing to boast about.

The fact is that in my own analytic experience the incidence of tracer elements has shown considerable fluctuation over the years. At periods of intense preoccupation with the matter—from 1947 to 1953, when my interest had been receiving added stimulation through monthly meetings with a group of likeminded colleagues in the American Society for Psychical Research—the pages of my diary were dotted with entries of the type discussed in the preceding chapter. Other members of the ASPR group, such as J. Eisenbud, M. Ullman, G. Pederson-Krag, J. Meerloo, and G. Booth have gone on record with similar observations. At other times, psi incidents seemed to recede into the background or were completely in abeyance. In recent years, with a gradual change of my personal style in psychotherapy, such anticipatory, "intuitive," or telepathic responses to my patients as described in the preceding chapter have come to the fore.

The emergence of specifically labeled tracer elements is, however, only one of the four faces of psi in the pyschotherapeutic situation. The second face is less readily identifiable but has major significance in psychoanalytic theory and practice. The basic observations have long been familiar to students of the history of psychotherapy. We know that virtually every school finds a wealth of confirmatory evidence to bear out its thesis. Freudian patients are said to be in the habit of dreaming "Freudian" dreams, Adlerian patients "Adlerian" dreams, Jungian patients "Jungian" dreams—at least as far as the manifest content is concerned. More generally speaking, we find that the patient's productions tend to meet his therapist's wishes and expectations concerning the validity of his doctrine or of the school of thought to which he owes allegiance. This is what I have described in *Psychotherapy: Myth and Method* (Ehrenwald 1966) as doctrinal compliance by the patient with the therapist's emotionally charged theories. Doctrinal compliance may in effect be responsible for some of the telepathic tracer elements and the clustering of telepathic dreams discussed here. In addition, doctrinal compliance may have been involved in some of the uncontrolled erotic manifestations of positive transference in the early days of psychoanalysis. The same principle applies to the confessions an exorcist may extract from his victim at witch trials, to Mesmer's or de Puységur's somnambulists, to Charcot's patients in the Salpêtrière, to certain manifestations of the mediumistic trance, and so on and so forth. Also, doctrinal compliance, telepathic or otherwise, may have been one of the conditioning factors in some of the dreams discussed on an earlier page. So-called demand characteristics are part and parcel of the hypnotized subject's response to the hypnotist, and it may be at least half of the story in the productions of patients undergoing hypnoanalysis. We have seen that, by the same token, doctrinal compliance plays a decisive role in the original prototype in the doctor-patient or hypnotist-subject relationship: in the relationship between parent and child.

It is an interesting historical footnote that in a letter to Fliess, dated 1897, Freud asked whether or not the "pressures of [his] technique" were apt to elicit potentially misleading responses from his neurotic patients, much the same way as did the subjects of the medieval exorcists. In 1919, Freud freely admitted that "the gold of psychoanalysis" is often alloyed with "the copper of suggestion." Suggestion itself is indeed a virtually ever-present ingredient of the treatment relationship. Doctrinal compliance as it is described here is, however, another matter: it is *unintended suggestion emanating from the therapist who is usually unaware of its operation.*

Yet this should not be taken to indicate that doctrinal compliance is exclusively due to telepathy between therapist and patient. It may be aided by suggestion; by Skinner's "operant reinforcement" or by other nonverbal or preverbal cues. Still, to the extent to which a telepathic factor is involved in doctrinal compliance, it represents the second major aspect of psi in the psychotherapeutic situation.

There is another implication of doctrinal compliance which goes far beyond the telepathic contamination of the patient's productions. It derives from the fact that doctrinal compliance, so long as it is not recognized for what it is, may generate its own evidence, as it were. The therapist, like the witch-hunter of a past era, always tends to be right. Unless he is thoroughly aware of this potential source of error, his "doctrine" may indeed be borne out by his findings. A classical example is Mesmer's discovery of "animal magnetism"—and its subsequent "confirmation" by all his patients.

It is needless to say that this state of affairs is apt to have far-reaching repercussions upon the formulations of diverse theories of psychotherapy both Freudian and non-Freudian. In the early days of psychoanalysis Freud himself had been disturbed by such a possibility and sought to guard against being misled by the confabulations of his "neuroticas." He was well aware of the possibility of hidden suggestions, telepathic or otherwise, emanating from the therapist, which might influence the patient's productions. In any case, he made it his business to forestall such a contingency by the proper analytic training and indoctrination of his disciples.

On the other hand, I noted in the introductory chapter of *Psychotherapy: Myth and Method* that Ernest Jones, his biographer and close associate, was frankly dismayed by Freud's flirtation with the "occult." Some years later, Paul Schilder cautioned that the acceptance of the telepathy hypothesis may shake the very foundations of psychoanalytic theory, if not of the behavioral sciences in general. Yet it should also be noted that Schilder's or, for that matter, Jones' apprehensions had been exaggerated. Doctrinal compliance, observer-contamination, telepathic leakage, or whatnot do not, in themselves, vitiate basic psychoanalytic propositions. They leave untouched the validity of a vast body of documentary evidence which has been recorded long before the advent of Freudian—or Jungian—analysis. A good example is the myths and legends that have come down to us from the dawn of history. The Oedipus complex is not Freud's nor even Sophocles' invention—it is an integral part of Western man's intellectual history and cultural heritage. So are Shakespeare's tragedies, or the tortured writings of Franz Kafka. Nor are the data derived from Freud's studies of the Schreber case, or from Jung's study of psychotic patients in general, likely to be marred by doctrinal compliance.

Nevertheless, making due allowance for the occurrence of doctrinal compliance as a possible source of error in the making of our theories has remained a challenge to the student of human behavior since Freud's earliest encounter with the problem. It requires continued soul-searching and self-scrutiny by psychoanalysts and psychotherapists of all denominations. It is a problem confronting workers in all branches of the behavioral sciences, who are becoming increasingly aware of the pitfalls of what Robert Rosenthal described as "observer bias" or "observer contamination" (1966).

Yet the fact is that in the past decades modern theoretical physics has been confronted with a similar challenge. It goes back to Heisenberg's principle of uncertainty and the discovery that, on the microphysical scale, the very act of observation is apt to affect the physical event under observation. P. W. Bridgman put it succinctly when he stated that "the act of acquiring knowledge itself distorts the object of knoweldge" (1952). It was only the availability of sophisticated mathematical reasoning, in conjunction with Niels Bohr's principle of complementarity, which bailed the physicist out of his predicament.

Unfortunately, no such expedient is available to the behavioral scientist. Doctrinal compliance, involving both sensory and extrasensory clues, could therefore legitimately be described as the *uncertainty principle in psychiatry* and the behavioral sciences in general.

However, it goes without saying that contamination by the therapist's unconscious wishes and expectations need not necessarily be confined to doctrinal compliance. On the contrary, it can rightly be expected that a substantial part of his motivation is directed toward effecting cures. Indeed, we shall see in Chapter 25 that the doctor's therapeutic motivations, conscious and unconscious, including faith in his much-maligned omnipotence or personal myth, meeting halfway the patient's hopes and expectations to be cured, play an important part in his personal impact upon the patient, regardless of his school of thought or of the particular technique used in his approach. Many authorities in the field of hypnosis and hypnoanalysis have arrived at the same conclusion. Thus, the circular pattern of mutual reinforcement of the therapist's and the patient's emotionally charged reciprocal attitudes constitutes the third aspect of psi in the psychotherapeutic situation.

It should be noted, furthermore, that in actual clinical practice the three faces of psi—if they are not masked beyond recognition—are closely intertwined and indeed inseparable. Or else they tend to alternate, with either one or the other occupying the center of the stage. In my own experience, during periods of prevailing interest in the factual evidence for ESP, tracer effects tended to "oblige" by making their appearance in the therapeutic situation. At other times, when I was chiefly preoccupied with problems of psychoanalytic theory and technique, evidence of doctrinal compliance seemed to be the order of the day. At still other times, I am happy to report, it was my patients' positive therapeutic responses which took the place of such artifacts as tracer effects or doctrinal compliance.

A fourth aspect of psi in psychotherapy is more conjectural: the part played by psi-missing. Psi-missing has been attributed by J. B. Rhine (1952), K. R. Rao (1966), C. Tart (1976), and others to selective blocking, deliberate inattention, or resistance to a given ESP target. All this is supposed to take place on the unconscious level. Whatever its modus operandi, it results in statistically significant negative scores, suggesting an apparent avoidance of the ESP target.

The paradox is that psi-missing nevertheless presupposes something like an unconscious recognition of the target prior to its being missed by the subject. Failing this, the subject would be unable to miss it at a statistically significant rate. Thus, the process of psi-missing is perhaps even more baffling than psi-hitting.

Nevertheless, it is interesting to speculate about the relationship of psi-missing to the process of repression and resistance in the psycho-analytic sense. Unfortunately, speculations along these lines run into another problem: the problematic nature of the concept of repression itself. We have to realize, moreover, that the concept of repression as used here cannot be strictly equated with the classical Freudian term. Freudian repression is concerned with pushing what has once been in the field of consciousness into the unconscious. In contrast, repression of heteropsychic material, that is, of telepathy and related phenomena, is directed against material which has never been in consciousness in the first place. The common denominator between the two uses of the term is therefore the dynamic aspect of repression, as against its familiar topographic aspects in terms of Freudian metapsychology.

According to Freud, the essence of repression lies simply in the function of expelling and keeping something out of consciousness. This "something" may be an incompatible idea, impulse, memory, instinctual drive, or, more generally, various derivatives associated with them.

However, such formulations still leave a gap in our understanding of the processes involved in repression. Assuming that the offending idea is indeed wholly unacceptable to our conscious self—to our ego— how, then, can it be picked out by the ego for subsequent disposal through repression? At this point the concept of perceptual defenses proposed by experimental psychologists comes to our aid (Bruner and Postman, 1961; Payne, 1959, and others). Payne suggests that there is a filter mechanism which cuts out excessive stimuli (p. 247). Bruner and Postman found that experimental subjects can be conditioned to block the admission of a given stimulus into conscious awareness while at the same time responding to the stimulus on a subliminal level. Psy-chologists talk about "pre-perceiving perceivers" and suggest by way of explanation that a subject, in order to know what to avoid "must first recognize the stimulus which is to be avoided" (Eysenck 1961, p. 266).

Much the same problem is raised by the findings of psi-missing. There is massive evidence indicating that under "ordinary" conditions ESP operates on the unconscious level. As a general rule, the subject does not know whether he hit or missed the target. A hit indicates that here, for once, ESP impressions can break through the barriers sepa-rating ego from nonego, or the autopsychic from the heteropsychic sphere. We have seen that in the treatment situation an occasional tele-pathic "hit" or "breakthrough" is facilitated by the symbiotic aspects of

the doctor-patient relationship. It sets the stage for the telepathic meeting of their minds or for the interpenetration of their respective heteropsychic and autopsychic spheres. But I also noted that such incidents
still remain the exception, and the warding off or "repression" of heteropsychic material is the rule.

If this is true, psi-missing is in effect an example of a far wider
range of subliminal perceptions or "unperceived" psi responses in everyday life.

What, then, is the equivalent of psi-missing in the psychoanalytic
situation? Every experienced therapist is familiar with temporary stale-
mates in the therapeutic process, when the patient seems to close his
mind to all attempts at communication, verbal and nonverbal, with his
doctor. Interpretations miss the point or are misinterpreted by the patient. So are the analyst's neutral comments or even his silence. In turn,
the lack of feedback from the patient may have a disconcerting effect
on the therapist, unless his training and analytic insight give him the
strength to weather the crisis.

More often than not, the difficulties can be resolved by analysis of
the patient's resistances in the treatment relationship. But in more severely disturbed cases—especially in paranoid schizophrenics or borderline patients—the cause for the blocked communication lies deeper.
There is the patient for whom regression to the symbiotic level of communication seems to hold more than the usual threats. He recoils from
the intimacy of therapeutic contact on the psi level. But here, again, we
have to realize that the operation of an unconscious psi ability is required to insure the efficacy of the act of repression. Indeed, this require-
ment applies with equal strength to psi-missing, as well as to repression
in the psychoanalytic sense. Psi seems to be their common denominator.

Yet, as I have noted, despite these similarities, we have to bear in
mind that the two processes—they can be described as autopsychic
versus heteropsychic repression—cannot be equated without qualifica-
tion. One is directed at pushing what has once been conscious into the
the unconscious; the other seeks to prevent the intrusion into consciousness of mental content—of Jungian archetypes, if you like—that has
never been there in the first place.

The modus operandi of these dual defensive attitudes is still ob-
scure, especially so long as we insist on arriving at explanations in terms
of topographic Freudian concepts or of analytic ego psychology. The
fact is that we cannot tell *how* the ego is capable of "recognizing" (and
warding off) an ego-alien idea invading it from either the autopsychic
or the heteropsychic sphere without first bringing it into the purview

of consciousness. Still, we are perfectly satisfied when we are told by the biologist that, on the level of immunological processes, an antibody is capable of seeking out, attaching itself, and in the end neutralizing an antigen invading the organism from the outside world. The fact is that, except for cases of serious illness, antibodies can do just that, without holding a degree in biochemistry or molecular biology—indeed, without even looking. The same may be true for the operation of psi phenomena, including psi-missing in the laboratory as well as in the therapeutic situation.

7

Predisposing and Conditioning

Factors

THE preceding chapters were concerned with some of the psycho-dynamic aspects of psi phenomena. Ruth's telepathic dream expressed her secret desire to move into a new apartment whose existence she could not have been aware of by the ordinary means of cognition. Her dream spelled out her positive transference on the therapist as a father surrogate. Mrs. D.'s dream, highlighting her identification with me, is another variation on the same theme. Dreams of this order, including the telepathic element woven into the manifest dream content, are essentially need-determined. They provide symbolic fulfillment of the dreamer's desire for symbiotic closeness with the parent figure. Many spontaneous incidents in the waking state are likewise geared to meet emotional needs of those involved. Indeed, Gardner Murphy has noted that this is one of the basic characteristics of psi functions (1943).

But such a hypothesis is difficult to reconcile with forced choice, micropsychological incidents of the card-calling type under laboratory conditions. Nor can it account for all aspects of the manifest dream content in a given case.

Mr. G., a patient aged forty-seven, saw in his dream a key with the numerals 117 printed on it. It turned out that they were an imperfect match with the numerals 10117 printed on my office key. Analysis showed that the dream expressed his wish to take possession of a symbol of my professional status and phallic prowess—the key. Thus, its markings can be viewed as a near miss on an imperfectly perceived ESP target. I have described the case of Mr. G. in more detail elsewhere

(1955). Suffice it to say in the present context that his dream contained several additional clues supporting a telepathic interpretation. My interpretation was in effect based on a combination of the criterion of psychological significance with the criterion of uniqueness and the presence of tracer elements.

Yet a skeptic may rightly ask at this point: "Suppose we are prepared to accept the imperfect match of the two sets of numerals as a legitimate telepathic or clairvoyant tracer effect, why, then, should the patient choose such a trivial item as his ESP target? How can such a capricious choice be reconciled with a psychodynamic reading of the case? Why did the dreamer pick a set of emotionally neutral numerals in the first place—while at the same time failing to score a bull's-eye with his supposedly telepathic response?" The answer is that his near miss cannot, without farfetched psychoanalytic or numerological speculations, be brought in line with a strictly need-determined psychodynamic scheme.

Does this mean that the case for ESP should therefore summarily be dismissed in this instance? Not necessarily. On changing our frame of reference from the analytic to the experimental, the patient's near miss would merely amount to one single, wholly inconclusive, "call" made in the course of what should preferably have been an experiment with a large number of randomly selected and mathematically definable targets. Failing this, and in the absence of a dependable criterion of uniqueness, the significance of Mr. G.'s near miss is indeed negligible. What we are left with is a cluster of need-determined responses (patient identifies with therapist, assumes his phallic prowess, and so on), meeting the criterion of psychological significance, while tracer elements or other telltale clues of telepathic correspondence (117 versus 10117) are at best equivocal and fall short of the criterion of specificity.

But the skeptic may raise yet another question at this point: "Why," he may ask, "would the dreamer—or indeed any experimental subject involved in an ESP experiment—show the slightest interest in scoring a bull's-eye on such uninspiring items as numerals, letters of the alphabet, or the five geometrical figures printed on Rhine's Zener cards? Why should he do any better or even as well as Mr. G. in his telepathic number's game with his therapist?"

The question is indeed justified. It points to the limitations of purely psychodynamic considerations in trying to account for parapsychological incidents of the card-calling type. The fact is that even though our dreamer had failed to reach the passing mark as far as the target numerals on my key were concerned, a large number of experimental subjects confronted with equally uninspiring target materials pass their tests with flying colors, scoring far in excess of chance expectation. Clearly, ESP responses of this order are not amenable to explanation along psychoanalytic lines. It is true that experimental subjects— like analytic patients—may try to oblige their experimenter and produce occasional results by doctrinal compliance, but such a blanket statement does not explain why Mrs. Gloria Stewart, one of Dr. Soal's champion subjects, tended to function best under telepathic conditions, while Basil Shackleton, his other star "guesser," seemed to specialize in precognitive scores. Nor does it give us any clues why Pavel Stepanek, the subject of the Ryzl-Pratt experiments, excelled in producing what they described as the "focussing effect" on a selected set of target materials.

The same considerations apply to the highly idiosyncratic performances of the Dutch sensitive G. Croiset, who tended to score bull's eyes on such trivial items as a hole in a (future) agent's socks, the figure 5 versus 6 in a woman's housekeeping records, or a "bu-bu" on a person's left big toe (Tenhaeff 1962). Similar capricous responses have been recorded by the psychiatrist Oscar Fischer (1924) in Prague with Raphael Scherman, the psychographologist, or by B. E. Schwarz, with Jaques Romano, the American sensitive (1968). They duplicate on a macropsychological scale, as it were, the exploits of successful subjects in micropsychological mass experiments of the ESP type.

The same problem is posed by the Ullman-Krippner experiments in the REM state, mentioned in Chapter 1 (Ullman, Krippner, and Vaughan 1973). In these experiments the sleeping subject was shown an emotionally charged picture as the telepathic target. The dreamer, in the REM state, was indeed able to pick out a number of trivial details from the target picture, even though the details were lacking any appreciable vital significance or emotional interest to the subject. In that respect they were comparable to Mr. G.'s near miss on the number 117 in our previous example.

Observations of this order, coupled with the quantifiable laboratory tests with ESP cards, suggest that in these cases the psi response is not necessarily correlated with the percipient's personal needs and goals. As a matter of basic principle, it cannot be accounted for solely by reference to psychodynamic factors. Rather, it is *flaw-determined*: that is, due to what can be described as an existing minus function, to some minor organic or functional deficit, global or circumscribed, lasting or transient, in the agent's or percipient's personality makeup (see Chapter 20).

What is the nature of these minus functions? They range from such altered states of consciousness as sleep, absentmindedness, and the suspension of rational reasoning in meditation, hypnosis, or mediumistic trance to such minimal brain damage as was responsible for the reading disability of Ilga K. or Little Bo. We shall see in Chapter 19 that it is in effect some minor cracks or fissures in the screening function of a subject's ego which open what Aldous Huxley called the *doors of perception* to the occasional influx of psi phenomena. In some cases it seems to be the subject himself who opens the door, a little or a lot. In others the door—or the protective screen of the ego—stays open much of the time. In others again, the screen seems to be more or less selective, deciding in a more or less random way what specific spatio-temporal configurations (geometrical figures, numerals, and so on) are permitted access through the screen, while barring entrance to other configurations. This selectivity may in turn determine whether a would-be psychic will function better under telepathic, clairvoyant, or precognitive conditions.

Basil Shackleton tended to score consistently above chance some two and a half seconds *before* or *after* the agent had looked at the target card. We shall come back to this puzzling form of temporal scatter in Chapter 19. Mrs. Gloria Stewart, on the other hand, worked best under telepathic conditions and showed no tendency to scatter or displacement. By contrast, Croiset's screen seemed to be riddled with tiny scintillating lacunae that brought into focus clusters of events geared, of all things, to a chair which a specific randomly selected person would occupy at some future time. As in Schackleton's case, this aspect of Croiset's performance was likewise flaw-determined, thought raised to the level of striking proficiency and accuracy.

Similar considerations apply to the still controversial observations of psychokineses in Mrs. Kulagina; to the even more astonishing "thoughtographic" exploits of Ted Serios, studied in painstaking detail by Jule Eisenbud; or to some of the subjects with the out-of-the-body experiences discussed in Chapter 15. In all these cases, need-determined, psychodynamic factors were obviously part of the picture. They are responsible for the striking organizing power characteristic of the human mind. But they also bear the stamp of their idiosyncratic, flaw-determined origin.

It goes without saying that such formulations are only a crude approximation to a far more complex state of affairs. They include changing moods, mental sets, and diverse cultural and situational factors. We have learned from Heraclitus that we can never bathe in the same stream twice. Nor can there be any doubt that sooner or later the metaphors used here will be replaced by more exact neurological, microbiological, or electrophysiological terms. Yet in the meantime it is safe to say that in an individual case it is neither a given set of need-determined nor a given set of flaw-determined predisposing factors alone which accounts for an individual psi event. Rather, it is a combination of the two: a combination of flaw-determined and need-determined (or psychodynamic) factors, aided by the organizing quality inherent in the psi level of functioning.

The medical reader will perhaps recall at this point that, in this respect, psi phenomena follow a pattern well-known in the field of neuropathology and psychoanalysis. A lapse of memory, a faulty action, or a slip of the tongue may be of either psychological or organic origin. It may be goal- or flaw-determined—like a person's susceptibility to psi; or it may be determined by a combination of both. It is true that a simplistic, either-or explanation would be more appealing to a clinically untutored or unsophisticated mind. But who says that psi phenomena should be easier to explain than a creative act, a neurotic symptom, a reading disability, or an organic speech impediment?

There is one more set of predisposing and conditioning factors of psi phenomena which has received growing attention in recent years. They are attempts by Charles Tart (1976) and his associates at the University of California, Davis, to improve experimental ESP scores by giving immediate feedback to the subject, signaling him whether he had hit or missed the target in a given guess. Tart found that such a procedure is indeed conducive to high extrachance results—provided that the subject possesses any ESP talent at all. In somewhat circular reasoning, Tart suggests that ESP can be reinforced in talented subjects by methodical training. This is in contrast to the dreary routine of the standard test procedure that inevitably leads to the extinction of whatever innate ESP talents a subject may have had in the first place. Surprisingly, some of Tart's high-scoring subjects tended to produce psi-missing instead of psi-hitting. Total failure of ESP performance Tart attributed to a total lack of innate ESP potential.

Nevertheless, Tart holds that immediate feedback and reinforcement is a sine qua non for obtaining positive results in all forced-choice

ESP tests, and he is confident that his approach will open up a new era in ESP research.

Rex Stanford (1977) is less sanguine and finds fault in Tart's experimental design and reasoning. Other critics note that diverse procedures using such altered states of consciousness as meditation, relaxation exercises aiming at increased alpha wave activity, or partial sensory deprivation under so-called *ganzfeld* conditions (Honorton and Harper 1974) (eyes shielded with half Ping-Pong balls; "white noise" to eliminate distraction by structured auditory stimuli) are likewise conducive to high extrachance scores even in the absence of special reinforcement techniques. The fact is that despite differences in procedure and rationale, all these sundry approaches have proved to be successful in the hands of their initiators, even though none has passed the acid test of a replicable experiment so far.

Viewed in the present context, the reason for this state of affairs lies in the basic difficulty of transforming essentially flaw-determined incidents of the card-calling type into psychologically significant need-determined events. The problem is not one of devising more and more sophisticated experimental techniques but of creating authentic emotionally charged motivations, a proper mix of interpersonal relationships, in which subjects, experimenters, and bystanders alike (preferably Schmeidlerian sheep) are united for a common purpose. Tart himself rightly pointed to the pitfalls of trying to transplant a given experimental setup from one laboratory or from one nondescript research team to another.

Yet I believe that a major difficulty encountered by Tart and his associates derives from another source: from the very performance-oriented learning paradigm of their approach. We have to realize that attempts specifically aimed at better ESP scores are essentially geared to conventional, left-hemispheric functioning. But we shall see in Part Four that psi phenomena have a much closer affinity to the right than to the left hemisphere. The left side of the brain is the scholar, the intellectual, the logician, concerned with grammar, syntax, and quantifiable material; the right side, generally considered intellectually inferior, is the artist, the poet, the dreamer, geared to symbols, metaphors, intuitive hunches—and to the need-determined aspects of psi. Trying to force the right hemisphere to adopt functional patterns characteristic of the left— or the other way round—is therefore likely to be counterproductive.

If this is true, it explains, among other things, why some of Tart's "best" subjects happened to produce psi-missing instead of psi-hitting:

the right hemisphere seemed to balk at the unfamiliar task, even with the "left-handed" assistance of its opposite number. In either case, what Tart describes as "motivated" psi-missing may have been due to resistance from either the right or the left hemisphere, if not from both.

However that may be, some of Tart's subjects did seem to confirm his working hypotheses at least some of the time. Still, the question is whether or not his overall results are amenable to alternative, no less plausible, explanatory hypotheses. Indeed it can be argued that they resulted not from one but from a concatenation of three predisposing and conditioning factors: (1) the extrachance scores had indeed been boosted by the technique of immediate feedback and reinforcement; (2) in addition, they were aided by the well-nigh ubiquitous tendency of "good" telepathic percipients to doctrinal compliance; and (3) this may have been further reinforced by the tendency to clustering and telepathic contagion characteristic of psi pehnomena in general.

This is illustrated by a wealth of observations culled from the history of parapsychology. There are the minor epidemics of mediumistic phenomena, mental and physical, in the heroic days of psychical research in late nineteenth century England. There is the little group of high-scoring percipients in Rhine's early ESP experiments at Duke. There is the clustering of telepathic incidents in the psychoanalytic situation among members of the Medical Section of the American Society for Psychical Research between 1947 and 1951. There is evidence of a similar clustering touched off by the Targ-Puthoff experiments (1976) at the Stanford Research Institute in the 1970s. And there is the contagious spread of Uri Geller's spectacular spoon-bending exploits to scores of "mini-Gellers"—the spoon-bending children described by John Taylor (1975) in Great Britain.

Whatever be the psychodynamics of the epidemiology of contagion along these lines, it stands to reason that in the absence of the requisite psychological factors, initial ESP successes are bound to peter out even in the face of good experimental designs and impeccable laboratory techniques.

In sum, we have to realize that, other things being equal, the triad of doctrinal compliance, clustering, and telepathic contagion has to be added to Tart's learning paradigm of "learning to use extrasensory perception." Working in concert, it is their combination that provides the predisposing and conditioning factors necessary for the origin of psi phenomena. It may well be that the very training of the left hemisphere for its idiosyncratic intellectual functions has jeopardized its ability to process ESP. But that should not preclude the possibility that the right hemisphere may step into the breach without losing its pristine innocence as a result of Dr. Tart's enthusiasm for its training and domestication.

It should also be recalled, however, that there is no all-inclusive technique for designing "psi-conducive" conditions. We have seen that they are widely divergent for need- versus flaw-determined phenomena. The added contribution to ESP and the ESP experience by what I described as the existential shift will be discussed in Part Three. Our next order of business, however, is a brief digression into the purported parapsychological effect of drugs.

8

Drugs, Dreams, and ESP

AMONG the flaw-determined predisposing factors of psi phenomena, psychedelic drugs have recently received growing popular attention. Yet any informed discussion of this problem must make allowance for the fact that the experimental effects of any drug—including the psychedelics—are dependent on at least four factors. First, there is the chemical composition of the drug itself. Second, there is the personality of the subject taking the drug. Third, there are the personal idiosyncracies of the doctor, experimenter, or "guide" dispensing and supervising the action of the drug. Fourth, there is the psychological set, or *Einstellung*, and the specific "field characteristics" of the experimenter-subject relationship. Medical men and psychiatrists in particular are fully aware of the part played by these factors in determining drug effects. They have learned to make allowance for experimenter bias, for placebo effects, or for what I have described as doctrinal compliance by patient or subject with the doctor's or experimenter's wishes and expectations, conscious or unconscious, regarding the efficacy of his remedy or of his particular therapeutic approach. These experimenter attitudes, as I have stated, are especially apt to be effective when they are met halfway, as it were, with the subject's corresponding hopes and expectations.

It goes without saying that placebo effects or doctrinal compliance should be a major challenge to psychical research. There is no field of experimental inquiry which runs a greater risk of contamination by experimenter bias or doctrinal compliance than parapsychology itself. If it is at all true to its own premises, it should be an ideal proving ground for telepathic leakage, or paraexperimental telepathy (Ehrenwald 1948), as a potential source of error.

This may be one of the reasons why reliable and wholly convincing experimental observations of ESP or spontaneous psi occurrences in the drug state are few and far between. R. E. L. Masters and Jean Houston, in *The Varieties of Psychedelic Experience* (1966), report on four out of twenty-seven LSD subjects, three males and one female, whose responses in ten runs through a pack of ESP cards were far in excess of chance expectations. Instead of 5–5–5 . . . as expected by chance, the results were as follows:

M–1: 9–8–6–10–12–13–9–5–3–4
F–1: 8–13–10–11–8–11–9–10–6–5
M–2: 11–9–8–11–13–10–10–10–7–4
M–3: 8–7–10–12–9–11–4–6–4–3

The experimenters noted that the subjects were in an empathic state with their "guide" and had from the outset been on personal and friendly terms with Miss Houston. They also found that in all subjects, scoring in the last few runs tended to decline, sometimes below chance, showing Rhine's familiar decline effect, presumably due to boredom or fatigue.

Unfortunately, the Masters-Houston experiments do not measure up to the rigid technical standards demanded in modern ESP tests. Yet the high scores obtained in their first series are reminiscent of the results obtained in the pioneering experiments carried out by Rhine and Pratt in the 1930s with their champion subjects A. J. Linzmayer and Hubert Pearce. It is significant that these striking exploits occurred during the heroic days of the Duke experiments and were not sustained in the succeeding years.

It should also be recalled that clusters of telephathic incidents in the psychoanalytic situation were recorded by members of the Medical Section of the ASPR between 1947 and 1951, showing a similar pattern. They grew into a minor epidemic of psi phenomena but tended to decline with the gradual waning of the shared excitement and interest that had initially animated the group.

The same principle may apply to ESP tests under the influence of psychedelic drugs. The positive findings of A. Puharich, Duncan Bluett, and other workers did not live up to their early promise. A study by Emilio Servadio and Roberto Cavanna (1964) with LSD subjects yielded no extrachance results. Nor has the psychedelic experience proved to be the rich source of creative inspiration which such enthusiasts of the drug culture as Allen Watts, Timothy Leary, or Andrew Weil claimed it to be. According to literary critics, Aldous Huxley's last novel, *The Island*, reportedly written under the influence of LSD, does not measure up to the standard of his previous writings. Art critics and reviewers are generally unimpressed by productions issuing from the drug state. It appears that instead of improving the esthetic quality or the originality of the output, it rather tends to impair the artistic judgment of the drug user. In a similar vein, it may be the impairment of judgment which accounts for the many unsupported claims of ESP under the influence of LSD, mescaline, or marijuana (Tart 1971, Krippner and Davidson 1974).

More recently, the Italian chemist Professor Salvatore Guarino (1975) served as his own subject in experiments with vitamins B_1 and B_6 and adenosine triphosphate. He claimed high extrachance results when the vitamin or ATP level was building up; contrariwise, reduction of their levels was supposed to produce the reverse effects. He attributes these results to his newly discovered "thermodynamic radiation." Unfortunately, Guarino fails to make allowance for doctrinal compliance and does not include controls in his experimental design; his experimental technique itself has been criticized by a reviewer.

John Lilly's account of out-of-the-body experiences under the influence of sensory deprivation and LSD will be discussed in Chapter 15. Unfortunately his claims of spectacular veridical events under these conditions are not amenable to verification in terms of "consensus reality." The same is true for claims of the same order made by Timothy Leary and other enthusiasts of the drug culture as well as for some LSD observations reported by Stanislav Grof (1975). A precognitive dream reported by Stanley Krippner (1973) may or may not be an exception. The dream, supposedly presaging the assassination of President Kennedy, occurred after ingestion of Psilocybin. That alcoholic intoxication may become a rich source of divination and ecstasy is an age-old feature of legend and folklore, a stock in trade of diverse Dionysian cults. Similar claims have been made by early workers in ESP. Whether or not the "thoughtographic" exploits of Ted Serios were facilitated by his heavy drinking must remain a matter of speculation.

My own observations are confined to a few dreams and other spontaneous occurrences in patients undergoing prolonged analytic psychotherapy who were habitual users of marijuana; that is, they had smoked "pot" at least once or twice a week over the years. (Only a few occasional users of LSD are in my files.) Contrary to expectations, the yield of psi incidents in a cumulative total of some fifty "patient years" has been poor. In a sample of twenty-six drug patients, the yield was not larger than in a comparable sample of nonusers.

A characteristic example is the following case. Mrs. W. is a professional women of twenty-six who developed a psychotic episode following her divorce the preceding year. She felt she was losing her identity and was afraid of being unable to control her actions, of "going crazy." She was plagued by violent destructive impulses against her father and against men with whom she happened to be sexually involved. After a year and a half of analytic psychotherapy, combined with small doses of a tranquilizer (Librium 5–10 mgm., three times daily), her condition showed a marked improvement. Yet on February 24, 1970, after smoking two or three marijuana cigarettes, she suffered a sudden relapse. She came to her next session still "high" from the drug. Her mood fluctuated from euphoria to sullenness and depression. She reported that she had slept with A, one of two men with whom she was having affairs, and had felt the urge to kill him, then and there: "I wanted to bite through his jugular vein . . . The more sexually potent the man—the bigger his penis—the more I wanted to crush him. . . ." The next day she was sullen and darkly threatening: "I am in a melodrama . . . I feel homicidal with you too. . . ."

It was obvious that the patient was one of those cases in which the drug experience had triggered off a psychotic episode. In her next session, on March 3, she was deeply remorseful over her "misbehavior." Yet at the same time she was greatly relieved: "All the witches are exorcised," she stated. "I received nothing but good vibrations. I also enjoy sex more." She indicated that following the incident with Mr. A (and his close brush with murder), she had continued her affairs with both A and B. She was visibly relaxed and I noted on her case sheet: "Emerges from another marijuana episode. She had experimented with marijuana and LSD once or twice before her present illness and it is possible that they contributed to its origin."

Three days later, on March 6, she reported the following dream:

> It's about you and your wife. It's not here in your office . . . space and time are mixed up . . . we sit on a couch, I and your wife. It's a social occasion, not a session with you. Lots of other people are present, perhaps thirty. Is it group therapy? No, it's your birthday. There is a beautiful girl, with short brown hair . . . also several couples. Also some girls I know from grade school. You decided to give a birthday party—yes, yours. Yet I saw no gifts for you as far as I can recall. . . . Frankly, I regard birthdays as a pain in the neck. But you know all the answers. (Laughs.) Then all left, except me, and the scene shifted. I was out in the open, in a backyard with trees around. Two men were fixing a swimming pool. They asked me to pay for the repairs—$10. I got angry with them. Also, you didn't bother to be there. . . . As a child, at grade school, we had a park

where we played . . . there was a swimming pool . . . there were trees and hills around it . . . and little waterfalls. In winter there were sleigh rides. (About the swimming pool in the dream?) Repairmen were fixing it, but it was just like a bathtub . . . quite small.

She went on to remark about the party: "I'm against birthday parties. . . . Funny, everybody came in for a group session . . . I was surprised though. . . ." (My entry in her case sheet at this point: "Relaxed, friendly, feels well. Out from under the marijuana cloud. Advised to avoid 'pot' in the future.")

Except for her derisive remarks, the patient had no more associations in connection with the birthday party, the group session, the missing birthday gifts, or the shift of the dream to the outdoors. Yet she connected her reference to the two repairmen "fixing" the swimming pool with the two men with whom she had been sexually involved. They were supposed to straighten out her frigidity which she, in turn, associated with two minor surgical operations recently carried out on her genital organs: cauterization of the cervix and removal of several benign growths (condylomas) from the genital region. Her anger with the repairmen was thus connected with her resentment about medical fees, presumably including those she had to pay to me. Apart from these, her associations were unrevealing.

As usual, more light can be thrown on the dream on turning attention to my side of the picture. First and foremost, the dream occurred one week *prior* to what in actual fact happened to be my birthday. It was an anniversay that marked the turning of one decade into the next. Despite my personal idiosyncracies in regard to such occasions, it gave me pause and made me wonder whether my family and friends would respect my wish to let the day pass without the usual fanfare and gift-giving rituals. Indeed, my aversion to what I considered a socially sanctioned regression to childhood had long been a family joke which involved my wife, my daughter, and my old friend Richard. Whether or not this attitude served to cover up a lingering nostalgia for times long past, when birthdays and birthday parties had been joyous events in the child's life, must remain a matter of conjecture. In any case, the dreamer's remark, "frankly, I regard birthdays as a pain in the neck," did reflect my conscious feelings about the matter.

Needless to say that the patient had been unaware of the particulars of my vital statistics as well as of my personal idiosyncrasies in regard to birthday celebrations. Mercifully, March 13, the critical day, came along without fanfare. It fell on a weekend and, as usual, my wife and I left the city for our summer home, accompanied by our granddaughters—Debbie, age eight, and Lisa, age six. On our arrival Debbie's first order of business was to run to the shore of our lake. She proceeded to dam up the flow of a little "waterfall" emptying into the lake through a twelve-inch pipe. "This is going to be our swimming pool," she remarked. In actual fact, it could at best have passed for a doll's bathtub.

I may add that the lake is surrounded by trees and hills. In this respect it is reminiscent of the park and swimming pool featured in the dreamer's associations.

The rest of the day was uneventful. It culminated with the children helping me to unwrap the only birthday gift my wife had taken upon herself to buy in defiance of the family rule. It was a penknife to take the place of one I had lost a few weeks earlier. This was not, however, the last item on the agenda of the abortive birthday celebration. Two weeks later, my friend Richard committed another breach of the rule and made arrangements for a surprise party for me in his home. It was attended by fifteen or twenty people, most of them members of Richard's and my own extended families. Among them was my daughter, fitting the description of "a beautiful girl, with short brown hair" which was frosted with blonde and white strands on that occasion. There were no presents, except for a large scrapbook containing photographs taken, thoughtfully arranged, and annotated by Richard himself.

On appying the principles outlined in Chapter 5 to Mrs. W.'s dream and to the two installments of subsequent events in my life, the correspondence between the two fragments of her dream and the two series of real events following in its wake is unmistakable. There is, first, the theme of the birthday itself which was, at the time of the dream, much on my mind. There is, second, my (overtly) negative attitude toward such anniversaries, echoed by the patient's remark, "Birthdays are a pain in the neck." There is, third, the dreamer's reference to "no gifts" which, by current American standards, is an understandable slight to the sentimental value of the penknife and the photo album presented to me on two subsequent occasions. There is, fourth, the shift of the scene to the outdoor "swimming pool" (which was in effect a doll's pool) and, fifth, the setting in the second fragment—a swimming pool surrounded by trees, hills, and "little waterfalls." It was a scene which took the patient back to the time when she herself had been Debbie's or Lisa's age.

On interpreting Debbie's actual participation in the scene as a stimulus for the patient's identification with my granddaughter, it would

79

in effect amount to a sixth point of correspondence between dream and reality. There is, furthermore, the patient's reference to some thirty persons attending the party, although this admittedly overestimates the number of those present in Richard's home. There is, last, her mention of the "beautiful girl, with short brown hair" which, as I stated, can be applied both to my daughter and to the dreamer herself. In a similar vein, her friendly conversation with my wife in the opening phase of the dream illustrates in a graphic manner her own participation in the proceedings.

As noted in Chapter 5, the correspondence of such a multiplicity of distinctive features, in conjunction with the criterion of psychological significance, cannot reasonably be attributed to chance alone. The argument in favor of such a reading is by no means weakened by the fact that it implies both telepathic and precognitive correspondence between dream and reality. We shall see in Part Four of this book that the psi syndrome, by its very nature, is independent of the spatial and temporal order of things. It is also interesting to note the patient's remark that in her dream "space and time are mixed up." This certainly applies to most "ordinary" dreams; but Mrs. W., in reporting her dream experiences, had never before made a comment to that effect. This is particularly true for the precognitive aspects of her story.

Another intriguing item is Mrs. W.'s remark on emerging from her bad trip that "all the witches are exorcised." This happened to correspond closely with my own thinking about her as another "witch of our time." I hinted that describing her behavior toward men in terms of a "castrating" woman was more than a mere figure of speech: it was part of her overt clinical behavior. It has to be viewed, furthermore, in conjunction with the wartlike growths in her genital area which had recently been removed. Finding such minor anomalies in the "private parts" of an unfortunate victim of the medieval witch trial was considered an ominous sign and was often reason enough to convict her of consorting with the devil. Thus, in the context of the present study, the patient's reference to witches speaks for itself. It can be interpreted as yet another manifestation of either doctrinal compliance or straight telepathic leakage or both.

One more comment on the "two men fixing the swimming pool" is in order at this point. I noted that this had to be taken as a symbolic reference to the two men with whom she had been sexually involved at the same time and who were supposed to "fix" her damaged sexual organs, or relieve her "frigidity." Thus the dream element in question was overdetermined: it was derived in part from the patient's own, or autopsychic, experience and in part from telepathically received hetero-psychic material, woven into the fabric of the manifest dream content. A further determining factor was her resentment against two other men who had to be paid for their services: her gynecologist and myself. All this was brought into focus by Debbie's swimming pool as an external reference point.

Nevertheless, despite the patient's occasionally avowed resentment, her positive transference on me was unmistakable. It was perhaps this gamut of conflicting emotional attitudes which prompted her to "tune in" on my birthday party in a telepathic way, to join my wife, my daughter, and my granddaughters in the "group session" and to become, at least for a fleeting moment, a member of my family.

What, then, was the drug's contribution to Mrs. W.'s telepathic or precognitive dream? On the face of it, the evidence is inconclusive. She had smoked marijuana—presumably a potent Mexican variety—on February 24. The dream occurred two weeks later, on March 5. She had, in the meantime, passed through another fairly severe psychotic episode marked by homicidal impulses, sadistic fantasies, anxiety, and inappropriate affect and behavior. Such delayed reactions—or flashbacks—are rare in emotionally stable persons, but have been frequently described in neurotics or borderline schizophrenics. (One of my patients, a seemingly well-adjusted college graduate, attacked and bit his wife in the neck while under the influence of "pot." Another became confused and suicidal and had to be hospitalized for a brief period.) Yet the striking fact is that Mrs. W.'s telepathic dream occurred when she was *emerging* from her bad reaction to the drug. The dream was therefore either unrelated to the marijuana or associated with the recovery phase from her psychotic episode.

Similar observations in schizophrenic patients, discussed in Chapter 11, point in the same direction: they provide added evidence in favor of the latter assumption. Schizophrenics tend to produce telepathic dreams when they emerge from periods of autistic withdrawal from their social environment, when they let go—at least temporarily—of their insulating screen (or chemical buffers) which are protecting them from overwhelming external stimuli, including heteropsychic experiences. The same may be true for some of the psi phenomena claimed to be associated with the use of mescaline or LSD.

A similar process may have been initiated in Mrs. W.'s recovery phase from her "flashback," superimposed as it was on her underlying psychopathology. It was a phase when she relinquished her belligerent stance toward and hostile withdrawal from the world and reached out for closeness with the therapist and his family. If this is true, marijuana in this case had indeed triggered off a psi response. But it did so within a complex biphasic pharmacological, clinical, and psychodynamic context, closely attuned to certain features in my own emotionally charged preoccupations at the time the dream occurred. Thus the emergence of psi, though aided by the recovery phase from a minor psychodelic drug, was predicted on a well-defined interpersonal configuration of the symbiotic type. It was conditioned, but not "caused" by a chemical agent.

This is also borne out by the fact that six weeks after the drug experience the patient had another precognitive dream, complete with tracer effects, the criterion of uniqueness, psychological significance, and so on, without having used marijuana again.

Still, such advocates of the mind-stretching effects of psychedelic drugs as R. G. Wasson, Aldous Huxley, Timothy Leary, and Alan Watts have hailed the "sacred mushroom," mescaline, peyote, LSD, or Psilocybin as means for achieving spectacular ecstatic experiences, ineffable religious raptures, "instant salvation," and mystic union with the godhead and the "Ultimate Ground of Being." If Freud called the dream and free associations the royal road to the exploration of the unconscious, the partisans of psychedelic mind stretching see in the drug culture the master key to a state of superconsciousness, opening the doors of perception to a new, hitherto unexplored psychic reality.

Such claims have a familiar ring. They hark back to the age-old techniques of trial and error, to the random practices of ancient and medieval herbalists in the search for the fountain of youth or the philosophers' stone, in the quest for magic omnipotence and its reenactment in the fantasy life of the child or the neurotic and in the "divine madness" of the psychotic patient.

But we have seen that the actual exploits of subjects in the drug state are inconclusive and difficult to dissociate from purely psychological factors: from subject and experimenter expectations, doctrinal compliance, and placebo effects. Pahnke, Masters and Houston (1973), Krippner (1973), Krippner and Davidson (1974), Tart (1971, 1977), and others have made due allowance for this state of affairs. W. Pahnke (1967) has shown that a Psilocybin trip staged on Good Friday in a church setting and accompanied by suitable organ music transported ten theology students serving as his subjects into a world of lofty religious experience. One of two controls who were given a placebo produced much the same response.

By contrast LSD, given in a mental hospital setting, is merely conducive to bizarre hallucinations, terrifying changes of the body image, and delusions of persecution or grandeur. In my own clinical experience I have come across several cases of this kind. Some are borderline schizophrenics whose condition was aggravated by the drug. Another case in point is Bill F.'s episode of "possession" discussed in Chapter 12.

All these observations suggest that *need*-determined psychological factors are at least as important in the origin of supposedly drug-induced, *flaw*-determined, psi phenomena as are chemical agents. Reliable double-blind techniques to study the problem in more detail have not as yet been developed. Yet it should be recalled that telepathic leakage or paraexperimental telepathy will perhaps always be a potential source of error in experimental psi research, if not in the behavioral sciences at large. To state the obvious: the decisive factor in parapsychology, as in human affairs in general, is man himself, propelled by his wishes, needs, hopes, and expectations. It is he who determines the ways in which his technical tools, mechanical skills, and chemical appurtenances shape his behavioral repertoire and inner experiences.

Whether or not marijuana and its recently discovered depressive effect on the left cerebral hemisphere was an added factor in facilitating Mrs. W.'s telepathic-precognitive dream must remain a matter of conjecture. It should, in any case, stimulate further pharmacological research along such lines.

9

Precognition or Self-fulfillment

in Dreams?

MY FIRST ENCOUNTER with a presumptively precognitive dream reflects my lingering doubts and mental reservations in the matter. The case, first published in 1951, had a question mark tagged to its title (Ehrenwald 1951). Today, some twenty-five years later, the question mark still clings to the issue. Nevertheless, or rather for that very reason, it is in order to go over once more an abridged version of the original account.

The patient, Mr. S., was a man of thirty-eight at the time of our first contact. He was married, the father of a boy age seven and a girl age five. He worked as a floorwalker in a big dime store. He reported that during the past year he had been subject to increasingly severe anxiety attacks when in the subway, bus, and so on. More recently the attacks also occurred when he crossed busy streets, in a restaurant, or even at the fountain counter of his store. In addition, he had always been plagued by obsessive-compulsive symptoms. Analysis revealed that most of them were in the nature of defensive mechanisms directed against unconscious homosexual impulses which were aggravated in the feared situations.

After initial difficulties, Mr. S. made good progress in treatment. He gradually became able to face repressed material without untoward emotional reactions and to overcome many of his anxieties, although he was still not able to go about his business without being accompanied by a friend.

Precognition or Self-fulfillment in Dreams?

It was in the fourth month of psychotherapy that he reported the following dream:

> I was in the store. There was a guy who apparently worked for us. I had the feeling he was after something, ready to hold up the place. He had a large flip-open knife, opening it, closing it, suggesting he is a dangerous fellow. I got scared, called for Mr. X and Mr. Y to catch the man. I myself retreated into the telephone booth to call the police to get him. All of a sudden the whole situation seemed to have dissolved. The guy was sitting there and I was talking to him. It was a much more friendly conversation. He took out the knife, flipped it open. It was not large any more—just half an inch or maybe one inch long. I thought how foolish it was to be afraid of the knife. It was not nearly as dangerous as it looked. It was very small.

The patient's associations made the homosexual nature of the holdup situation obvious. The phallic symbolism of the knife needs no further elaboration. The two men mentioned in the dream—Mr. X and Mr. Y— were his colleagues who used to accompany him in the subway or bus. His call for the police stood for his invoking the help of the therapist in overcoming his unconscious homosexual impulses. Again, the sudden change of the scene in which the large knife turned out to be quite small and harmless was an obvious reference to the therapeutic progress made, to his feeling that he was no longer afraid of his homosexual tendencies. I felt the time had come to offer an interpretation to the patient to this effect. This I did during the same session. At the same time, I encouraged him to try actively to overcome his phobia. He left greatly relieved, while I had the impression that an important step had been made toward his recovery.

Two days later, the patient was some five minutes late for his session. He reported with an embarrassed smile that when he was on the bus he saw a black man sitting next to him take a knife out of his pocket and open it quite unconcerned. "It was a little penknife, just like the one in the second half of the dream." The patient added, "I felt quite uneasy, ready to get panicky any time, keeping an eye on him. Then he took an apple out of his pocket, cut it, and started calmly eating it."

The patient was puzzled by the apparent correspondence between parts of his dream and the subsequent event in the bus. "The knife," he added, "was like taken out of the dream. But please don't think I am suffering from hallucinations. Never before has a similar thing happened to me." He further added that he had missed the previous bus by a few seconds. This was the reason for his being late for our session.

85

Remarkable though the existing points of resemblance between the two sets of events may appear, they are not stringent enough to warrant any far-reaching conclusions. Yet one week later—that is, twelve days after the dream—Mr. S. recounted a second real incident involving a knife:

> Yesterday morning I was on the floor of the store when some character walked in. He looked like a real tramp, with a battered hat, disheveled shirt, holes in his shoes. He looked fierce, like a maniac. I knew him from before. He had come to our place about three or four times before. I always watched him [to see] whether he was not out for stealing. But as a rule he bought something—stationery, pencils, or soap. This time he walked straight to the cutlery counter. I was just two counters away and saw that he picked up a large kitchen knife four or five inches long and said something to the girl at the counter, though I could not hear what he was saying. At that he turned around toward me, looked at me, and with a savage gesture brandished the knife toward his throat. I got very uncomfortable—in fact, I ran downstairs to the basement. After a while I pulled myself together and went back to the girl at the cutlery counter. "What happened to your boy friend?" I asked jokingly. "Did he buy the knife?" The girl answered in the affirmative—adding, still somewhat taken aback, "He said 'when that guy bothers me I'll cut his throat open.' Then he paid and walked out with the kitchen knife."

I repeated to the patient my previous interpretation of the dream and suggested that both the first and second waking incidents involving a knife may have been due to his increased awareness of such objects in his environment and, therefore, largely to his own state of mind. This explanation, I said, should dispose of any superstitious misinterpretation of his experience and also account for the apparent "duplicity" of the cases described.

But the question is, does it really do so?

It will be noted that in telescoping together the two waking incidents and disregarding the actual chronological order of events in the dream, we treat them as though they were "residues" (*Tagesreste*) derived from days both preceding and following the dream. The dreamer seems to "remember" both the past and the future, as Dr. L. E. Rhine once put it. On taking this liberty with our material and on comparing the manifest content of the dream with the two supposedly corresponding sets of actual events, matching references to seven different items can be found:

1. A "guy" plans an aggressive action.
2. He carries a large knife in a menacing way.
3. The dreamer seeks to escape.
4. A change to a friendlier setting occurs.

5. The dreamer and the previous pursuer sit near each other.
6. The latter holds a much smaller knife in his hand, flips it open, showing a blade only an inch or so long.
7. The dreamer is greatly relieved and sees how foolish it was to be frightened of the knife.

Although it is admittedly impossible to estimate the odds against such correspondence in mathematical terms, they certainly involve a "multiplicity of distinctive features" that we invoke as one of our criteria for the occurrence of ESP. Also, here again an equally important argument in favor of a paranormal interpretation of the dream is the criterion of psychological significance. Disregarding for the moment its puzzling precognitive aspects, such an interpretation is in good keeping with the overall dynamics of the case: with the patient's latent homosexual trend, with his fear of "knaves and knives" and other phallic objects.

It should be noted, furthermore, that the dream occurred at a turning point in the analytic treatment: at a high-water mark of positive transference, involving what I described as an existential shift. We know that many things can happen at such a point—above all, striking improvement in the patient's condition.

This is precisely what happened in our case. It will be recalled that Mr. S.'s symptoms severely curtailed his freedom of movement. He was unable to ride in a subway or bus by himself. He had to take a taxi when he came to my office. Yet after my interpretation of his dream, I felt he was ready to take the first active steps toward overcoming his difficulties— and I told him so. Three days later he came to his session by himself, riding on a bus for the first time in many months, and reported the incident which had occurred in the bus.

All these considerations admittedly tell us nothing about the most puzzling, precognitive, aspects of the dream. Evidently, our reference to its essentially need-determined quality is not enough. It may well be that in view of the serious pathology involved in his case—Mr. S. was certainly sicker than Basil Shackleton—flaw-determined factors have contributed to the precognitive elements contained in the manifest content of his dream.

In 1958, eleven years after the dream occurred, the patient reappeared in my office for a few more consultations. This provided an opportunity for a reappraisal of his case. Mr. S. had been free of phobic symptoms since the termination of the treatment. His wife had died several months earlier. He was depressed and remorseful for having given her a "hard time." Above all, however, he complained of difficulties with his son and daughter, now age eighteen and sixteen, respectively. It transpired that Mr. S. had been engaged with them in an insidious struggle of wills, characteristic of the authoritarian parent. His son and daughter, who had now to bear the brunt of his still persisting obsessive-compulsive trend, rebelled violently against him. They too were evidently victimized by his pathology. Despite their resistance, they were hopelessly enmeshed in their father's residual neurosis and tended to act out—vicariously, as it were—some of his repressed "complexes."

It is this ominous tendency, discussed in greater detail in Chapter 14, which may provide a clue for the apparent self-fulfillment of Mr. S.'s anxieties and phobic expectations woven into his supposedly precognitive dream.

We know that patients of this type have an uncanny need (and often the capacity) to exercise control over their next of kin and their social environment at large. However, more often than not, they merely succeed in antagonizing their fellowmen in the process. Their behavior in this respect is the photographic negative of the behavior characteristic of paranoid patients: they affect their friends and relations in much the same way as the paranoid patient thinks he is affected by his pursuer. He turns into a "persecuted persecuter," as it were. Here, as in the case of children acting out their parents' neurotic complexes, the key factor may be telepathy, duplicating the symbiotic pattern. This, then, may account for the picture of both compliance and rebellion that Mr. S.'s antics had provoked in his offspring.

By the same token, it can be conjectured that a similar or derivative symbiotic pattern may have been at the root of the two knife-wielding characters' behavior in Mr. S.'s waking experiences. As M. Ullman has pointed out (1969), dreams can be described as internal or intrapsychic communications in which the dreamer's vital concerns are expressed in metaphorical language. In the present case, it could be argued that the two knife-wielding characters happened to act out Mr. S.'s dream metaphors. For some unaccountable reasons they may have become telepathically sensitive to the patient's repressed fears and expectations—and they promptly acted upon them with whatever paraphernalia happened to be available to fit the occasion. If this is true, Mr. S. did not act as a "percipient" of future events; rather he played the part of an agent who was instrumental in bringing the events about.

It will be noted that such an interpretation tends to replace precognition with telepathic self-fulfillment, however improbable such a freakish interaction between perfect strangers may be. It is an interpretation which is in effect satisfied with describing two sets of interrelated incidents in terms of a psi syndrome, without insisting on removing the question mark from our chapter heading.

Freud, Zulliger, Hitchman, and other psychoanalysts (see Devereux 1953) have been satisfied with the conventional self-fulfilling interpretation of such dreams without reference to a psi factor. But such a reading is hard to apply to J. W. Dunn's much-quoted studies of precognitive dreams which seem to presage various natural catastrophes (1927); to Ian Stevenson's (1970) collection of several premonitory dreams surrounding the sinking, in 1912, of the Titanic; and to some of Jule Eisenbud's observations of precognition in the psychoanalytic situation; to say nothing of Gerard Croiset's "chair tests" in the waking state described by Tenhaeff (1962), Bender (1957), Eisenbud (1973), and others.

Nor is the hypothesis of self-fulfillment applicable to the following observations: Dr. Richard G. is an old friend and classmate from my medical school in Prague. On August 2, he took his usual afternoon off from his practice. He was in high spirits, spent his time at the beach, took a swim in the ocean, played a game of bridge in his cabana, and drove back to New York City to have dinner with his wife. On opening the refrigerator in his home to help himself to a drink, he collapsed on the floor and was pronounced dead by the physician called in by the family.

At his funeral, his daughter, Charlotte, aged thirty-seven, told me of a nightmare she had on Tuesday night, August 1, while she was vacationing in Puerto Rico. "I woke up in the middle of the night in a sweat, full of anxiety. I dreamt that daddy was stricken with a brain hemorrhage . . . I thought he was dying, but he came to and recovered again." In the morning, Charlotte told her husband about her nightmare. He confirmed her story to me in all details.

I may add that the attending physician left the question open whether Richard's sudden death was due to a massive brain hemorrhage or to an acute coronary attack. In any case, he was stricken while in apparent good health, with no premonitory symptoms, cardiac, cerebral, or otherwise. Unless we discuss the dream as mere coincidence, it was frankly precognitive, involving a time span of eighteen or twenty hours. Cases like these abound in the literature of psychical research. They are plainly inexplicable in terms of telepathic self-fulfillment. Such an explanation would merely shift the argument from parapsychology to the domain of witchcraft. Alternatively, we would have to presume the dreamer being capable of "diagnosing" clairvoyantly the impending breakdown of her father's diseased coronary or cerebral arteries, before they had led to the fatal outcome.

Such a feat would presuppose a virtually omniscient Laplacean mind with an attending unlimited capacity for precognition. In the circumstances, precognitive telepathy from Richard's mortal crisis to his daughter is still an at least equally plausible—or implausible—assumption. In either case, the dream is one more example of ESP in the child-parent relationship, both need- and flaw-determined, on the part of agent and percipient. At the same time, Charlotte's dream work incorporated the telepathic message in the manifest content and used denial—denial of her father's death—as a defense against its impact. I may add that Richard himself had had a number of psi experiences in his lifetime and that both he and his family had always shown sympathetic interest in my preoccupation with the topic.

It is the cumulative evidence of cases like these, coupled with the experimental findings of Soal and Goldney (1943), Schmidt (1969), and many others which suggest that psi phenomena, in whatever form they make their appearance, do constitute a break in the closed, virtually self-sealing system of our standard "Euclidean" mode of experience. It is true that Mr. S. and, for that matter, most patients described in the psychoanalytic literature, were not immediately aware of the paranormal aspects of their dreams. Nor do experimental ESP subjects "know" whether or not they have scored a hit. But whenever a paranormal event does happen to be consciously registered on a person's mind it carries a powerful emotional charge. It may shake him to the very roots of his being. Like Macbeth's encounter with the Weird Sisters, it may make his "seated heart" knock at his ribs. It may throw him into an ecstatic rapture; it may strike him as a theophany or as a stirring mystical experience. It may imbue him with a sense of fusion with the rest of the universe, of a messianic mission that sets him off on the path of a prophet or religious reformer. It may open up to him vistas of a new psychic reality, illumination, and freedom of action.

It is these, essentially need-determined, existential dimensions of psi phenomena of a higher order of complexity to which we will address ourselves in the next chapter.

10

Precognition or Self-fulfillment

in Prophecy and Myth?

Is IT PERMISSIBLE to trespass from the parapsychologist's laboratory
or from the psychoanalyst's office to the vast field of prophecy and myth?
Can we carry over the insights gained from the study of self-fulfilling
dreams to the priestly oracles of classical antiquity or the major prophetic
utterances of the Old and New Testament? Can the principle of self-
fulfillment be applied to the cluster of scriptural prophecies presaging
the coming of Christ, the ingathering of the children of Israel in the
Promised Land, or the return of Quetzalcoatl in Aztec mythology? Has the
rise and fall of Hitler's Thousand-Year Reich been a veridical dream that
failed to come true, or a nightmare acted out on a world stage by a crazed
leader in search of greatness or suicide?

The problem of prophecy versus self-fulfillment runs the whole gamut
from the sacred to the profane, from the ridiculous to the sublime, from
what is testable in the laboratory to historic events of cosmic magnitude.
It is needless to say that the answers to these questions go beyond the
ken of the present inquiry. But they will at least be brought into focus in
the pages that follow.

The story of divination, prophecy, and precognition over the ages
reflects faithfully the vicissitudes of magic and its latter-day derivatives in
our culture. We have seen that magic, in any form, has become increasingly repugnant to Western man, incompatible with his habits of thinking
and his whole orientation toward the world. Yet the desire to fathom, to
foretell, and to influence the course of future events has apparently been
particularly hard to relinquish. This is why any lingering hope in the

possibility has fallen into growing disrepute. It has been decried as superstitious, subjected to cultural repression, or relegated to the lunatic fringe of our culture. As a more sophisticated expedient, divination and prophecy, stripped of their magic connotation, were made the subject of quantitative laboratory experiments under a less offensive name.

The fact is that virtually every culture, at various stages of its life cycle, has dealt with the problem in its own way. In the present context I propose to focus attention on two major variations on the theme: on prophecy in Greco-Roman and Hebrew antiquity.

Prophecy and Divination in Ancient Greco-Roman Tradition

For obvious reasons, there is a close historical affinity between the classical Greco-Roman tradition and current Western thinking. Five major strands run through the ancient approach to divination, and they are, as we shall see, much the same as those that still engage the attention of modern students.

The first strand goes back to Homer, Hesiod, and other pre-Socratics. It consists of a loosely knit cycle of anecdotal accounts concerning the exploits of soothsayers such as Calchas, Tiresias, Mopsus, and scores of other legendary characters. According to Homer, Calchas was the wisest of them all. "He knew everything that has been, now is, or shall be in the future." Yet when Calchas challenged the soothsayer Mopsus to tell him the number of figs growing on a tree nearby, it turned out that Mopsus "outguessed" Calchas. In the ensuing competition between the two, Calchas lost out once more and died from a broken heart.

Tiresias, the blind seer, received the gift of divination to make up for his loss of sight. His exploits were of a more sophisticated, need-determined order than those of Calchas or Mopsus. He predicted that the plague that had struck Thebes would cease when the murderer of its slain king Laius was apprehended, and he divined further that the killer was none other than Laius' unfortunate son, Oedipus. It was Tiresias who foretold to Alcmene the heroic deeds of Heracles and who prophesied what the future held for Narcissus, Odysseus, and other figures of Greek mythology.

Professor E. R. Dodds (1964) describes feats of this order as inductive divination from omens, characteristic more of the Iliad than of the

Odyssey. They are still largely steeped in the tradition of magic. Some are playful elaborations of primitive lore: variations on the theme of the omnipotent shaman or medicine man. Others prefigure themes which are more characteristic of the classical Greek experience, as for example the motif of Greek tragedy, the downfall of the hero. The hero's death was understood to be predetermined by the Moirai, in Roman mythology the Fates, whose power over the lives of men was supposed to be greater than that of the gods themselves. This is why the tragic playwrights considered man's destiny as foreordained and beyond the individual's power to change.

This belief in inexorable destiny constitutes the second strand that runs through the Greek concept of prophecy. It is best illustrated by the pathetic figure of Cassandra, who correctly predicted the disasters that befell the city of Troy but was unable to make her hearers heed her warnings. The same fatalism pervades the gloomy forecasts by the Delphic oracles of the misfortunes which lay in store for Oedipus and all the descendants of the house of Laius or Atreus.

The oracles of Delphi and Dodona, presided over by Sibyls and Pythias, represent a third strand. They were inspired by Apollo or Dionysus, who spoke through their vocal apparatus much in the way that "spirit controls" are supposed to sound off in mediumistic trance states. We are told by Dodds that Apollonian mediumship chiefly aimed at knowledge of the future or the hidden present, while Dionysiac techniques aimed more at inducing shared ecstasy in which prophecy happened to be a more or less accidental by-product. In any case, both forms were attributed to divine interventions or possessions. Plato, in *Timaeus*, described them as "prophetic madness."

A fourth strand is represented by the vast literature on dreams and dream interpretation found in ancient Homeric texts and such later writings as those of Antiphonus of Athens, Artemidorus of Daldis, Aristander, and many others. Dreams, especially those entering through Homer's "Portal of Horn," were viewed as "images of truth," holding the promise of visions "manifest of future." Dream interpreters were called upon to unravel the hidden meanings of such visions. Dreams lacking such significance were regarded as "mocking dreams" and held no interest for either dreamer or interpreter.

Several dream lexica, cataloging the hidden meaning of premonitory dreams, have come down to us. Artemidorus (1965) claimed that, as a general rule, the dream of sleeping with one's mother presaged the death of the dreamer. But an artisan dreaming of intercourse with a living mother could be confident of success and steady employment in his craft.

For a statesman the same dream presaged a gain in stature or power since, figuratively speaking, the mother symbolizes one's motherland.

On the whole, ancient Greek dream interpretation chiefly favored the fortunes of the powerful and the rich. When Alexander the Great laid siege to Tyros, he dreamed of a satyr dancing on a shield. Called in to decipher its portent, Aristander interpreted the dream as an acronym— *Sa Tyros*, "Tyros is yours"—presaging Alexander's eventual conquest of the town. The Greek conqueror took the city after a siege of seven months.

By contrast, Artemidorus follows this account of Alexander's dream with the sad story of Syros the slave, who dreamed he had no soles under his feet. He was burned alive "shortly after the dream."

On an earlier page, I described as doctrinal compliance the characteristic tendency of today's patient in psychotherapy to confirm with his productions the therapist's emotionally charged wishes and expectations concerning the validity of his doctrines. This tendency, I stated, may in effect introduce an embarrassing source of error in formulating theories of psychotherapy.

In antiquity, doctrinal compliance seems to have operated in the reverse direction: it was the dream interpreter who tended to comply with the emotionally charged wishes and expectations of his well-heeled client. He who paid the piper called the tune.

The mercenary spirit of the dream interpreters of the time is illustrated by Artemidorus' admonition to his son and successor in the mantic arts to limit the copies in circulation of his magnum opus so as to preserve their market value for the benefit of his heirs.

The fifth strand in ancient Greek tradition is of particular interest in the present context. It reveals the searching curiosity and remarkably open mind with which philosophers like Heraclitus, Plato, and Aristotle had approached the problem of alleged "god-sent," or veridical, dreams. According to Dodds, it was Plato who first recognized the internal, intrapsychic origin of dreams, as opposed to their origin in the world of outer reality as was previously held.

In a similar vein, Aristotle contested the notion that all dreams originated from the gods. As alternative explanations, he stressed that some dreams brought about their own fulfillment; that others—for example, those informing the dreamer of his own state of health—simply focused on symptoms ordinarily ignored in the waking state; and that still others were due to chance alone. Nevertheless, Aristotle held that divination and the production of premonitory dreams sprang from an innate "faculty of the soul." This general concept was in effect later reaffirmed by Moses Maimonides (1956).

What may be one of the earliest recorded examples of an experimental approach to the problem appears in a much-quoted story told of King Croesus of Lydia. To test the reliability of six different oracles, the king asked them to divine what he was doing, in his palace at Sardis, at a particular time. One of the oracles produced a "near miss." The others failed, with the exception of Delphi, who won the contest. This is what, according to Herodotus, the Delphic oracle said:

> I can count the sands and I can measure the Ocean.
> I have ears for the silent, and know what the dumb man meanest.
> Lo, On my sense there striketh the smell of shell-covered tortoise
> Boiling now on fire with the flesh of a lamb in a cauldron.
> Brass in the vessel below and brass the cover above it.

The fact is that Croesus was having a barbecue at the self-same hour.

Herodotus tells of a similar, though unsuccessful, test made by Xerxes in the wake of a dream that urged him to embark on his fateful war with the Greeks. Democritus, the first proponent of an atomic theory of matter, likewise tried to put the veridical power of dreams to the test. Simulating laboratory conditions, he isolated himself in "cemeteries and desert places" remote from the influence of his fellows, and waited for prophetic inspiration.

Democritus' theory proposed that "images" continually emitted by objects may carry representations of the thoughts, characters, and emotions of persons connected with them. Similar concepts were expressed by Plutarch and Epicurus, among others. Poseidonius, the stoic philosopher, held that veridical dreams resulted from the "community of the human with the divine reason." In a striking metaphor Plotinus described all of mankind and the world as "one great animal." Its "sympathy" abolishes distance, enabling distant members to influence each other without affecting intervening parts.

Cicero, himself influenced by Stoic philosophy, wrote a celebrated treatise on divination. One of the most quoted ancient source books in the field since its appearance, it has long served as a guidepost on the tortuous road from magic to science.

Ancient Hebrew Prophecy

Even this sketchy survey of the ancient Greco-Roman tradition of divination, prophecy, and precognition should make it sufficiently clear that the classical attitude is worlds apart from the Hebrew tradition of prophecy, messianic or otherwise.

Although ancient biblical and talmudic texts are studded with vestiges of magic current in the Middle Eastern orbit of the time, Jewish prophetic tradition was chiefly preoccupied with the ethical aspects of prophecy rather than with its scientific implications or modus operandi. Eliahu Auerbach (1966) stresses that "the lighthearted bantering tone with which Homer describes the weaknesses of the Greek gods was entirely foreign to the spirit of Israel as expressed in prophecy." The prophets did not "precognize." They foretold events in a conditional way and they were in deadly earnest about what they had to say.

Isaiah, the prototype of the great prophets of the Old Testament, "predicted" that Assyria would be the instrument through which punishment would be visited on the children of Israel to purge them of their sins. He foretold "merited disaster." Yet we are reminded by Cecil Roth (1965) that Isaiah's prophecies also had a comforting side. "The triumph of a foreign power was not to be final." Together with his denunciation of moral shortcomings, Isaiah drew the picture of brighter Messianic days to come. He prophesied that ultimately the moral imperatives of his people would prevail and that "dedication to perfection rather than to power shall be the driving force of Judaism."

> And it shall come to pass in the last days that the mountains of the Lord's house shall be established at the top of the mountains, and shall be exalted above the hills, and all nations shall flow into it. And many people shall go and say, Come ye and let us go up to the mountain of the Lord, to the house of the God of Jacob; and he will teach us of his ways, and we will walk in his paths, for out of Zion shall go forth the Law and the word of the Lord from Jerusalem.* (Isa. 2:2–3)

This passage from Isaiah's prophecies culminates with an ecstatic vision of the time when "they shall beat their swords into plowshares and their spears into pruninghooks; nation shall not lift up sword against nation, neither shall they learn war any more."

The prophecies of Amos, the herdsman from Tekoa, likewise presage disaster, to be followed by a better world to come:

> And I shall draw out my people of Israel from slavery, and they shall build the waste cities, and inhabit them; and they shall plant vineyards and drink the wine thereof; they shall also make gardens, and eat the fruit of them. And I will plant them upon their land, and they shall no more

---

* Quotations from the Old and New Testament are taken from: *The Holy Scriptures According to the Masoretic Text* (Philadelphia: The Jewish Publication Society of America, 1964); the *Holy Bible*, King James Version; and *The Jerusalem Bible* (New York: Doubleday Co., 1966).

be pulled up out of their land which I have given them, saith the Lord thy God. (Amos 8:14-15)

Jeremiah, the prophet of doom and disaster, made his prophecies expressly conditional: "For if ye thoroughly amend your ways and your doings, if ye thoroughly execute judgments between man and his neighbor; if ye oppress not the stranger, the fatherless and the widow and shed not innocent blood . . . then will I cause you to dwell in this place." And he quotes Yahweh's explicit command: "Obey my voice, and I will be your God and ye shall be my people." (Jerem. 7:23)

Such dramatic utterances throw into sharp relief the contrast between the activistic, ethical commitment of Jewish prophetic tradition and the Greco-Roman fatalistic acquiescence with a foreordained, inexorable destiny. Viewed against the religious fervor of the great prophets of biblical times, the showmanship of the Greek soothsayers and the cryptic ambiguity of the oracles pale into insignificance. In retrospect even Moses' or Joshua's occasional excursions into the miraculous appear as aberrations from the classical prophetic tradition of Judaism. Like Jesus of Nazareth, these prophets seemed to resort to miracles largely in order to establish their supernatural credentials in the eyes of people who needed tangible proof of the prophetic mission. Their psi exploits were largely need-determined, and there can be little doubt that the contemporaries of Amos, Isaiah, or Jeremiah would have been unimpressed by the tricks of Homer's soothsayers. On the other hand, we know that the religious zeal with which the Hebrew prophets, including Jesus of Nazareth, sought to change the human situation was equally foreign to the rational Greek or Roman temper.

It is true that the ancient Greeks produced such social reformers or "philosophical ethicists" as Pythagoras, Empedocles, Socrates, and Plato. Still, Max Weber (1964) has rightly pointed out that their contribution to the religious idea of salvation in the Western sense was of little consequence. Even Socrates never laid claim to a "directly revealed religious mission." His *daimonion* reacted only to "dissuade and admonish." Martin Buber (1963) stresses that Socrates' voice advised him only as to what he was not supposed to do. Buber also notes that Plato, to whom Western man owes the concept of the philosopher-king, resigned himself to an attitude of philosophical detachment from the field of social action. In effect, Buber describes Plato's role in world affairs as a "glorious failure" compared with the example and the message of the Hebrew prophets, and he contrasts the nagging voice of Socrates' *daimonion* with the voice of the Lord that awed Isaiah and Jeremiah in their raptures. The prophets' myth and their message, though "misunderstood, misinterpreted, and mis-used" in their lifetime, proved to be "effective" after all.

It is interesting to note that Henry Kissinger, the jet-propelled phi-losopher of history and political pragmatist, seemed to hew closer to the Hebrew prophetic tradition than his critics would have expected him to do. Like Isaiah or Jeremiah before him, he too had been decried as a prophet of doom foretelling the Decline of the West and the threatening ascendancy of the West's Eastern adversary. But it may well be that Kissinger's Spenglerian pessimism, like the gloomy forecasts of his biblical precursors, were merely indicative of Kissinger's particular brand of re-verse psychology. He too made negative pronouncements for positive ends. He predicted failure of his mission to one or another trouble spot in the world in order to improve his chances of success. He too was ethically committed and predicted "merited disaster"—unless the children of Israel and the rest of mankind mended their ways. That his reverse psychology was not always successful, and his ethics still *sub judice*, is another matter.

Prophecy and the "Effective Myth"

If the divergence in their respective attitudes and traditions is so pro-nounced, one may well ask whether it is altogether permissible to attempt a comparison of the ancient Hebrew concept of prophecy with the concept of divination or precognition as it was understood in classical antiquity. The Greek seer "foresaw" and "foretold" the future, preordained as it was by the will of Zeus or by the fateful handiwork of the Moirai. Prophecy in the Hebrew tradition had a different objective. It was meant to be instru-mental in changing the future. The prophet scolded the people for their waywardness and pleaded, if need be, with Yahweh, imploring him to alter the impending course of events.

But despite the differences in approach, ancient Greek and Hebrew prophecy did have one thing in common: in a sense which shall later be more closely examined, they both proved historically effective. Aristander's prediction of a triumphant outcome for Alexander the Great's assault on Tyros undoubtedly reinforced the conqueror's determination to continue the siege. Cassandra's gloomy forecasts, although ostensibly unheeded by the people of Troy, could very well have weakened their will to resist nevertheless. Similarly, but with a wholly different impact, Isaiah's mes-

sage of the Messianic Days to come kept alive the hope of scores of generations of the children of Israel that "the remnant shall return" and that
the people who "walked in darkness" would see the light, and that "the
light will shine upon those who dwell in the land of the shadow of death."

There can be no doubt that these prophetic words have made a major
contribution to the ensuing historic events that led to the Zionist movement and culminated in the founding of the Jewish state.

A slightly different dimension of the self-realizing power of predic-
tion is illustrated by another prophecy associated with the figure of the
"First Isaiah": the famous passage on which the Christian doctrines of the
Immaculate Conception and the Virgin Birth are based. This is how the
King James Version of the Bible introduces the subject:

> Therefore the Lord himself shall give you sign. Behold, a virgin shall
> conceive, and bear a son, and shall call his name Immanuel. Butter and
> honey shall he eat, that he may know to refuse evil, and choose the good.

The 1613 Revised Version carries essentially the same text. Luther's
translation says "Siehe, eine Jungfrau ist schwanger und wird einen Sohn
gebären, den wird sie heissen Immanuel. . . ." Translations into virtually
all modern languages—except for the Masoretic text—contain the same
reference to the miracle of the Virgin Birth.

The key word in this passage is the Hebrew *almah,* meaning "young
woman." The critical phrase in the Masoretic text reads therefore: "The
Lord Himself shall give you a sign; behold, the young woman shall conceive, and bear a son, and shall call his name Immanuel. . . ." According
to Jewish biblical scholars, the reference is to a child destined to secure
the dynastic succession of the kings of Israel.

The 1966 edition of the *Catholic Jerusalem Bible* comes close to the
same interpretation. It refers to the "sign" given by the Lord as follows:
"The maiden is with child and will soon give birth to a son whom she will
call Immanuel. . . ."

In short, the editors of the *Catholic Jerusalem Bible* remain non-
committal as to the literal translation of the crucial passage. Yet they add:
"The solemnity of the oracle and the symbolic name [Immanuel—"God is
with us"] given to the child show that the prophet sees more in this royal
birth than dynastic continuity." In a footnote they refer the reader to the
famous passage from the Gospel of Matthew: "The virgin will conceive
and give birth to a son and they will call him Emmanuel." Thus is the
continuity of dogma maintained.

In effect, according to Christian tradition, it is the hidden prophecy
contained in Isaiah's oracle of the birth of Christ upon which the doc-

trine—or the myth—of immaculate conception is based. It is what Protestant theologians call an "effective myth" (Wieman 1945).

Here, again, there is no need to point to the far-reaching historical repercussions of a visionary pronouncement. The Christian reading of Isaiah's prophecy has indeed become an effective myth on a grand scale. Viewed in this light, it does not make much difference that the myth itself was occasioned by an early mistranslation of the Hebrew word *almah*. The crucial point is that the doctrine of the Virgin Birth became one of the cornerstones of the whole edifice of Christian tradition, especially of the Catholic creed. This also may explain why Catholic theologians have placed great emphasis of the predictive quality of Jewish prophetic tradition.

It is interesting to note that the annotations of the Jerusalem Bible often refer to such passages in terms of oracles. The reason is obvious. The exultant poetic language of the Old Testament allows for latitude of suggestion concerning past and future events just as did the cryptic utterances of the Greek oracles. It is this very ambiguity and obscurity which over the millennia have given rise to a wide spectrum of emotionally charged interpretations. We have seen that in the case of the passage from Isaiah the interpretations ranged from the advent of the Messiah and the Return of the Remnant to the Ingathering of the Children of Israel and the Immaculate Conception of the Christ Child. A similar prophetic significance has been read into a moving passage from Isaiah as a prefiguration of the suffering of Christ: "Despised and rejected of men, a man of sorrows and acquainted with grief . . . and Jehovah hath laid on him the iniquity of us all."

Myth and Antimyth

If myths have been described as the collective daydreams of mankind, it could be stated that their apparent self-fulfilling power duplicates the self-fulfilling quality of dreams discussed in the preceding chapter. Although we know full well that this is by no means the only function of myths, their power over the minds of men has been amply borne out by the course of subsequent historic developments. Myths and mythmaking are in effect central features in the dream laboratory of history; both myths and dreams may or may not contain an element of psi. Some are validated by the events they were supposed to presage: they prove to possess positive survival value for those espousing the myths. Other myths are doomed to failure and carry their upholders down to destruction. The pattern of circular feedback between a healer and his client or between an analyst and his patient, described on an earlier page, may sustain the effect of a viable myth. Alternatively, it may hasten its demise and the downfall of its makers.

The belief in the mystery of the Virgin Birth and the prophecies of the advent of Christ illustrate the prodigious power of myth generated among the Catholic faithful by the clergy, who saw to it that the reality of the myth was kept alive in the believers over the centuries. In the case of Isaiah's prophecy concerning the return of the children of Israel to their homeland, we can see the operation of a similar pattern of feedback, projected across the dimensions of historical space and time. In the end, it was the concatenation of Isaiah's myth with world events—extending from biblical times through the advent of Christianity to the ultimate triumph of the Zionist movement—which made his prophecy "come true."

Yet the very self-fulfilling potential of myth is not without its dangers. People and events may obstinately refuse to be molded by its persuasive power. Christ was put to death on the cross and Christian martyrs were thrown to the lions. Prophets and saints were burned as heretics or witches. The same point is brought home to us by the process of circular feedback triggered off by the myth of the Jewish messiah. Its propagation in ever-growing circles beyond the ranks of a numerically small people dispersed all over the globe gave rise to what can best be described as an antimyth. The nations of the world, after adopting in some cases substantial portions of the Jewish message, refused to go all the way on the path to Jerusalem. They rejected Isaiah's claim that "out of Zion shall go forth the Law." The myth encountered the resistance of those who did not want to be swayed and who raised barriers against its effectiveness. Indeed, it was the very power and persuasiveness of the Judaic myth— from Moses to Isaiah, Jeremiah, and the minor prophets—which became a spiritual threat to the "gentiles" and which helped to generate the intermittent tide of equally powerful and persuasive rationalizations of anti-Semitism as a worldwide phenomenon.

Anti-Semitism, viewed in this light, is an irrational yet wholly consistent reaction (or reaction formation) to the threat of Judaism's severe moralistic (or superego) demands. Some of these demands were recast in gentler and more palatable terms by Judaism's more ingratiating offspring: early Christianity. This may be the reason why the older, more exacting creed was to become the loser in one of history's most spectacular and most pernicious popularity polls. Judaism set limits to the self-fulfillment and further propagation of its own myth. In the end it jeopardized the very survival of its own adherents.

Is There a Unifying Bond?

One may well question at this point the relevance of these considerations to problems of precognition studied by the parapsychologist under either experimental or more or less spontaneous conditions. Is there a reasonable connection between psi phenomena seen in the analyst's office (or the flaw-determined variety cultivated in the laboratory), and the panoramic vistas of prophecy, divination, and the effective myth discussed earlier?

I submit that here, again, we are dealing with one of the manifestations of the psi syndrome. And, here again, the emergence of psi is predicated on the prohpet's or experimental subject's openness to psi in one or another of its modalities. In particular, we shall see in Chapter 21, the part played by the brain's right hemisphere in both cases. Equally important is the specific interpersonal configuration between the prophet and his tribe resulting in a circular pattern of feedback of emotionally charged wishes and expectations of the self-fulfilling type. It is such a pattern of communication which is responsible for the self-fulfilling quality of dreams. In a similar vein, it is emotionally charged experimenter expectations meeting halfway the subject's desire to "oblige" which are involved even in many flaw-determined ESP responses seen in the laboratory.

But we have to realize that psychodynamic factors or meaningful configurations of this order do not suffice by themselves to account for the emergence of experimental psi incidents of the forced choice or card-calling type. As I have noted, even a highly motivated subject has no earthly reason to score a hit on one specific target card in preference to another—and to do so "perchance" a second or two *ahead* of time. It is at this point that neurophysiological or flaw-determined factors enter the experimental situation. They are determined by the subject's anatomical or structural makeup and by minor imperfections in the reticular formation of his brain or other neural sites. They are factors largely independent of his personal preferences or emotional needs.

If this is true, precognition in life or laboratory shows the same basic dichotomy as is characteristic of the psi syndrome in general. To that extent there is indeed a unifying bond, admittedly a tenuous one, between the two types. This is a conclusion that may run counter to our need for tidy, esthetically appealing generalizations. But the need for simple answers fails to make allowance for the complexity of the human situation. It ignores the basic fact that our whole mental organization, including psi functions and dysfunctions—from ESP and PK to self-fulfilling dreams, myths, and prophecies—can only be understood within a dual need- and flaw-determined frame of reference. We shall come back to this point in Part Four of this book.

Part Three

PSYCHOPATHOLOGY

You cannot believe in parapsychological observations before they are confirmed by theory.

Sir A. S. Eddington's dictum about astronomy—paraphrased.

11

Schizophrenia and Psi Pollution*

IT IS an old maxim of medical research that organs, organ systems, and patterns of behavior are subject to disturbances which throw their underlying structures or lawful operation into sharper perspective. Freud once noted that it is the broken surface of a crystal which reveals its hidden molecular organization. Pathology is apt to throw light on physiology in both medicine and in the behavioral sciences.

Psi phenomena are no exception to this rule. Indeed some authorities are inclined to consider psi itself as an abnormal or "paranormal" variety of physiological adaptation. If this is true, one may, on purely theoretical grounds, expect psi functions to show at least some affinity to psychopathology—regardless whether or not we subscribe to the "medical model" of psi phenomena. The fact is that they frequently occur under stress, in crisis situations, and in such *minus-functions* of the ego as sleep, trance, absentmindedness, or transcendental meditation, coupled with the tendency to compensation or overcompensation of the minus state. On the other hand, it may be their occasionally spectacular, numinous features which have, from times immemorial, struck fear, awe, or reverence in the hearts of observers. The ancient Greeks considered epilepsy as a sacred disease, and Plato distinguished divine madness from other types of insanity. Similar notions are still reflected in the writings of Aldous Huxley, Alan Watts, and Timothy Leary.

But what about the schizophrenic reactions or the full-fledged picture of paranoid schizophrenia of modern clinical psychiatry? What about

---

* A first draft of this chapter was submitted for publication to the *British Journal of Medical Psychology* during World War II. The MS was lost in an air raid on London. A second version was submitted to the *Psychiatric Quarterly*, New York, 1958, but subsequently withdrawn by the author because he felt its publication was premature at that time.

such drug-induced alterations of consciousness as LSD, mescaline, or major marijuana trips? Do they lend substance to the widely held belief of a positive correlation with demonstrable psi phenomena? Let me state from the outset that the evidence is inconclusive. Nevertheless, we shall presently see that the clinical observer keeping an open mind to the phenomena is occasionally faced with spontaneous incidents strongly suggestive of psi.

Two of my clinical observations go back to the early years of my career as a psychiatrist. Florence C. is a schizophrenic girl at an advanced stage of the process, with marked catatonic features. She is negativistic and given to impulsive outbursts, exposes herself, and exhibits various mannerisms and antics. I first saw her on June 21, 1942, shortly after I had commenced work in an institution in England.

I was about to make the routine six-monthly notes in her case-sheet and cast a brief glance at her particulars before proceeding to her room. The case-sheet contained the usual data, such as her name, age, address, and date of admission. Admitted in 1935, she was thirty years of age at that time, that is to say, thirty-seven at the time of the interview. However, I mistook the significance of "1935" in a moment of absentmindedness and jumped to the wrong conclusion that she was thirty-five years old, that is, seven years my junior. This mistake is perhaps better understood if I mention that having been born in 1900 I had made it a habit to calculate other persons' ages by comparing their birth date with my own year of birth. After my casual glance at her papers I entered the patient's room and put the routine question: "How old are you?" No answer. Wanders about the room; grimaces. "How old are you?" "Don't ask silly questions . . . you are seven years older than me. . ." No further conversation was possible. She took no notice of my presence and remained resistive to examination. Her apparent reference to the erroneous result of my calculation struck me only when I had left the patient. Her statement about our respective ages was certainly off the mark. Yet it was all the more significant that it reflected my own absentminded error in figuring.

The next observation was made shortly afterward in the same institution. Catherine J., aged twenty-four, a schizophrenic with marked paranoid features, watched a fellow patient of about her own age, Betty H., breaking out of her room, smashing a window pane, and sustaining slight cuts to her wrist which necessitated stitching. Betty was a difficult patient and had failed to respond to insulin shock treatment. The day before I had remarked to the ward sister that I felt even my cautious attempts at humoring her might have had a paradoxical effect and only helped to bring about her recent outburst. After attending to her wounds I found Catherine J. waiting for me in front of the side room door. Reproachfully she turned to me: "*You* have done that to her . . . You made her do it!"

She ignored my explanations and maintained her charge. "You should have the courage to admit that you have made her do it. Why don't you admit it?"

The telepathic interpretation of this case is open to more than the usual objections. But accepting it for the sake of argument, we would have to assume that in Catherine's case it was an ill-founded (though psychologically intelligible) feeling of guilt on my part which was "sensed" and promptly reproduced by the patient.

There are several more cases of this order in my files. They all involve references made by schizophrenic patients to more or less emotionally charged preconscious material in my mind. This factor played a particularly significant part in the two incidents reviewed here. They occurred in 1942, during my wartime exile in England. It was a time when I had barely recovered from the shock of emigration and from the hardships imposed on myself and my family by the London blitz. The war went badly. I had just found employment as an assistant medical officer in a state mental hospital and I felt my job was a letdown from more prestigious positions I had held in Prague and Vienna. My English was poor. I disliked the rigid, authoritarian ways in which the hospital was run. To make matters worse, on my first day in the wards I was physically attacked by one of the assaultive patients. All this contributed to a considerable feeling of insecurity and vulnerability on my part. It must have been this vulnerability and lingering anxiety which was picked up by the patients. Here, for once, they were faced with a doctor who had fallen grievously short of the smug, self-assured professional man—and they let him know about it in no uncertain terms. By the same token, it may be the unusual circumstances surrounding the two cases which account for the rarity of telepathic incidents of this order in my own experience—or for that matter, in the well-ordered routine of my psychiatric confreres.

This also is the reason for the altogether different complexion of telepathic incidents involving schizophrenic patients at a later period of my professional career, when I was again safely ensconced in private practice and in more congenial hospital positions in the United States. The following observation is a case in point:

Mr. M. is a gifted commercial artist of twenty-nine who developed a paranoid trend and phobic symptoms which on one occasion made a brief hospitalization necessary. He felt persecuted by big burly men who spied on him, tried to break into his apartment while with a girl friend, kept him awake at night by making suspicious noises, and the like. He showed slight disorder of thinking and flatness of affect, suggesting the presence of latent or borderline schizophrenia.

Mr. M. had previously been treated by Dr. Y., a distinguished psychiatrist, who referred him to me for further therapy. As it happened, the patient made such good progress while under my care that Dr. Y. decided to refer his own son, Peter, aged twenty-five, to me for psychotherapy. On the evening of April 1, Dr. Y. made a surprise call to my office in order to discuss his son's problem. They were, in effect, in many ways similar to those of the patient, Mr. M., who had been referred to me by Dr. Y.

I must explain here that it was Dr. Y.'s first visit with me in the course of many years of professional association and that during our conversation I was greatly inconvenienced by a small vesicle which had just developed on my left eyelid. Dr. Y. first inquired about Mr. M., the patient he had referred to me for treatment. I informed him that progress continued to be good, that I had reduced the frequency of his visits, but that the patient was still coming to see me "off and on." I also pointed out that success in Mr. M.'s case might be partly explained by my more permissive, nonauthoritarian approach. "In the patient's eyes I am the passive, permissive one; you are the active, forceful one," I remarked. What I did not tell Dr. Y. is that I considered this very difference in personalities as a good augury for my proposed therapeutic management of his son.

Two days later I saw Mr. M. in my office. He reported a dream which had occurred the night after my meeting with Dr. Y. These are the salient points of Mr. M.'s dream:

> I came to a psychiatrist. But in fact there were two of them, a woman and a man. The woman had a pimple or mole on her left eye. I was very mad at her because she said I did not come regularly for my sessions whereas I had only missed a couple of sessions during a whole year. The woman reminded me of Aunt Sally, mother's sister, who always had gone on my nerves. The male psychiatrist reminded me of Charlton Heston who played the role of Janus in the Broadway play of the same name.

Without trying to go into the deeper dynamics of this dream, it shows certain unmistakable correspondences with some of the details of my meeting with Dr. Y.: (1) The dreamer's reference to two psychiatrists amounts to a statement of actual fact. (2) His reference to one woman and one man psychiatrist seems to paraphrase my reference to myself as the passive, permissive one, and to Dr. Y. as the active, forceful one. (3)

The patient's mention of Janus, the two-faced mythological figure, seems to lend further emphasis to my remarks concerning our contrasting personalities. (4) The dreamer seems to have caught me at telling a half truth about him and expresses his resentment in no uncertain terms. The truth is that he had always been irregular in keeping his appointments with Dr. Y., but that he had been coming regularly to see me throughout the past year. His main objection was apparently to my phrase "He is still coming to see me off and on." (5) The dreamer seems to be aware of the discomfort caused by whatever was wrong with my left eye.

So much about the presumed telepathic aspect of Mr. M.'s dream. Yet if we are satisfied with the reality of this aspect we arrive at the same time at a fairly satisfactory understanding of the dynamics underlying the dream. First and foremost, the dreamer seems to inject himself into my meeting with Dr. Y. as a "participant observer." He is annoyed with my reference to his alleged irregular attendance. This annoyance seems to be out of proportion to its trivial cause. Viewed from the psychoanalytic angle, one could speculate that the patient equated the reality situation with what analysts call the primal scene. If so, he would be witnessing in a telepathic way my encounter with Dr. Y. At the same time the dreamer seemed to transform me into a passive, permissive mother figure, while Dr. Y. played the role of the aggressive father.

There is, however, a more compelling reason for the dreamer's anger. If we are satisfied with the telepathic interpretation of his dream, it stands to reason that he resented the intrusion of a new sibling figure, Dr. Y.'s son Peter, into our relationship. The fact is that one of Mr. M.'s problems did spring from an intense sibling rivalry with his older brother. No less significant is the fact that in his childhood years he too, like his "sibling rival," had been under the dominance of an authoritarian father and a controlling, possessive mother.

Summing up, Mr. M.'s dream brought a highly complex transference situation into focus, involving both his former and his current therapist, each representing one particular aspect of the patient's relationship with his parents. At the same time, the telepathic element contained in the manifest content of the dream expressed his excessive concern with a feared and beloved father figure, the prototype of his paranoid pursuers. Certainly, this does not amount to a telepathic confirmation of his ideas of persecution. But we have seen that, interwoven with the manifest dream content, there are a few points of information—including the half-truth regarding the alleged "betrayal" by his doctor—which could not have been obtained through any of the usual channels of communication. On the face of it, my remark was trivial and harmless enough. Owing to the patient's underlying pathology it was nevertheless apt to feed into and reinforce his delusional trend. It was thus more the result than the "cause" of his basic paranoid orientation.

The following observation is of a yet different order. It is concerned with a telepathic incident in the waking state, experienced by Mrs. J., a paranoid patient aged forty-one whom I had seen in the outpatients' department of Roosevelt Hospital in New York City. One October morning at 8:45 A.M., on my way to the hospital, I stepped into the elevator of my apartment house. My next door neighbor, Mrs. V., a noted child psychiatrist, was in the same elevator, taking her daughter Edna, aged six, to school. In the ensuing brief small talk I commented on Dr. V.'s early rising, whereupon she retorted in what I felt was a somewhat critical tone of voice: "Why, do you think a little girl of six should be allowed to go to school all by herself?"

Mrs. J., my paranoid patient, was scheduled fror a therapy session at 9:15 A.M. She opened our conversation with the abrupt question: "What do you think, doctor, of parents who let their daughter of six travel all alone?" Mrs. J. explained that as a child of six, in order to get to her village schoolhouse in Indiana, she had to go by bus several miles away, that neither her father nor her mother "gave a damn" what might happen to her, and so on. The patient's attitude toward me was colored by marked resentment over what she felt was too little attention paid to her by her therapist. It was a direct reenactment of her old grudge against her parents over emotional deprivations in her early childhood.

Here, again, the patient seems to have caught a telepathic glimpse of an apparently trivial incident involving her therapist, this time immediately preceding the therapeutic session. Yet here too, as in the previous incidents, the existing psychological constellation was of far greater psychological significance than met the eye. If we take the telepathic nature of her remark for granted, Mr. J. obviously identified with the other "little girl" of six who had all the advantages of a sheltered childhood which she, the patient, had been deprived of in her early years. That little Edna, the object of her identification, happened to be the daughter of a child psychiatrist, lends added significance to the patient's reaction.

As far as her therapist is concerned, the psychological situation is less transparent. As it happened, I found myself in the crossfire between two minor rebukes: one which I myself may have projected into Dr. V.'s casual remark, the other coming from the patient, who accused me of misunderstanding and disregarding a child's needs. It was perhaps this hidden implication of Dr. V.'s utterance which happened to touch a vulnerable spot in my mind. In turn, it was apparently this very vulnerability which the patient's telepathic production had seized upon.

What, then, is the relevance of these observations to our issue? Whatever views we may hold about the nature and causation of schizophrenia or schizophrenic reactions, there is a striking similarity between the patient's—and especially the paranoid schizophrenic's—delusions of persecution, of grandeur, of thought or action at a distance, and some of the basic propositions of parapsychology. They suggest that the theories of parapsychology, as well as certain features of the schizophrenic's, the child's, and the magician's superstitious beliefs, are essentially derived from the same roots: from the symbiotic matrix of all human experience or, to be more specific, from the original unity or fusion of the newborn infant's ego with that of his mother.

I noted that at this early stage, the inner experience of the normal child is dominated by the feeling of magic control over his mother's personality and the world at large. At the same time he takes for granted his mother's mastery and omnipotent control over his own body. The schizophrenic child, I stated, responds to this state of affairs in an exaggerated way: in terms of autistic withdrawal and negativism or in terms of passive compliance and surrender to the overpowering parent figure which, he feels, has invaded the boundaries of his ego. It is these contrasting reaction types which have been described as the autistic versus the symbiotic child psychosis (Mahler 1968).

In view of these similarities—both in overt symptomatology and psychodynamics—one would expect schizophrenics to produce a wealth of psi incidents. But my own observations, as well as those of my confreres, indicate that, by and large, schizophrenics are neither more nor less susceptible to spontaneous or, for that matter, experimental psi phenomena than so-called normal persons. The fact is that several older studies of the ESP type recently reviewed by Scott Rogo (1975) proved to be inconclusive. Schizophrenics did not tend to score consistently in excess of chance expectation.

At first sight such a conclusion would tend to cast doubt on the close affinity between psi phenomena and schizophrenia. It seems to be inconsistent with the thesis that paranoid delusions do contain a grain of truth, that the patient's complaints of persecution are fashioned after the model of the symbiotic child's experiences of control by a supposedly omnipotent parent, and that it is therefore no coincidence when his belief in magic, in "thought transference," or in action at a distance duplicates theories of modern parapsychologists.

However, the dearth of clinical evidence to support such a proposition is only apparent. My observations indicate that while the paranoid process in fact tends to increase the patient's sensitiveness to flaw-determined psi influences, it also reinforces his ego defenses against them. Indeed, the schizophrenic's and preschizophrenic's whole personality makeup seems to be aimed at canceling out his vulnerability to what can be described as *psi pollution*. It may in effect be conducive to a tendency to psi-missing and to a striking lack of empathy with, and ordinary social responsiveness to, his fellowmen. Above all, it may set the stage for what all too often becomes a losing battle against the deleterious effects of conflicting demands and injunctions—the notorious *double bind*—emanating from his parents.

Clinical psychiatry has long been aware of this state of affairs. The textbook description of the schizophrenic has always been one of a withdrawn, shut-in, autistic type of personality. He may shut himself in and surround himself with Wilhelm Reich's "armor plating of character"—to become virtually immobilized by its excessive burden. Or else he may lay himself open to the "slings and arrows" of outrageous fate like Saint Sebastian of Christian hagiography. The resulting behavior may amount to a paradoxical blend of the Princess on the Pea and the Indian Yogi, resting serenely on his bed of nails. Clearly, his characteristic tendency to projection alone cannot account for this state of affairs.

The fact is that many analysts, from Freud (1959) and Fenichel (1945) to Frieda Fromm-Reichmann (1950) and Silvano Arieti (1955), have stressed the schizophrenic's excessive sensitivity to his social environment. He is particularly prone to ferret out repressed or subdued hostility in his friends and relations. This tendency is likewise illustrated by some of the case histories reviewed here. The patient's behavior may alternate between the autistic and symbiotic patterns of child psychoses. He may show all shades and gradations of the two contrasting personality types, ranging from violently hostile to passive-compliant reactions. Or else, they may amount to a combination of both. This statement is also borne out by the distinctly ambivalent attitudes my own unintended telepathic agency had elicited in some of the patients. Obviously I too represented a magically endowed, soothing or threatening, parent figure to them.

However this may be, the schizophrenic patient's refractory—if not allergic—response to psi appears as an exaggerated version of Western man's familiar attitude toward experiences of this order. It expresses his frantic attempt to deny, to ward off, and to repress what is incompatible with our prevailing sociocultural mode of existence. Indeed the roots of our resistance to psi may well go deeper than culturally acquired idiosyncrasies; they may be due to what Freud described as *organic* repression, that is, to a tendency inherent in the evolutionary process itself.

An apparent breakdown of organic repression reaching back to man's evolutionary past is illustrated by the following case. Lydia H. is a highly creative women of thirty-one. During an acute schizophrenic reaction, she saw herself, first, as an amorphous embryonal "blob," then as a tadpole, then as a weird "subhuman shape." Her experience was not drug induced but shows close parallels to S. Grof's (1975) observations of ostensible phylogenetic regression triggered off by LSD in some of his subjects. I have seen dramatic evidence of profoundly repressed, if not atavistic, motor patterns in deteriorated schizophrenics receiving insulin shock treatment in the mid-1930s in Vienna. They produced automatic choreo-athetotic, grasping, clutching, and climbing movements of all four extremities, reminiscent of the behavior of our simian ancestors hanging from the trees.

On the other end of the time scale are the delusions of some agitated schizophrenics telling of their experiences of the end of the world. Such psychotic episodes often culminate in the experience of a cosmic catastrophy in which the earth, the solar system, and our whole galaxy are engulfed in an ultimate fiery holocaust. It should be noted at this point that such doomsday visions made their appearance long before the advent of the atomic age.

Another patient of mine, a physics major aged twenty, emerging from a bad LSD trip, insisted that his molecules, atoms, and electrons had gone through the same recurrent cycles of cosmic catastropies and for that reason he knew why another such happening was unavoidable.

Needless to say, the actual storage and persistence in the genetic code of archetypal or atavistic memories of this order is highly problematical, and its operation on the subatomic level is pure science fiction. Nevertheless, organic repression may well be one of the prerequisites of our sanity—if not of our being human.

Be that as it may, the schizophrenic breakdown signals the failure of the process of organic repression. It is contingent on the breakdown of ego barriers designed to ward off the intrusion of both autopsychic and heteropsychic material into the patient's consciousness. Viewed in the longitudinal perspective, the struggle against such a contingency is life-long and unrelenting. We have seen that it may culminate in the patient's total surrender to a possessive, engulfing, or devouring mother figure. Alternatively, it may lead to the disruption of communication with her and with the rest of his social environment—to autistic withdrawal or catatonic stupor. Yet I emphasized that the shifting balance between compliance and resistance is not merely confined to overt verbal and non-verbal cues, pressures, and prohibitions. It includes the same alternative responses in relation to a wide spectrum of psi influences impinging upon the infant or the growing child.

Yet to the would-be schizophrenic the continued influx of parental influences of this order assumes an increasingly threatening quality. Put in analytic terms, what Bychowski (1956) described as the parental introject becomes predominantly bad and hostile, the storm center of future paranoid persecution. Whatever vestiges of telepathy are still attached to it share the forbidding qualities of ego-alien instinctual drives, of rejected parts of the body image in left-sided hemiplegia, of fecal matter or poisonous food. Indeed, there is only one step from the vehement rejection of such ego-alien material to the attitude of the paranoid schizophrenic in relation to his enemies. It is a step which may be determined by an underlying organic pathology, by the existing personality disorder, or by both.

Thus, the schizophrenic's defensive posture toward psi is merely an exaggerated version of Western man's prevailingly hostile attitude toward it. Telepathy, both as an actual perception and as an operational concept, has remained a foreign body in our everyday experience and in our culture at large. Like non-Euclidian geometry or quantum physics, it is outside our classical, spatiotemporal, causal-deterministic frame of reference.

Still, despite the schizophrenic's allergic reaction to what is here described as psi pollution, he cannot help but maintain the reality of the uncanny powers that threaten to overwhelm him. To him their reality is not just one of new insights or conceptualizations. It carries a deep existential meaning and significance. Regressed as he is to a prelogical, paleological, or symbiotic level of experience, he regards telepathy not merely as a metaphor nor as a faint echo of an intrapsychic type of communication reverberating from the past. Telepathy to him is a persistent psychic reality, blissful and terrifying at the same time. It is an attempt at restoring his lost contact with his fellowman, while his success in doing so may constitute a threat to his very sanity. Hence his frantic attempts to ward off and deny influences of this order (Ullman, 1975).

Yet the psi factor comprises but one—presumably narrow—segment of psychic reality to which the schizophrenic patient responds in his characteristic way. We know that human closeness and intimacy in any form and on any level of experience are potential threats to his vulnerable ego. To him the outside world—including the unconscious of his fellow-men—is fraught with the same dangers as his own unconscious drives. Both the outside world and the unconscious of his fellowmen have become immediately transparent to him, merging imperceptibly with his personality. The therapist himself cannot help being caught up in this fateful pattern of lost boundaries, of shifting and overlapping perspectives. Whatever he seeks to convey to his patient on the level of ordinary discourse is apt to be contaminated by psi pollution or drowned out by "noise" in the schizophrenic's overloaded channels of communication. To the schizophrenic the therapist's unconscious speaks louder than his words. This is why communication between the two is the greatest challenge to the therapist's skill and the supreme test of his personal integrity and dedication to his calling.

12

Possession and Exorcism:

Delusion Shared and Compounded?

VIEWED in historical perspective, demoniacal possession is a variation on the theme of Plato's divine madness, of primitive man's fear of evil spirits, ghosts, and poltergeists, or of what Pierre Janet (1894) or Morton Prince (1906) have described as secondary personalities in hysterical dissociation and in the spiritualistic trance. Stripped of its malignant, diabolical aspects and dressed in the costume of eighteenth or nineteenth century romanticism, if not in more up-to-date modern attire, possession has reappeared on the contemporary scene in the spiritualistic séance room. It is one more example of what in Chapter 4 was described as the metamorphosis of witches. Indeed, in a few sporadic cases, it has reverted to its original prototype.

Here, again, as in medieval or Renaissance accounts of witchcraft, the part played by genuine psi phenomena is difficult to determine. It will be recalled that we encountered the same difficulty in the clinical picture of schizophrenic reactions—to say nothing of out-of-the-body experiences, the Salem disturbances, or the poltergeist incidents to be discussed in the chapters that follow.

Here are a few observations of my own:

Mrs. H., aged fifty-one, is the wife of a high-powered Argentinian business executive, two years her junior. Childless and neglected by her husband, she became addicted to alcohol eight or ten years ago. For a while she had dabbled with the Ouija board and had taken part in spiritualistic séances. She was referred to me when she became subject to bizarre attacks of what she and her husband described as possession by some sinister power. While in my office, she spontaneously lapsed into a trance state. She fell back in the easy chair, rolled up her eyes, and moaned and groaned as if in the throes of severe pain and anguish. This was followed by a phase of convulsive and jerky movements of her entire body accompanied by howling, barking, yelping, and grunting noises which soon turned into an unmistakable take-off of canine antics and posturings. Reversing the biblical story of the swine of Gadara who were invaded by the demons cast out by Christ, she was "possessed" by dogs, if not by a herd of farm animals, and acted out their parts. This bizarre behavior continued for the better part of our first session and could not be interrupted by my attempts to establish communication with her. On coming to, she was slightly dazed and vaguely apologetic for her conduct and asked for the whereabouts of her husband, who had been waiting outside my office. When restored to her usual self, she had a spotty memory of what had transpired, and was fully oriented and capable of observing social amenities but tearful and plainly asking for sympathy.

Her neurological examination revealed halting, slightly slurred speech, tremors of the hands, uncertain gait, and a coated tongue. Previous consultants had put her on tranquilizers and vitamins and diagnosed her condition as chronic alcoholism with episodic confusional states. Significantly, her EEG showed evidence of diffuse cortical damage in the parieto-occipital region of both hemispheres. The changes were attributed to her years of alcoholic abuse.

Thus, Mrs. H.'s diagnosis suggests a combination of organic damage and massive hysterical acting out, hallucinations, and delusions involving possession by assorted animal "spirits."

Whether or not Mrs. H.'s delusional and hallucinatory trend was affected by her alcoholism must remain a matter of conjecture. But in other respects it closely resembles the characteristic syndrome of demoniacal possession as it is described in the literature—from the Dominican monks Kramer and Sprenger in the Middle Ages to Pierre Janet (1894), T. K. Oesterreich (1921), Freud (1932), Mircea Eliade (1964), D. M. Yap (1951), and many others. On the other hand, possession by animal spirits is unusual in Western culture, though it is a recurrent feature in Japanese and Chinese folklore.

As in most cases of this order, there was nothing in Mrs. H.'s personal history to suggest the involvement of genuine psi phenomena. Thus, from the parapsychological point of view, her case was unrewarding. All the more revealing was the psychological inquiry into her problem. She gave a history of years of frustration and rejection by her husband. She felt he had treated her like a dog; her barking and howling signified her helpless rage against him, and her masochistic groveling was an appeal for his forgiveness and love, as well as for the attention he was ready to bestow on his house pets and racehorses but not on his wife. Thus, her exhibitionistic performances were clearly aimed at getting her husband's sympathy while at the same time punishing him for his callous indifference toward her. Mr. H., in turn, fed into her delusional trend by condoning and seemingly endorsing her claims of being the victim of external powers beyond anyone's control—especially, his own. Wittingly or unwittingly, he went along with his wife's bizarre performances because they relieved his own sense of guilt. Doing so demonstrated both to himself and to the world his continued loyalty and loving concern for her.

Unfortunately, this was in the way of her receiving proper psychiatric help. She did not respond to my attempts to talk "directly" to the animal spirits by which she felt she was possessed. When I pretended to address her barking and yelping pooch and ask him whether he would like to go with me for a walk, she shook her head in violent protest. Obviously, it was not mine but her husband's attention she wanted to obtain. Her husband, in turn, refused to accept my recommendation to resume conventional psychiatric treatment and insisted on my trying some newfangled form of exorcism with his wife.

My next case is what in clinical parlance could be described as an incomplete, or *forme fruste,* case of possession in a young man of thirty-two. It was triggered off by a series of marijuana trips in an otherwise well-integrated personality and occurred in the waking state.

Bill F., a successful advertising executive, is married to a charming woman some ten years his junior. They have two small children. Bill has smoked "pot" on four or five occasions in the company of his wife, their friend Helen—a "big, hefty woman" of thirty-eight—and one or two others. When I saw him he was in a state of acute anxiety and agitaton. He had flown some 1,200 miles to consult me.

> I have read Ouspensky, Suzuki, Castaneda . . . I have tried mental telepathy experiments with Helen. It was all nonverbal . . . I made some psychic discoveries of my own . . . It was fantastic and we exchanged thoughts, feelings, and moods; we switched to different memory tracks . . . I had new perceptions . . . But suddenly I got an actual physical sensation of Helen's presence deep in me, wanting to take over. I was fright-

ened, my whole body shook—then I felt the buildup of energy in me . . . I drew it from her, from Helen . . . Then it was as if she had left me, yet she wanted to repeat it again. I felt charged with her energies, it was like an illumination, an inside glow! Now life had a purpose and we can have an impact on the universe! But then she did not let go of me. I yelled "Stop it," but she wanted to do it again. Then I developed a paranoid feeling about her, tried to escape from her power. I began to hallucinate. Reality became ambiguous; I got increasingly frightened. I feared I would transmit by anxiety to the kids. Even my little daughter had a sinister influence on me—or I on her? Helen's little dog cowered in a corner, barked and ran away from me . . . The telephone rang and then conked out . . . There were mysterious voices breaking in on my tape recorder; the whole world became chaotic and disorganized.

Bill never had similar experiences before, but his mother, aged fifty-three, suffered from recurrent episodes of depression alternating with periods of hyperactivity and elation. "At such times," Bill said, "she would be brimful of energy—like Helen." Bill's wife, who had accompanied him on his visit to my office, had absorbed most of her husband's delusions. They were both frightened and perplexed by his "possession." Yet after passing through the height of initial confusion, his sensorium cleared. When first seen, he was still terror-stricken but fully oriented and in contact with his environment. In the course of several two-to-three-hour sessions, he gained growing insight into his condition, yet still stubbornly clung to the reality of having been under the control of, or possessed by, Helen's powerful personality. He was also convinced of having been in close telepathic contact with her. At the same time, he was ready to acknowledge the part that marijuana had played in his experience. He also wondered about the contribution of his maternal heritage to the problem. "Apparently I cannot win; according to you, doctor, it's either due to marijuana or to my genes."

Despite his growing insight and gradual recovery, Bill was still reluctant to give up the idea that he had gone through a state of what theologians have described as possession from *above* as opposed to *below*, and I saw no reason to challenge this position. Instead, I called his attention to his ambivalent feelings toward Helen and hinted at her apparent infatuation—if not her ulterior designs, on him. He realized that her controlling personality was in many ways remniscent of the controlling, emotionally unstable mother of his formative years. She had, in effect, all the characteristics of what Rheingold (1967) and other analysts described as the witch-mother, eclipsing the nourishing, benevolent aspect of the "good" mother figure. Thus, Bill's experience of mystic union with Helen—together with his attending terror and fleeting sense of elation—was indeed a symbolic representation of symbiotic fusion with the nurturing and devouring mother figure of his early infantile experience. It should be noted that apart from the drug-induced changes of consciousness, Bill never went into a trance. Thus, according to the old nomenclature, his case would have to be described as one of "lucid," by contrast to "somnambulic," possession. Two years after his acute episode Bill was fully recovered though still afraid of its recurrence.

Whether or not a genuine telepathic interchange took place between Bill and his reincarnated and externalized mother surrogate is an open question. His accounts of some of the incidents in which he felt he was telepathically attuned to Helen might have contained a grain of truth. His preoccupation with the paranormally tempered tapes was centainly purely delusional. In this respect, Bill's purportedly paranormal claims are indeed closely akin to some of the characteristic features of schizophrenic reactions discussed in the preceding chapter. The patient's persecutor represents in part a projection into the outside world of his own repudiated instinctual drives, in part the internalized image, or caricature, of a hated and beloved parental figure. In possession, the same repudiated hostile-destructive or deviant sexual impulses are attributed to a malignant external influence that has invaded the victim's personality.

In the Christian world, such sinister influences are traditionally personified by the devil, with the resulting macabre picture of what theologians have called possession from below. Alternatively, superhuman, divine, benevolent attributes are bestowed on the possessing agency, infusing the subject with a sense of elation, mystic rapture, or ecstasy. This is what has been described as possession from above. The particular clinical manifestation of the possession syndrome in a given case are then determined by the subject's personal history, his psycho pathology, his religious background, his cultural conditioning, and the beliefs held by him or his social environment. While an East Indian "demoniac" may have felt possessed by the terrible goddess Kali, a medieval faithful may have thought he was victimized by Beelzebub, and the nuns of Loudun by their father confessor Urbain Grandier. Some of of the hysterical children of Salem accused the unhappy Reverend George Burroughs or John Procter of similar ungodly mischief.

It was in the wake of eighteenth century enlightenment that the demon was expurgated from demoniacal possession and replaced by benevolent, heroic, or romantically inclined "secondary personalities" or spirit controls of the spiritualistic trance. Nevertheless, in whatever shape, form, or costume they made their appearance, analytically speaking, they are dissociated aspects of the medium's personality, personifications of her "complexes," or instinctual drives. They are externalizations of what Gustav Bychowski (1956) described as "introjects," that is, internal representations of a controlling father or mother figure who had invaded the subject's personality structure. Bill's feeling of possession by Helen, the reincarnation of his psychotic mother, is a case in point.

Thus, the psychodynamics underlying both the possession syndrome and secondary trance personalities are indeed closely related. There are, however, several points of difference between so-called spirit controls in the trance state and the classical picture of diabolical possession.

Trance personalities, though they too are dissociated parts of the medium's personality, live in a state of relatively peaceful coexistence or complementarity with her. By contrast, in the typical possession syndrome the possessing entity is felt as an ego-alien, hostile intruder, a demon, an evil spirit, the devil incarnate. Although it is derived from a dissociated fragment of the patient's personality, it has to be banished, cast out from its confines.

The same is true if it is a derivative of an introjected parental figure: a tyrannical father or a "witch-mother." Thus, the mechanism of defense underlying the trance is mental dissociation and externalization—that is, an essentially hysterical reaction. By contrast, possession is largely based on paranoid projection, that is, an essentially psychotic pattern of response. Another feature differentiating possession from secondary or trance personalities is the fact that the phenomena of hysterical dissociation rarely amount to a total take-over of the medium's personality by the so-called spirit control. It leaves the rest of it unimpaired, or it restores her personality to her previous state immediately on her emergence from the trance. The same is true for so-called motor or sensory automatisms seen in habitual users of the Oijua board or the planchette, even though they usually amount to little more than a harmless parlor game.

My third case comes closer to the syndrome of spirit possessions than the cases of Mrs. H. or Bill F. We shall presently see that there are two reasons for this state of affairs: the patient is of Jamaican origin, and her experiences of possession had been initated and encouraged by a native *curandero* or witch doctor.

Alma Y., aged twenty-seven, has studied graphic arts in Europe and at a leading art institute in the United States. Her studies were subsidized by foundation grants. Her first bouts with the "occult" occurred at age twelve while she was still living in Jamaica.

> I liked to listen to music. Suddenly I felt some strange vibrations . . . I may have gone into a trance. . . . Then, at nineteen, my grandmother died. I was praying at her coffin, when all of a sudden I again felt vibrations in my body. . . . Grandmother talked to me. She said: "I am alive, not dead." I became quite upset and went to a medium for help. He told me, he saw the spirit of grandmother next to me. He said, grandmother wanted the help of my body to express herself . . . she wanted to send messages through me to her relatives. I said: "I am afraid to do so" . . . But I went into a trance. Gradually I felt her emanations . . . her personality was invading me. Mother said: Yes, the way I looked and expressed myself was quite like grandmother. I felt, I was not me any longer . . . It lasted perhaps half an hour . . . He, the witch doctor, pushed me into it . . . I did not want to go into a trance.

Besides grandmother there were also other relatives who had occasionally invaded her body: Nine or ten spirits, or even more.

> On one occasion I heard my uncle call from a neighboring village: "Mother help me." Three hours later, I learned he had a heart attack. Then my face got contorted—like uncle's face. I felt he too had invaded my personality. Yes, there were both good and bad spirits in our house . . . my parents confirmed it . . . One night I saw mother's apparition in a white tunic. Next morning she said she was chasing bad spirits out of the house.

When Alma graduated from high school and moved to an art college on the mainland, she had a novel type of experience. There was a woman teacher, Ethel, some forty years old, who exerted an uncanny influence of her.

> One night I felt Ethel wanted to call me on the phone. I felt a magnetic force like an iron band around my head. Then Ethel appeared . . . she had a gadget in her hand to suck my soul out of my body—to steal my soul from me. I asked: "How can you do that to me?" She said: "I thought you are a woman—but I see you are just a baby" . . . and I heard voices saying: "Yes, she want you as a woman. It's a shame since you are her pupil."

It transpired that Ethel had become her homosexual pursuer while Alma was at college in X. She had assiduously sought her teacher's favors but had pulled away from her whenever Ethel seemed to take more than a professional interest in her student. Yet during a preceding one year's stay abroad, Alma had actually been involved in two homosexual relationships. "The first time, it was an older woman who made me drunk and seduced me." However, Alma had also a number of casual affairs with men at the same time, without any deeper emotional involvement with them. It was obvious that she had used such relationships as antidotes against her homosexual inclinations. In the wake of her early exposure to the primal scene, she considered men as brutal attackers of the female and associated love and tenderness only with female partners. She had never made the break from her original attachment to her grandmother, the matriarch of the family, and from her mother, whom she likewise described as a strong personality.

Thus Alma's possession by the spirit of her grandmother and subsequently by Ethel, her college teacher, had in effect dramatized her inner struggle with a thinly veiled homosexual trend. Her trance states facilitated and symbolized her passive surrender to the mother figure. On the other hand, her frantic remonstrations against her personality being invaded by her homosexual attackers expressed her struggle against a repudiated instinctual drive. Thus, in her case, the possession syndrome dramatized her alternative use of an essentially dissociative, hysterical pattern of defenses instead of a more ominous projective, paranoid pattern.

In this respect, Alma's psychodynamics resemble those of the previous patient. The major difference between the two is obviously due to their vastly different cultural backgrounds. While the existing intrapsychic conflicts could have set the stage for the same hysterical or paranoid acting out in both cases, Alma's Jamaican heritage helped to produce the typical snydrome of spirit possession, and Bill's psychotic episode was aided by his drug experience, though here, too, its specific coloration may have been provided by the then current fascination of the American public with spirit possession and exorcism. Thus, the juxtaposition of the two patients suggests that the manifest content of the possession syndrome is largely a cultural artifact, superimposed on an existing genetic predisposition, internalized conflicts, and other idiosyncratic factors. Similar considerations apply to Mrs. H.'s more elementary attention-getting psychodynamics, combined with her underlying organic pathology. It should also be recalled that the productions of trance mediums in the spiritualistic séance room are virtually "coproduced" by their sitters. In a similar vein, I have pointed out elsewhere (Ehrenwald 1966) that the hapless victims of the medieval witch trials likewise tended to reflect some of the bizarre psychopathology of their time. This is what I described as doctrinal compliance.

Alma, like Bill, responded well to psychotherapy aimed at providing a modicum of insight into the origin of her experiences. The first order of business in Alma's case was to counteract, as tactfully as possible, the adverse effects of indoctrination by her witch doctor. Doing so was facilitated by her own long-standing critical attitude toward the superstitions of the "voodoo people." The next step was to bring her ambivalence toward mother figures into focus. This was followed by confronting her with her overriding homosexual conflicts. Here, for once, the sexual permissiveness of her upbringing and the easygoing life style and the woman's lib movement of her generation helped to reduce the intensity of the conflict. She faced up to her homosexual tendencies and chose a "bisexual" solution which she felt was more congenial to her.

It is needless to say that such a purely clinical-psychiatric approach to the possession syndrome and trance phenomena does not tell the whole story. It glosses over the patient's occult claims and their parapsychologically most intriguing aspect: it leaves the demon out of demoniacal possession. It is Hamlet without the Prince; it stages Macbeth's banquet without Banquo's ghost and ignores the psi element—the psychic reality—which may or may not be involved in the popular image of demoniacal possession.

This aspect can only be brought into proper perspective when we realize the close psychodynamic affinity of mediumistic trance and the possession syndrome. I have noted that trance phenomena can be described as *formes frustes* of the ancient protoype of possesion, purged of its malignant, demoniacal ingredients. Yet if and when such trance productions happen to include genuine psi phenomena, they may give rise to a wide variety of mystical or religious interpretations, to a revival of the devil theory, or to the theory of survival after death, which is held by the church and is still attractive to many spiritualists and parapsychologists of our day.

I submit that an alternative interpretation in terms of telepathy or clairvoyance "pure and simple"—or, if you like, Rhine's "super-psi"—is more parsimonious, even though it admittedly requires an auxiliary hypothesis. It is predicated on the assumption that a gifted trance medium is able to do three things: (1) to pick up a telepathic cue from the sitter or his associates, (2) to weave such telepathic impressions into the fabric of her own "autopsychic" mental content, and (3) to pull it out again from the conjuror's hat, as it were, and to bring it to life as a seemingly autonomous "secondary personality." It is a performance reminiscent of a gifted actor conjuring up the living presence of a dramatis personae on the stage.

Possession and Exorcism: Delusion Shared and Compounded?

The hypothesis of dramatic impersonation and elaboration of such secondary personalities is indeed widely held by students of psychical research. It is supported, furthermore, by Gestalt psychologists and their concept of *closure* of incomplete configurations under experimental conditions. The process can be described as the hypothesis of telepathic grafting or seeding. Given the fertile soil of a medium's creative imagination, coupled with her need for identification and a gift for showmanship, minute telepathic cues or tracer elements seem to suffice to grow and to be fleshed out into the familiar form of a departed "dear one," of such imaginary personages as Mrs. Eileen Garret's Uvani or Abdul Latif, as the medieval knight Ulrich, von Grebenstein in a case studied by C. G. Jung (1902), or, in cases of classical diabolic possession, by the devil and his minions.

Whatever be the chain of psychological events touched off by such telepathic seeding, its veridical nature is then contingent on the bits and pieces of correct factual information which it conveys to the circle of sitters and other witnesses involved in the experience. Given the requisite atmosphere of awe, of "fear and trembling"—or plain credulity—the scenario of what would otherwise appear as an impressive trance manifestation may be miraculously transformed into the spectacle of diabolical or divine possession—shamanistic, medieval Christian, voodoo, or cabalistic style.

If this is true, the pitiful, or awesome, picture confronting us in possession, both from below or from above, is neither more nor less divine than Plato's divine madness, Hippocrates' sacred disease, or a contemporary schizophrenic reaction. The psychiatrist's or parapsychologist's interventions must therefore be guided by this basic understanding of the possession syndrome. Failing this, the psychiatrist is unlikely to make due allowance for the paranormal implications of a given case. On the other hand, the priest or "psychic investigator" turned exorcist may be at a loss to cope with the frankly psychiatric aspects of the picture. (Needless to say, the hazards are greater in the latter than in the former case.)

Indeed, more often than not, the primitive exorcist—ancient Egyptian, Babylonian, medieval Christnan, or Hasidic style—approached his client's delusions on the level of the deluded. He shared his terrors, projections, and fantasies in the guise of the devil or the divinity. His conjurations, prayers, chants, and incantations, his bloodletting of sacrificial animals, sprinkling of holy water, and flashing of the crucifix, tended to reassure both the exorcist and the victim of the demonic possession. They served to deliver both of them from the abominations of the devil

127

—and from whatever kindred blasphemous, sadistic, or otherwise deviant sexual impulses they might harbor in their unconscious. At the same time the exorcist's participation in the victim's plight tended to offer him a vicarious thrill and the opportunity for the guiltless acting out—*ad majorem dei gloriam*—of his own repudiated instinctual drives.

Evidently, such a scenario has an equal chance for good or for evil. Instead of calming the victim's agitation and relieving his terror, it may confirm his worst expectations. Analytically speaking, the ritual of exorcism may give an added dimension of reality to the internalized object—the demon. It may appear to the patient as consensual validation by the exorcist and by society of his hallucinatory experiences and thus may compound his delusional trend. I pointed out in Chapters 3 and 4 that the medieval witch-hunter's and his victim's shared delusions had frequently become the sources of minor or major epidemics of witch craze or of collective hysteria, as exemplified by the crazed nuns of Loudun and the hysterical children of seventeenth century Salem. The current wave of artificial, media-made hysteria about possession sweeping this country strikes the same theme, though in a minor key.

Indeed, despite the vast differences in the contemporary scene, the problems of possession are not unlike those which were encountered in less "enlightened" societies. Once again, we have to deal with scores of casualties of hysterical contagion originating from either primary sources of pathology or artificial, media-made sources. It is a pathology faithfully reflecting its archaic prototype. Yet if the modern psychiatrist is unprepared to descend—or ascend—to the level of the patient's delusional experience, unable to speak his language, to communicate with him on his own terms, and to "get into the act" when necessary he will fail to meet a major professional challenge and drive the patient once again into the arms of the primitive exorcist or the faith healer, if not the charlatan.

On the other hand, seemingly concurring with the premises of the patient's delusional system may merely reinforce his pathology. He must therefore never lose sight of his primary therapeutic objective: to pare down the delusional elements in the clinical picture. The major tranquilizers or even a placebo may be helpful. (Akihisha Kondo 1977). But more important is to help the patient to recognize his delusions for what they are: his tendency to externalize deep-seated emotional conflicts. Instead of escalating mental dissociation into paranoid delusions, the therapist must try to lower the grade of the existing pathology by reducing delusions to the level of hysterical symptomatology. This may bring the patient one step closer to insight and better reality testing. It may help him to recognize in the purportedly possessing entity the projection of his own repudiated instinctual drives.

At the same time, the therapist must do one more thing: he must keep an open mind to the possibility that genuine psi elements—PK, ESP, or even alleged xenoglossy (speaking a language unknown to the user) may be involved in the clinical picture (Stevenson 1974). He must make allowance for the fact that in such a case their very emergence may serve the patient as an indication of his sanity and a vindication of his mental health. Even more than in a schizophrenic's delusional system, this may have a modicum of restitutive value. But the therapist must also realize that either way, the influx of psi elements into the patient's "normal" waking experience is usually maladjustive: it is maladjustive as far as his standard mode of existence and reality testing is concerned. Even possession from "above" is more a matter for the saints, the mystics, or the creative artist than for the ordinary man or woman in contemporary Western culture.

It is this basic existential position which seems to be responsible for the profoundly ambivalent reaction of both religious and scientific orthodoxy to the syndrome of possession, demoniacal or otherwise. In a past era, possession and its paranormal aspects posed a grave threat to both the faithful and to the defenders of the "true faith." Both the exorcist and the victim of possession had to be protected at all costs from the "enormity" of witchcraft and heresy—if necessary by burning the recalcitrant victim at the stake. Fortunately, this ultimate remedy of the medieval inquisitor is no longer an option open to the modern psychiatrist when dealing with some of his more difficult cases.

13

Parent-Child Symbiosis

and the Revolt of the Poltergeist

REPORTS of the direct influence of the will upon physical objects without neural conduction or the mediation of the muscular system is so odious to common sense and our ingrained habits of thinking that I have for years refused to face up to such a possibility. My doubts in the authenticity of the phenomena were further enhanced by the frequent exposure of fraud and trickery in alleged materializations, levitations, and feats of table-tilting produced by so-called physical mediums in the séance room.

But we shall see in Chapter 19 that the occurrence of psychokinesis (or PK) as the motor counterpart of ESP, as postulated by the extension hypothesis, can rightly be expected on purely logical grounds. If the mother-child relationship in the symbiotic stage can be described as the "Cradle of ESP," it should be reasonable to explore the same interpersonal configuration as a potential breeding ground of PK.

Such a proposition provides at least a tentative frame of reference to accommodate both ESP and PK in our overall picture of the world, and it should lower our intellectual resistances against psi in general. Indeed, in my own case, it was the striking symmetrical relationship of ESP and PK—and especially of alleged poltergeist phenomena, or "recurrent spontaneous PK" (RSPK), involving parent figures and their rebellious offspring—which helped to tip the balance in favor of accepting PK as one of the possible manifestations of the psi syndrome.

The fact is that the evidence for PK, spontaneous and experimental, including so-called poltergeist incidents, is just as strong as the data pertaining to the more familiar modalities of ESP. Indeed, apart from experimental PK, anecdotal reports of capricious physical manifestations supposedly emanating from rebellious youngsters are more frequent in both occult lore and the parapsychological literature than are cases of telepathy between mother and child discussed in preceding chapters.

A typical account of RSPK reads as follows. A family living in a detached house or an apartment is disturbed by recurrent knocking or banging sounds coming from the ceiling or walls. Books fall from the shelves; crockery, ashtrays, or bottles of cleaning fluid fly through space and break on impact, apparently thrown by mysterious agencies. A broom or a lamp hurls through the room and lands in another location. Sometimes it is a large piece of furniture which is displaced or the contents of a drawer spilled on the floor. Light switches are turned on or off; the telephone or other electrical appliances are interfered with by forces not explainable in terms of ordinary breakdowns, fraud, or trickery.

If this is not enough to turn off the skeptic, he must be advised that in some instances genuinely paranormal phenomena of this order occur together with a mixed bag of tricks and childish pranks. The difficulties are further compounded by sensationalistic reporting, unreliable witnesses, or conflicting stories told by bona fide observers. Yet it must be said that there is an increasing number of recent, well-documented cases that have stood up to critical scrutiny.

The Seaford Case

This case was initially investigated by J. G. Pratt of the University of Virginia and W. G. Roll, project director of the Phychical Research Foundation (Durham, N.C.). An account of it appears in the *Journal of Parapsychology* (1958) and was subsequently published in more detail in an article by Roll in the *Journal of the American Society for Psychical Research* (1968). In this case the disturbances seemed to center around Michael, aged twelve, while his sister Nancy, aged thirteen, played no apparent role in their origin. The parents, Mr. and Mrs. Lessing (pseudonym), are both college graduates, middle-class, Catholic, and respected members of their community. Mr. Lessing, holding a responsible position, is described as a strict disciplinarian, an authoritarian personality. Mrs. Lessing is a permissive mother, protective of her son. Both children attend the local public school.

The disturbances were confined to the Lessings' home and occurred only when one or both children were present and not asleep. They were observed by the investigators, by a police detective, and by other witnesses. In one of the typical occurrences, a sixteen-inch figurine of the Holy Virgin in the master bedroom moved "spontaneously" from the father's dresser and knocked over the mother's picture. Only one hand of the plaster figurine was broken. Other objects displaced, seen flying through the air, or found broken on the ground were of such trivial nature as bottles of cleaning fluid, ashtrays, and so on.

For obvious reasons, the investigators gave first priority to collecting as much factual evidence as possible and were less concerned with interpersonal relationships in the Lessing family. Both parents were much disturbed by the occurrences and gave willing cooperation to the investigators; however, Mr. Lessing refused to submit himself or the children to a polygraph test, although he did permit extensive psychological studies to be carried out with both Michael and Nancy.

Michael is described as a bright, seemingly well-adjusted youngster with a verbal IQ of 127 and a performance IQ of 109. Yet his projective tests reveal a great deal of unconscious or repressed hostility. Dr. Gertrude Schmeidler of the City College of New York, commenting on some of his Rorschach responses, specifically noted a tendency to an "eruption of spontaneous, unconscious, depersonalized violence." In one of his responses Michael sees a polliwog or baby frog emerging from its egg jelly. "The space could be where it bored a hole so it could make its escape . . . sometimes the frog dies because he can't get out" (Roll 1968, p. 304).

Dr. Schmeidler suggests that Michael felt "he had a tender and loving home, even though its restrictions sometimes began to smother him" (Roll 1968, p. 304). Some of Michael's Thematic Apperception Test responses expressed his unconscious conflict with the father figure which was "killed in self-defense." On the other hand, Roll emphasizes Michael's rebellious, passive-demanding attitude toward his mother.

The Newark Disturbances

This is another interesting case studied by W. G. Roll (Roll 1966). It takes us from the seeming tranquillity of the well-to-do Lessing home to the troubled atmosphere of a housing project building. In this instance the suspected RSPK agent was a thirteen-year-old black boy, Arnold Brooks, living with his grandmother, Mrs. Susie Parks, whose husband had died a year or so previously. The series of sixty-four events again involved the usual assortment of trivial objects—bottles, ashtrays, saucers, light bulbs. Two lamps floated through the air and smashed; pictures swayed on the wall. Numerous objects fell to the floor and broke to pieces. On several occasions the incidents involved the mysterious disappearance and recovery of dollar bills. On another occasion a small bottle "grazed Mrs. Parks" and then hit the investigator "squarely on the head." This happened at the very moment when Mrs. Parks expressed her wish to have her grandson removed from the apartment. The investigator, pleading with her to let the boy remain, noted that "It doesn't hit people" after all. The boy had been sitting close to him "unmoving and stoical . . . as usual" (Roll 1966, pp. 137–38).

No events occurred when Arnold moved to his uncle's house for a week. On his return to his grandmother, the disturbances started up again. The kitchen cupboard, the refrigerator, the television set, and the washing machine all fell over. All this apparently became too much for Mrs. Parks to cope with and Arnold was placed in a temporary children's shelter. Ultimately he and Mrs. Parks were taken by Roll to the Parapsychology Laboratory at Duke University in Durham for further study. In this setting the phenomena seemed to peter out and were apparently replaced by childish pranks.

Polygraph studies carried out in this instance were inconclusive. The EEG findings were perhaps more significant. They showed a brief burst of 14-per-second positive spikes while the boy was drowsy—a pattern often seen in adolescents with behavioral problems.

Extensive personality studies included the Rorschach, the Thematic Apperception Test, the Minnesota Multiphasic Personality Inventory, and even an interview in hypnosis. Arnold's intelligence test indicated an IQ of 90. The psychodiagnostic studies, carried out by Drs. Paul and Altrocchi, showed an angry little boy "who felt completely helpless and unable to express or act upon his anger." They noted that his relationship with his grandmother was severely neurotic and indeed more pathological than either of them as "separate personalities." In any case, Arnold's prevailing defense was denial and repression, with a tendency to dissociated states. In addition, there was evidence of a paranoid trend and the possibility of a schizophrenic breakdown. All this led to "an increasingly intolerable relationship between Arnold and his grandmother." Mrs. Parks is in turn described as an immature personality "focusing more on her needs than onto Arnold" after the death of her husband, "thus placing more than usual stress on an already tenuous relationship" (Paul and Altrocchi 1966, p. 1965).

I may add at this point that Arnold's family history showed added features of severe pathology. His father, a boxer, had been repeatedly jailed. In one of the recurrent battles with his wife, she shot him to death and was subsequently sentenced to a jail term. Arnold had been brought up in at least four consecutive foster homes, the last one with his grandmother. In the end the New Jersey Board of Child Welfare placed him in a new, sheltered foster home where he reportedly made a good adjustment.

The Miami Disturbances

The Miami case was likewise investigated in great detail by Roll and Pratt (1971). In this instance there are well-attested reports of breakages and mysterious dislocations of objects stored on the shelves of a Miami warehouse. Certain of the objects were seen traveling some distance before crashing on the floor. In contrast to the Lessing and Newark disturbances, the RSPK agent was not a child but a nineteen-year-old Cuban shipping clerk. No information about his family life or his relationship to his employers is available. Yet personality studies carried out in Durham revealed "strong feelings of hostility, especially toward parent figures, which he could not express overtly and from which he felt personally detached. It appeared that he regarded the owners of the business in Miami as parental figures and the disturbances were a means to express aggression which could find no other outlet" (1971, p. 18).

This observation shows that the interpersonal configuration responsible for RSPK need not necessarily involve a parent-child conflict. The crucial point is that the relationship is patterned after the original parent-child prototype. This statement is further borne out by the following case.

The Rosenheim Poltergeist

This case was carefully investigated by Professor Hans Bender (1974) and his associates at the Institut für Grenzgebiete der Psychologie, in Freiburg. In this instance, a nineteen-year-old girl, Annemarie S., employed in a law office in Rosenheim, Bavaria, was at the center of the disturbances. They involved a variety of electric appliances such as neon lights, telephones, and a copying machine. Abnormal fluctuations in the electrical power supply were recorded by an electronic monitoring device. In addition, an Ampex video recorder was used to register objectively the seemingly spontaneous swinging of lamps and pictures on the wall and the simultaneous bangings and rapping noises.

Neither experts from the telephone company nor physicists called in from the Max Planck Institute for Physics and Plasmaphysics near Munich were able to account for the phenomena. The physicists F. Karger and G. Zicha remarked in their summary: "Although recorded with the facilities available to experimental physics, the phenomena defy explanation with the means available to theoretical physics" (1967, p. 35).

There is less information concerning the psychological aspects and interpersonal relationships of the suspected agent. Miss S.'s work-up with a series of personality tests showed, among other things, lability, irritability, emotional instability with low frustration tolerance, and sexual conflicts. An important feature stressed by psychologist John Mischo (1967) director of the Institut für Grenzgebiete der Psychologie, in Freiburg, Germany, was displacement of aggression and destructiveness, repression, and projection. In his summary he concludes that "psychokinesis . . . can function as an aggression release mechanism" (1967, p. 36). It is a mechanism in which "a momentary regression to magic-animistic attitudes and fantasies become[s] dynamically active."

Though there is no mention of the interpersonal configuration surrounding the Rosenheim case, it can be surmised that here too, as in the Miami disturbances, conflict with the girl's employer may have been the triggering factor.

This is also borne out by the fact that the Rosenheim disturbances ceased as soon as Miss S. left her first employer. Yet milder manifestations started again at her new place of employment. It is also interesting to note that apart from her RSPK, Miss S. was at times subject to fits and convulsions of the type of conversion hysteria.

Some Other Cases

Dr. Bender and his associates have studied some twenty-three poltergeist disturbances over the years. One is known as the Pursruck case, after a town near Nuremberg. It involved two girls, Helga, thirteen years old, and Anna, eleven. The noises, rappings, and other disturbances associated with them threw the whole community into uproar. A Catholic priest and psychotherapist was called in but no closer psychological study of the children is available. All we learn is that in this case the girls' anxiety dominated the picture. It should also be noted that dance therapy and rhythmic exercises introduced by the therapist relieved their anxiety and led to marked lessening of the RSPK.

In the Scherfede case investigated by the Freiburg team, puddles and later a deluge of water appeared mysteriously, first in the bathroom and later in other parts of the house occupied by the K. family. The suspicion of the investigators fell on Kerstin, a girl of thirteen. However, apart from the K. family home, two houses in the neighborhood were likewise plagued by this unusual "water poltergeist." On further inquiry it transpired that in addition to using the family bathroom, Kerstin had also been in the habit of dropping in at the bathrooms of her neighbors. A psychoanalyst consulted by Dr. Bender suggested that Kerstin may have been suffering from a "urethral neurosis." Put in Freudian terms, it could conceivably be described as a fixation or acting out of aggression on the phallic level. Yet it is needless to say that such an interpretation still tells us nothing about the modus operandi of this bizarre case.

One of the most spectacular examples of a poltergeist has recently been reported from Cambridge, England. The author is eighteen-year-old Matthew Manning, describing his own case in his precocious autobiography, *The Link* (1974). The disturbances started when he was eleven. They were studied by several competent investigtors, including the psychologist Peter Bander who served as editor of the book; Professor George Owen, Fellow of Trinity College, Cambridge; and others. A preface by Matthew's father and introductory remarks by Mr. Bander permit glimpses into Matthew's family situation, his personality makeup, and what may have been a smoldering conflict between him and his somewhat authoritarian father. A fuller discussion of the Manning case will be found in Chapter 17.

More recent observations have added a new wrinkle to the poltergeist puzzle. It is described as the energy focusing and lingering effect of the presumed energy involved in the disturbances (Joins 1975). Joins quotes the example of a compass needle being deflected by the PK agent. The deflection remains until the compass is removed from the immediate area. Yet "the needle returns to the deflected position when it is replaced to the original area" (p. 134). Similar observations in a poltergeist setting have been interpreted in terms of hauntings or of the survival hypothesis. Yet here again, the possibility of temporal, as opposed to spatial, scatter or displacement, which is characteristic of ESP responses, may be a more parsimonious explanation.

The French police officer Emile Tizané (1951) has amassed a vast number of alleged poltergeist observations over a period of twenty-five years. He ranks them in their order of "oddity" ranging from a bombardment by stones or other small objects impinging on a house from outside, to breakages or displacement of furniture indoors, to objects seen flying "round the corner"(!) along irregular trajectories. Among the more bizarre phenomena, he lists apparent materializations and dematerializations.

All these cases of RSPK differ from the less spectacular laboratory type of PK in that they involve movements of static objects, while experimental PK is mostly confined to deflecting the motion of falling or otherwise moving objects. They are usually of a dramatic nature, seem to be triggered by highly charged emotions, and invariably elicit corresponding emotional responses in their social environment. Psychodynamically speaking, they have their roots in a prolonged symbiotic pattern and in the "junior" partner's violent reaction formation against it.

These few representative samples of recent well-documented cases may suffice in the present context. Their condensed summary cannot possibly do justice to the wealth of technical data presented by Pratt, Roll, Bender, and their associates, to the interpretations offered by their psychological consultants, to the mathematical model suggested by Roll and Artley (Roll 1972), nor to Roll's attempts at delineating the curve of apparent physical attenuation effects supposedly typical of the phenomena, their presumed field characteristics, and so on. The interested reader may be referred to Nandor Fodor's (1959) pioneering contributions, to W. G. Roll's excellent monograph (1972), and to the classical study *Can We Explain the Poltergeist?* by the Cambridge University geneticist A. R. G. Owen (1964).

The current situation is well summed up by Owen. He notes that an above-chance incidence of hysteria or other psychoneurosis seems to be characteristic of poltergeist agents. He quotes Breuer and Freud's remark that human beings usually release nervous tension by active biological response, by a conscious psychological process of attrition, or by surrogate physical activities. In Owen's view, the poltergeist represents a surrogate paraphysical activity which is open to a few specially endowed people. But, like fever, the phenomena are a cure rather than a disease.

Yet to this we must add that poltergeist phenomena do not occur in an interpersonal vacuum, that they are not merely tempests in a sealed and pressurized teapot, the results of repressed or bottled-up undirected hostility seeking an outlet as first proposed by Fodor (1959). They derive from oppositional behavior, specifically aimed at parental figures or their surrogates, with the individual's home and family group turned into the proving ground for an existing family conflict (Ehrenwald 1963; Rogo 1974; Roll 1972). In the acting out children in the Seaford and the Newark cases, such an interpretation goes without saying. It is further supported by the Miami, Pursruck, and Scherfede cases; and it can rightly be surmised in the Rosenheim disturbances.

If this is true, the prevalence of children and adolescents involved in poltergeist cases is readily understood. They are pitting their rebellious, oppositional behavior against parental authority—or authority in general. In effect, their spitefulness, destructiveness, or violence merely betrays their frantic need to emancipate themselves from unyielding, coercive, controlling parental figures who seek to maintain a symbiotic grip over their offspring. The conflict was well put in capsule form by twelve-year-old Michael Lessing in his response to one of the Rorschach cards in which he identified with the baby frog emerging from the egg jelly: "Sometimes the frog dies because he can't get out." This is a graphic illustration of the individual's struggle for what Margaret Mahler described as separation-individuation or what I have termed psychomitosis (Ehrenwald 1954). Viewed in this light, RSPK does not so much amount to the cure of an existing disease as to a pathological acting out of an interpersonal conflict by means of an admittedly unusual mechanism of hysterical conversion, extending far beyond the confines of the individual's personality structure.

Thus the naughty, defiant, rebellious youngsters emerge as the exact counterparts of the passive, compliant, symbiotic children whose telepathic responses to parental do's and don'ts were described as the cradle of ESP. Such children will have none of the programming, remote-control, or formative influences impinging on them on either the conscious, unconscious, or psi level. Their need to stake out the boundaries of their personality spills over the physical confines of their organisms. Like Konrad Lorenz's frustrated stickleback, they deflect their aggression to a substitute target, animate or inanimate—a lampshade, a plaster figurine, or even an innocent bystander. We have seen in Chapter 11 that in trying to do so, they walk the tightrope between schizophrenic surrender and all-out rebellion. They shift from hysterical conversion symptoms on the one hand to spectacular eruptions of PK activity on the other. Indeed, there seems to be an extension to their tightrope that carries them off into Einsteinian curved space in which the classical laws of physics, geometry, and a closed personality structure are suspended and in which action as well as awareness at a distance is no longer merely a matter of wish-dream or fantasy.

Yet from all we know about the symmetrical sensory-motor organization of our mental makeup, the occasional emergence of such seemingly freakish poltergeist phenomena as the motor counterparts of the passive-compliant cases of ESP in children can only be expected. More than that: in the absence of verified observations of this kind they would just as well have to be invented—like a missing element in Mendeleev's tables or the quarks and charms of the nuclear physicist.

I hinted that the explosive acting out of such interpersonal conflicts is by no means confined to the garden variety of the child-parent, master-servant, or employer-employee relationship. This point is illustrated by the celebrated story of what has, somewhat loosely, been described as Jung's poltergeist in Freud's study. The episode occurred in 1909, during what was to be one of the last heart-to heart meetings of the two men. Jung tried to persuade Freud of the reality of certain parapsychological experiences which were close to his heart. "Because of his materialistic prejudice," writes Jung (1963), "he rejected this entire complex of questions as nonsensical and did so in terms of so shallow a positivism that I had difficulty in checking the sharp retort on the tip of my tongue." During that exchange, Jung states, he had a curious sensation: "It was as if my diaphragm were made of iron and were becoming red hot, a glowing vault." At the very same moment both men were startled by a loud report in the bookcase which stood next to them. "There," Jung said, "that is an example of a so-called catalytic exteriorization phenomenon" (1963, pp. 155–56)—that is, an example of PK.

Jung did not, at that time, change Freud's position. A few weeks later, in a letter to Jung, he wrote: "My credulity vanished along with your personal presence . . . it seems wholly implausible that anything of the sort should occur. . . . I therefore don once more my *paternal* spectacles and warn my *dear son* [italics mine] to keep a cool head and rather not understand something than make such a great sacrifice for the sake of understanding" (1963, p. 362).

Skeptics—including, at least until a few years ago—the present writer, will be inclined to agree with Freud's caveat. Yet on closer scrutiny of Jung's recurrent brushes with the occult, a parapsychological interpretation becomes somewhat more plausible. There is his spectacular account of the "splitting with a loud report, and for no apparent reason, of a solid walnut table top" in his and his mother's presence. Shortly thereafter a "big bread-knife snapped, and with an equally loud report, broke into several pieces." Both he and his mother were convinced that such mysterious events must have a deeper meaning. Unfortunately, Jung does not let us in on his secret.

The psychodynamics underlying his "poltergeist incident" in Freud's study is, however, fairly transparent. It epitomizes in a dramatic fashion the clash between two unique personalities: between Freud and Jung, between master and disciple, with the younger man seeking to reverse their respective roles. It was a barely restrained showdown in which the disciple contained his anger on the surface but wrought havoc in the master's bookshelves.

The distance between this dramatic event and the broken plaster figurine or the smashed crockery in the Seaford and Newark poltergeist cases is as great as the gulf separating a couple of disturbed teenagers from the two giants of twentieth century psychiatry. But the underlying psychodynamics is the same. Perhaps their juxtaposition makes the similarity even more impressive. In Jung's case, as in that of the rebellious children, an apparent PK incident was triggered off by the pressing need to put an end to the adult derivative of a conflict-laden symbiotic relationship.

The modus operandi of the poltergeist phenomena and the perplexing problem of the energies involved is another matter. It will have to be discussed within the framework of the psi syndrome in general. But it should be noted that whatever be the nature of the presumed energy, the major disturbances generated by the poltergeist children are of the same order as the minor anomalies involved in the Kulagina case or in the dice-throwing PK experiments. Drawing a parallel with physical processes, the minor bursts of PK in the laboratory can be compared with the crackling of static electricity when I put on my nylon shirt. By the same token, the major explosions of poltergeist activity can be compared with the impact of a bolt of lightning on a church steeple: both are fueled by the same energy source. But the usefulness of the simile ends at this point. Energy—electrical, electromagnetic, physiological, or otherwise—is an anthropomorphic concept. It has amply proved its value in practice and in the field equations of the theoretical physicists. But when applied to human affairs, it reverts to its original prototype and reveals itself for what it is: a metaphor, a figure of speech.

Another puzzling question is that of symptom choice or specificity of the poltergeist disturbance in a given family situation, as opposed to the absence of poltergeist disturbances in countless similar family constellations. We shall return to this problem in Chapter 17.

14

The Witch-Mother and

the Children of Salem

THE TRADITIONAL PICTURE of the witch is a malevolent old hag, the distorted mother figure of sexually frustrated monks of a past age. Or else she is the seductive female, the harlot, who is made the target of their anal-sadistic, homosexual projections and fantasies. But we shall presently see that such widely accepted psychoanalytic interpretations are not easily applicable to the Salem witch trials. The unfortunate women facing their accusers in the New England court rooms lacked the grossly sexual, lewd, exhibitionistic features of the crazed nuns of Loudun or Louviers. The same is true for their accusers. They were hysterical children and adolescents whose antics in a different setting would have made them rather than their victims liable to prosecution by the inquisitioners. If the Devils of Loudun ran the whole gamut of sexual perversions and aberrations, the children of Salem seemed possessed by the Evil One and shrieked their rebellious defiance into the faces of those who had stood for him, by proxy, as it were. Their behavior reflected a different cultural climate; it stemmed from the internalization of different mores, conflicts, and concerns transmitted to them from their elders. The feature performance in the Salem courtroom was bedlam rather than burlesque: the stage was set in seventeenth century Calvinist New England, not in the picturesque countryside of sixteenth century France.

A different interpretation of the Salem witch craze was offered by P. Boyer and S. Nissenbaum (1974). Their historical investigation of the socioeconomic conditions of late seventeenth century New England led them to the conclusion that the disturbances originated from the long-standing hostility between the inhabitants of Salem Township and Salem Village, with the hysterical children acting out the sadistic vendettas of their elders. It is also interesting to note that another historian, John Demos (1970), has pointed to a seventeenth century generation gap as one of the factors responsible for the Salem epidemic, while S. G. Fox (1968) reactivated the scapegoat hypothesis of the witch craze. A more recent theory points to the ingestion of bread contaminated with a fungus causing convulsive ergotism as the culprit. It is an assumption difficult to reconcile with similar outbreaks in both the new world and the old. Nor is it supported by evidence of organic illness in such cases.

The facts of the Salem trials have often been told and call only for the briefest summary in the present context. In the early fall of 1692, fourteen women and five men were convicted of witchcraft and put to death on Gallows Hill in Salem. Most of the women were respectable matrons, mothers, and grandmothers, churchgoing members in good standing with their congregation. Their ages ranged from the early twenties to the seventies. One woman is described as a tavern keeper, the local "village Circe" of doubtful reputation; another as a pipe-smoking tramp, wife of a common laborer, mother of a child of five who was likewise suspected of witchcraft. Still another is said to have engaged in such harmless sorceries as palmistry and fortune-telling.

Among the men convicted and hung was the tragic figure of John Procter, who rushed to the defense of his wife, accused of witchcraft. Another victim was the Reverend George Burroughs, who had once been parson of Salem Village. He was joined on Gallows Hill by several lesser figures of the Salem witch trials. A few more of the accused died in prison; Giles Corey was pressed to death during his interrogation in an open field.

Who Were the Accusers?

The story emerging from the Salem documents is at considerable variance with the traditional picture of medieval or Renaissance witch trials. Instead of such wild-eyed fanatics as the Dominican monks Kramer and

Sprenger or such mild-mannered but hard-headed demonologists as Jean Bodin of sixteenth century France or Joseph Glanvill of seventeenth century England, the prime source of the Salem disturbances were children—"babes, out of whose mouths the truth was supposed to be revealed"—Hansel and Gretel, pitted against a pathetic array of witch-mothers and other parent figures. Whatever were the reasons for the children's bizarre accusations, they were evidently worlds apart from the assortment of sexually, ideologically, or socioeconomically deviant factors which were at play in the world of their elders.

The question of motivation becomes more puzzling still when we realize that the accusers semed to pick their victims at random from among their parents' friends, neighbors, or acquaintances, without discernible reasons for their choice. There was Betty, aged nine, daughter of Samuel Parris, parson of Salem Village; her cousin Abigail Williams, aged eleven; and Ann Putnam, aged twelve, daughter of Thomas and Ann Putnam, Sr., close friends of the Parrises. The youngsters were joined by four or five adolescent girls: Mary Wilmott, sixteen; Mary Lewis and Elizabeth Hubbard, seventeen; and Elizabeth Booth and Susannah Sheldon, eighteen.

There was another accuser and accused who would play an important part in the proceedings: Tituba, half Carib Indian, half Negro, brought by Betty's father from Barbados to Salem. Tituba and her consort, John Indian, worked as slaves in the Parris household, with Tibuta playing the part of cook, nanny, and mother substitute to Betty, at that time the Parrises' only child.

The youngsters congregating around Tituba were apparently fascinated by her exotic personality and her colorful accounts of voodoo folklore brought along from her native island home. She was certainly worlds apart from the austere, puritanical discipline and cold emotional climate of the Parris household.

We are told by the historians of the Salem trials (Cotton Mather; Burr 1914; Upham 1867; Starkey 1969; Hansen 1969; and others) that in early 1692 Betty started to sicken with sudden spells of weeping, twitching, convulsions, and fits of screaming. She made choking noises or howled and barked like a dog. Soon her cousin Abigail followed suit, adding even more outlandish behavior to the picture. Scolding, exhortations, or prayers were of no help. Betty screamed wildly at the mere sound of *Our Father*; Abigail covered her ears, stamped her feet, and joined in the screaming to shut out the holy words. Once Betty, described as the most gentle of little girls, hurled the Holy Bible to the floor.

Next, Mary Wilmott and Susannah Sheldon developed the same mysterious afflictions as the younger girls. Presently they spread to the house of Thomas and Ann Putnam, where it affected their daughter Ann, Jr., a precocious girl aged twelve. She in turn infected the Putnams' maid-servant, an adolescent of seventeen. It happened at a time when, according to Upham, Ann's mother was plagued by the discovery of such mysterious "wrongs" as visions of her late sister Mary's dead children "standing before her in their winding sheets, piteously stretching out their hands. . . ." Ann, Sr., had been mentally disturbed and her illness had long preceded the Salem disturbances.

When diverse home remedies and the ministrations of the physician, Dr. Griggs, were of no avail, he threw up his hands: "The Evil Hand is on them," he stated, and passed the responsibility for further treatment to the clergy.

Who Were the Accused?

As noted, the striking feature of the Salem trials is the fact that with one or two exceptions, accusers and accused confronted each other along generational lines. Virtually all defendants were adults who could have stood *in loco parentis* to the afflicted children. Most of the women accused were middle-aged, potential mother figures. In a similar vein, the male suspects seemed to be handpicked with the view of defying and demolishing harsh paternal authority. It was only with the further spread of the witch craze that a few hapless men and women more closely approximating the traditional specifications of the witch were caught in the net of the witch hunters.

A typical case is that of the middle-aged Martha Cory, a respected member of the village congregation, though apparently unpopular because of her opinionated and outspoken ways and skeptical attitude toward witchcraft. When she was incriminated by one of little Ann Putnam's visions, she first tried to laugh the matter off. When pressed to give more information about her visions, Ann was asked what Mrs. Cory's apparition had been wearing. The child said she could not tell, the witch had cast a spell on her which deprived her of her eyesight. This kind of evidence, we are told, was Martha Cory's undoing. When the investigators visited her in her home she said with a knowing smile: "I know what you have come for . . . you have come for a talk to me about being a witch." To make matters worse, she asked, "Did she [Ann] tell you about the clothes I have on? Well . . . did she tell you?" Ann did—though Martha could not, in the opinion of her examiners, have learned by any normal means of that particular detail. It must have been based on supernatural knowledge and was therefore one more piece of telltale evidence against her.

Another victim was Rebecca Nurse, a well-liked grandmotherly woman, the oldest of three sisters who were all incriminated in the witch trials. They are described as women of good character, though their families are reported as having been at odds with the Parrises. In any case, once Rebecca was "cried out" by the Parrises' niece, Abigail Williams, she stood condemned in the parson's eyes. He testified that he himself had witnessed his niece being tormented by Rebecca's "spectral shape." On similar grounds she was accused of having murdered six children and hurt sundry other people. Nevertheless, the jury was at first inclined to acquit the woman of hitherto blameless reputation. But the ensuing outcry of the hysterical girls (who may have identified with the "murdered" children) threw the courtroom into an uproar and was construed as added evidence of her guilt. According to another version, "the very moment" William Phipps, the governor of Massachusetts, had signed the accused woman's reprieve, her devils had taken possession of the girls again. In the further course of events, their pitiful state moved the governor's heart to rescind the reprieve, and the "unrepentant" woman was sentenced to join the others on Gallows Hill.

Once more the twitches, howls, and convulsions of the afflicted children had created their own evidence. They lent substance to their accusations right before the eyes of the jury. Their hysterical symptoms were taken as incontrovertible "spectral" evidence against the defendants.

Some of the girls' reactions are reminiscent of command automatisms, seen in catatonic schizophrenia. When an accused woman shrugged her shoulders or rolled her eyes, the girls claimed they were forced to do the same thing. Worse still, when an accused witch bit her lips, the girls cried out in pain, complaining that they were being bitten by the prisoner. Ostensible bite marks were found on the bodies of the girls and clinched the evidence against the accused.

The case of Bridget Bishop is complicated by the suspicion that, apart from her bad reputation in general, she had come closer to practicing black magic than any of the other accused women. Bridget was said to have visited several men in her sleep, giving them nightmares and other hallucinations. She was charged with using charms and spells against her neighbors. Magic effigies or homemade dolls with pins stuck in them were found in her home. They helped to seal her doom.

Another piece of incriminating evidence against Bridget Bishop is the story that, on her way from prison to the courthouse in Salem, she cast the evil eye on the building, causing suspicious noises inside. Investigators looking into the matter found that "a board which was strongly fastened with several nails had been transported into another part of the building." Put in contemporary terms, this is a case reminiscent of psychokinetic episodes attributed to nineteenth century physical mediums or to poltergeist children of our day.

A particularly tragic figure of the Salem trials was Elizabeth Procter, wife of the farmer John Procter of Salem, mother and stepmother of his brood. Elizabeth seemed to be made to order to draw upon herself the vindictiveness of the afflicted girls. According to the documents, one girl exclaimed during the testimony of another suspect: "There, Goody Procter. There Goody Procter . . . old witch . . . I'll have her hung!" When the girls were told that they were lying, since no one "saw" the woman in the flesh, they admitted blandly that they did it for "sport."

When the similarly afflicted slave John Indian chimed in, testifying that Elizabeth had choked him in his sleep, the girls went through their hysterical routine once more. Mrs. Procter sought vainly to reason with Abigail: "Dear child, it is not so . . . there is another judgment." When her husband, John, tried to come to her aid, Abigail cried out against him too. "Well, he can pinch me as well as she!" He was pointed out by the children as "the most dreadful wizard" and hanged on August 29, 1692.

The Reverend George Burroughs, Samuel Parris' predecessor at the parish, was another target of the girls' ire. According to tradition, there was something exotic about the appearance of the short, muscular "black minister." In Hansen's view, the accusations of witchcraft leveled against him were not entirely without foundation. On one occasion he had claimed "My God makes known your thoughts unto me." Here, again, a purported sorcerer's claim of occult capacities is reminiscent of those of contemporary psychics or mediums.

In addition, there may have been a lingering professional rivalry between Burroughs and the Parris family, which had taken his place in the parish of Salem Village. If this is true, it may have reinforced the rebellious girls' undercurrent of resentment against the harsh, puritanical father figures he stood for. Their resentment was spelled out by little Ann Putnam when she exclaimed during one of her fits: "Oh, dreadful, dreadful! Here is a minister come. What, are ministers witches too?" She sounded like a contemporary teenager expressing her dismay on finding out the moral iniquities and fallibilities of a once revered parent.

We are told that Ann's father, Thomas Putnam, was likewise dismayed on hearing the Reverend Burroughs thus accused. But his wife, Ann Putnam, Sr., was not surprised. She had suspected George's deviltry for a long time. Abigail's testimony against him was one more nail in his coffin. He had killed three wives, she stated, and their spirits had come to haunt their victims in their sleep.

Abigail's and Ann's charges were seconded by the confessions of Deliverance Hobbs, who said she had seen the small black minister participating in the witches' Sabbath as the Grand Wizard of all Massachusetts. On August 19, 1692, Burroughs was hanged on Gallows Hill.

What do all these harrowing details add up to? They focus attention on the disturbed children's thinly veiled rebellious attitudes toward their elders. Whatever love and respect they had felt for their parents was canceled out by smoldering resentment of their unbending, repressive, authoritarian ways. The girls, having their cruel sport with Tituba (the counterpart of yesterday's southern mammie), displaced their repressed hostility against their mothers upon a more readily hateable target: a degraded mother surrogate. In addition, they earned their elders' sympathy and approbation for helping them to restore peace in their troubled community. Much the same considerations apply to their "telling on" male figures in authority. Analytically speaking, their affliction made it possible for them to act out their aggressive impulses, while at the same time cashing in on whatever secondary gains did accrue from their pitiful condition.

Bizarre show trials of this order were not, however, confined to the Salem inquiry. From many parts of the world have come reports of disturbed children bringing death to innocent people by accusing them of witchcraft. The story of the "Warboys witches" in England, which preceded the Salem disturbances by about a hundred years, is a case in point. The Warboys witches were three members of the poor and downtrodden Samuels family. They were charged with bewitching Jane Throckmorton, aged ten, and her three sisters, ranging in age from nine to fifteen, daughters of a well-to-do and well-connected landowning family. Here, too, the symptoms were hysterical fits, convulsions, and hallucinations, complete with various bizarre charges fabricated by the children. "Mother" Samuels, the principal butt of the children's conspiracy, was seventy-six years old.

In 1627, in Hagenau, Alsace, a thirteen-year-old boy, Peter Roller, who was first himself accused of witchcraft, implicated twenty-four people in the crime. They were burned as witches. Three others committed suicide in prison. Francis Hutcheson, an eighteenth century bishop and crusader against the witch craze, lists more than a dozen stories of supposedly possessed adolescents who sought to implicate their elders. Happily, most of these cases were dismissed before they could cause major harm to their victims.

Thus the record shows that the "babes" out of whose mouths truth was supposed to be revealed were frequent originators of minor or major psychological epidemics which spread from country to country and from community to community both in Europe and in the English colonies of America.

It is interesting to note that delayed reverberations, though in disguised form, can still be gleaned from such popular children's tales as those of Hansel and Gretel or of Red Riding Hood and the Big Bad Wolf. They go back to the early days of the witch craze in medieval Germany and have come down to us through the labors of the Grimm brothers. The story of the witch who tried to kill Hansel and Gretel but whom Gretel, the ringleader, managed to push into the oven, has been the subject of various conflicting interpretations. In the present context it can readily be recognized as the children's confabulatory version of their scheme to "do in" such hapless old ladies as Mother Samuels, Martha Cory, or Rebecca Nurse. They were, in effect, runaway children, taking revenge on their elders for parental harshness or neglect. Their message to the bad, unloving witch-mother is: "It is you who will be burned in the oven (or at the stake), not us." It is significant that Hansel had played a more passive, innocent part in the plot.

In a similar vein, the original version of Red Riding Hood's tale of woe may have been that grandmother, disguised as a wolf, had come in the dark of night to gobble her up, not the other way round. Red Riding Hood's story is in effect one of *lycanthropy:* of a witch turning into a wolf or werewolf but being brought to justice in the end by a kindly woodcutter, hunter—or witch hunter. Here again, the stories suggest that, on a deeper level, the children's ire was directed against the archetype of the all-powerful matriarch, the cannibalistic witch-mother of the fairy tale; against the terrible goddess Kali; against Lilith of ancient Hebrew tradition; against Medea in Greek mythology.

Thus, the available documentary evidence as well as fictitious and mythical elaborations of an ancient theme help to throw light on the deeper reasons of the children's crusade against their elders in Salem and elsewhere. They suggest that, in contrast to the phychopathology involved in the witch trials patterned after the *Malleus Maleficarum* (Hammer of Witches), theirs was a battle between the generations, not between the sexes. It had its dynamic roots in the profound ambivalence conflict of the youngsters brought up in the harsh puritanical discipline of a closed theocratic society. In the absence of more legitimate outlets, they displaced their resentment to the more readily hated cannibalistic witch-mother or the man-eating ogre of the fairy tale.

It is at this point that similarities with the cleavage between the old and the young—with the "generation gap" of our day—suggest themselves. It is a cleavage which is usually thrown into sharper relief in periods of revolutionary upheaval, of radical revision of social, religious, and political values.

This was certainly the case in puritanical New England at the close of the seventeenth century. In more recent times it was highlighted by reports of Hitler Youths testifying against their parents before the Nazi authorities, or by similar accounts of youngsters of the Chinese Red Guard, charging their elders with bourgeois deviationism. Such hostile confrontations have presumably always marred the relationship between the generations. In the Salem case the tension between them culminated in a violent acting out with deadly consequences. It was the acting out of a conflict in which a "commune" of Hansels and Gretels, of Anns and Abigails visited their vengeance on a perplexed group of grown-ups who did not know that they themselves were the primary sources of their children's afflictions. Their clash was in effect a dramatization of both the individuals' and the communities' miscarried resistance to the threatening return of what had been repressed culturally as well as personally—including whatever psi elements still happened to be embedded in it.

The extraordinary dramatic impact of the Salem scenario is another matter. It was due partly to the zeitgeist of late seventeenth century puritanical New England and partly to the remarkable men who were observers, participants, and chroniclers of the events. But we have seen that the trials and tribulations of Salem were by no means historically unique. The potential for similar "psychic" explosions is apparently ever present in the historic process. It happened, in a minor key and in a more harmless way, around the Fox sisters in 1848, in Hydesville, New York, and we have seen that sporadic outbursts continue to occur in some poltergeist or possession cases up to our day.

15

Out-of-the-Body Experiences

and the Denial of Death

OUT-OF-THE-BODY (OOB) experiences, astral projection, and traveling clairvoyance are esoteric terms which cannot easily be translated into the language of psychology or clinical psychiatry. They denote a person's subjective experience of being outside his body and perceiving his environment from a vantage point other than where his physical body happens to be. The experience differs from an ordinary dream in that the subject's consciousness and his critical faculties seem to be the same as in his waking state. At the same time it is held to differ from hallucinations or delusions through such veridical elements as telepathy, clairvoyance, or precognition associated with it. The experiencer perceives the world from a bird's-eye view, as it were, and some of his perceptions are said to contain information which he could not have obtained through the ordinary channels of perception.

Both older and more recent parapsychological literature contains a wealth of observations of this kind (Hart 1954, 1956; Crookall 1961; Green 1967; Rogo 1976; Palmer and Vassar, 1974; and many others). While originally little effort was made to separate hallucinatory or frankly delusional accounts from common hypnagogic or eidetic imagery of the type seen in primitives, children, and artists, Hornell Hart emphasized the need to distinguish veridical from nonveridical cases. Nevertheless, phenomenologically, all these observations present the same clinical syndrome. The differences lie in the wide variety of dramatic elaboration and embroiderings of the underlying experience. We shall see that it ranges from neurotic depersonalization and derealization to autoscopic hallucinations with the appearance of the patient's double—or even duplication of his double—to claims of apparitional sightings and diverse ghostly activities which are attributed to PK or to direct intervention by the person embarked on an OOB "trip." Experimenters like R. L. Morris and his associates (1973) even used behavioral responses of cats or gerbils to presumed "visitations" by their masters as animal detectors of psi.

On the other end of the scale are the recent Targ-Puthoff experiments (1976) at the Stanford Research Institute in which a number of experimental subjects produced spectacular feats of "remote viewing." In these experiments the subject is supposed to visit or to reach out to distant places and scenarios without the characteristic trappings of trance or other features of the OOB state.

K. Osis, J. L. Mitchell and their associates of the American Society for Psychical Research (1975) have been engaged in a similar OOB project with Ingo Swann and other subjects. One of their objectives was to adduce experimental evidence of "direct viewing." The studies included EEG monitoring in the OOB and non-OOB condition.

While OOB experiences have so far remained literally "outside the body" of modern clinical psychiatry, they are a recurrent theme of folklore, cultural anthropology, and the history of religion. They go back to primitive animistic beliefs concerning the nature of the soul—a belief that it is possible to leave the body during sleep, reenter it on awakening, and leave it for good at the moment of death. Beliefs in the immortality of the soul, in an astral body, and in spirits roaming heavenly or demoniacal regions are closely linked with such systems of thought.

They are found in the Sacred Books of the East, in ancient Egyptian papyri, and in Plato's *Phaedo* and *Symposium* (Grosso 1975) and are a recurrent theme in the Judeo-Christian and Muslim traditions. According to Morton Smith (1973), author of *The Secret Gospel*, biblical accounts of Christ's ascent to heaven and resurrection are variations on the same theme. The mystical books of Hekalot features prayers, incantations, and the recitation of magical names that transport the faithful into the heavens and the presence of God. Israel Baal Shem Tob, the great Hasidic rabbi of the eighteenth century, claimed that he repeatedly had ecstatic experiences of this order and could induce them by his own volition. More recently, C. G. Jung went on record with an OOB experience of his own (1963).

Siberian and North American shamans developed elaborate techniques to put themselves into states of ecstasy which enabled them to take off on their renowned shamanic flights. According to Mircea Eliade

(1964), the Yenisei Ostyak shaman prepares himself for his ecstatic journey by fasting and various harrowing rituals. He leaps off the ground and cries, "I am high in the air; I see the Yenisei a hundred versts away." The Kazakh Kirghiz shaman's preparatory ceremonials include firewalking, touching red-hot irons, and slashing his face with razor-sharp knives.

The ancient Yoga tradition of *Kundalini*, recently revived by the Kashmiri mystic Gopi Krishna, is another case in point. It is based on meditation and culminates in states of ecstasy and depersonalization; "I experienced a rocking sensation and felt myself slipping out of my body. I felt the point of my consciousness that was myself growing wider and wider . . . while my body . . . appeared to have receded into the distance" (1971, p. 13). This dramatic episode seems to have brought about the same "bodyless" sensation he once had at the age of eight. Later on, such experiences were accompanied by an unspeakable terror and feeling of total mental and physical prostration and disintegration, carrying him right to the "point of death." Yet ultimately it was mortal crises of this order which gave him the feeling of supernatural powers and enlightenment, or samadhi.

Gopi Krishna frankly describes his condition as a delirium. The fact is that his experiences closely resemble those of a delirious patient whose delusions take him into a hallucinatory world peopled with figments of his imagination, divorced from the perception of his body image, or accompanied by its total disintegration. The following clinical vignettes illustrate the same point:

Bozena, age twenty-three, was seen in psychiatric consultation in a medical ward. She was at the height of a delirium with pneumococcal pneumonia. "How do you feel, Bozena?" I asked her. "I am not Bozena," said the patient. "Bozena is dead. They are doing the postmortem on her in the dissecting room. I am someone else." Put in the jargon of the customary clinical chart, she was disoriented in time, place, and personality. Hers was a case of profound depersonalization due to the existing toxic condition.

Another patient of mine, a woman of thirty-three, suffering from an organic brain syndrome, felt likewise severely depersonalized. Her limbs were "swollen," "distorted"; they did not belong to her; they had turned into snakes. She saw her face in front of her. It looked like a statue and grew bigger and bigger. At times she felt her limbs were rising and falling, or she herself was falling out of a window (Ehrenwald 1931a).

A third patient experienced the split in a nightmarish dream. She saw herself suspended in midair, above a big round table. She was up, hundreds or thousands of feet. Below she saw several sinister looking old men, Hasidic rabbis, huddled around a table. She felt an invisible thread was pulling her down toward them, while she was desperately trying to get away. Somewhere there was a baby floating around in space.

The patient was a borderline schizophrenic. Her father was a rabbi to whom she was tied by a symbiotic bond of love and hate. She was a homosexual, torn between her fixation on the father figure and female love objects whom she latched onto on the rebound. The baby, she stated, was a projection of her own infantile self. Her condition is thus far removed from the first patient and does not "fit" into the organic, medical model. Yet in her case sleep and the associated REM (rapid eye movement) state supplied one of the requisite predisposing factors for the OOB experience.

Celia, a fourth patient, is an unmarried woman of twenty-four. When first seen, she presented the picture of an acute schizophrenic reaction. A college dropout, she had been on drugs, including hashish, mescaline, and LSD for several years. Two years ago, she joined an ashram of a Sikh commune run by an American practitioner of Kundalini Yoga. As part of her training she learned to go into OOB experiences. On one occasion she projected herself into the house of her brother some 500 miles away. To her horror she was overpowered by the urge to kill her brother and his two children with a knife. "I must have been possessed . . . perhaps by the devil," she stated. She made a frantic telephone call to her brother's home and learned that all was well with the family. Bewildered and incredulous, she ran away from the ashram and was picked up by the police who ultimately referred her to a psychiatrist. Unfamiliar with the esoteric aspects of her case, he put her on tranquilizers which she refused to take.

There is no evidence of a psi factor involved in her experience. It was evidently of a purely delusional nature. But by contrast to fixed paranoid delusions, Celia readily accepted a tactful interpretation of her experience as falling short of the "real thing," that is, of true OOB projection. Apparently such ideas were grafted on her by contagion from the ashram community, and she could ultimately be steered toward better reality testing. Yet her emotional conflicts, her feelings of alienation, depersonalization, and dual personality persisted. "It may have been Guru Dan, my double, not Celia who tried to do the terrible thing," she remarked. Celia is still undergoing intensive psychotherapy.

Paul Schilder (1923) interpreted such cases of depersonalization and splitting as the patient's miscarried attempts to escape both from himself and harrowing external reality. It is an interpretation which applies with equal strength to organic cases, neurotic situations, and schizophrenics with their frequent hallucinatory experiences of a "double."

R. D. Laing (1965) noted more recently that "depersonalization is a technique which is universally used as a means of dealing with the other [part of the "divided self"] when he becomes too tiresome or disturbing." Depersonalization of the type reviewed here brings this tendency into sharper focus. It can be described as an attempt at dissociating oneself from a debilitated, mangled, perishable body, and in so doing *denying* the reality or possibility of death.

This overriding concern, coupled with fantasies of omnipotence, can readily be seen as the hidden motivation underlying OOB experiences in both illness and health reported in the anthropological literature. It is less obvious in our culture. But we shall presently see that many subjects, as well as investigators, tend to regard OOB experiences as arguments in favor of the actual separation of body and soul and, by implication, of the soul's survival after death.

Whatever be the nature of the assumed cleavage between the two entities—and whether we adopt a psychiatric, parapsychological, or theological interpretation—both patients and nonpatients experiencing the "split" are often in a quandry to decide to whom they should turn for aid. Most of the older cases published in the parapsychological literature —from those studied by Eastman (1962), and Palmer and Vassar (1974), Hornell Hart, and associates (1956), up to our day—were never brought into the psychiatrist's purview.

The following is a typical example of OOB seen in clinical practice.

The Case of Martin H.

Martin H., a college graduate aged twenty-five, was referred to me by Dr. R. K., a psychoanalytic colleague of mine who was puzzled by the patient's recurrent dreams in which he felt that his "astral body" had left his physical body to visit far away places, while the latter, asleep or in the waking state, was lying in his bed.

During his first session he gave a vivid description of one of his earliest childhood memories:

> I was two or three years old when I fell ill with croup . . . I had cramps; I choked, got blue in the face, and nearly died. They put me in a hospital for a few days. On my return, the first night at home, I had a dream: I was lying in bed, dreaming I was awake . . . at that I started

to rise . . . above the house. I could see the three floors of the house . . . I saw my parents inside the house—and myself lying in bed. It was fairly light outside. . . . Then I saw two men entering . . . they had a whispered argument—whether to kill anybody or just knock them out. I watched all that, terrified, and was wakened by a tremendous crash on my head. . . . I really [thought I had] developed a lump later and expected [to find that] my parents too had been knocked out. . . . No, they were not—it was just a dream. Yet somehow I felt my conscious life had started from that point.

On subsequent occasions he confirmed his account that his first OOB experience occurred in the wake of a serious respiratory illness, culminating in a coma. In a later session he reported a recent OOB experience:

I was lying in bed before going to sleep, trying to make myself have an OOB experience. Suddenly I felt the bed "flip." The foot of the bed moved up in a semicircle. It moved smoothly, but so fast that my body and my bedding were held to the bed by the centripetal force. Suddenly my body seemed to yield to gravity. From my upside-down supported state I slipped downward again; then I was reunited with the body lying in the bed, some three feet above the floor . . . the bed rocked up and down . . . it was like an earthquake. I was terrified. Still, I repeated it three or four times, but feared I would lose control over it. It is the astral body that wants to get out . . .

Under hypnosis he reproduced his usual pattern of OOB experiences with little difficulty. He was convinced that in addition to his capacity for OOB experiences he was endowed with diverse supernormal powers. He reported that he repeatedly succeeded in projecting his "astral body" to distant friends who subsequently corroborated his "ghostly" visitations. In several hynotic experiments carried out in my office, he failed to produce evidence of ESP or of clairvoyant or telepathic perception of two target pictures which were exposed some two miles away in the premises of the American Society of Psychical Research.

However, on the morning following this negative outcome, Mrs. F. K., one of the officers of the ASPR, reported to me over the phone that at the exact time of the hypnotic experience (at 6:25 P.M.), she was surprised by a mysterious "presence" in the house and specifically asked me what had happened in my office at the critical time.

There is nothing in this observation to substantiate the patient's claims of genuine "astral" exploits. Still, it is strongly suggestive of a psi factor being involved in the case: Mrs. K.'s response may have been due to a dramatic elaboration of a telepathic cue emanating from Martin H. He had "flunked" his test in ESP, or clairvoyance, but succeeded in adducing at least some evidence of related psychic abilities. This, to him, was added confirmation of his fantasies of omnipotence, of his belief in the reality of his OOB "travel," of the soul as an entity separate from the body, and, by implication, of its survival after death. For Martin H.—as for many workers in the field—such an interpretation was in fact a strong argument for immortality and for the denial of death.

This age-old tendency to denial is presumably the underlying psychodynamic determinant in most OOB experiences, regardless of whatever paranormal claims are associated with them.

The fact is that in most cases experiences of this order seem to be triggered off by episodes of illness, mental or physical, if not by mortal crises brought about by self-mortification, days of fasting, or drug-induced ecstatic or comatose states. It can be readily understood that such harrowing experiences are then interpreted as a successful challenge to the power of death—or, at least, as a heroic attempt at denying its reality.

Nevertheless, the paranormal exploits of some subjects of OOB experiences published in the literature are quite impressive. Miss Z., an apparently schizophrenic girl, studied by the California psychologist Charles Tart (1968), showed unequivocal psi abilities. She was able to "read" a five-digit number presented to her above eye level while she was lying on the couch hooked up to an electroencephalograph. Her EEG tracings showed increased alphoid activity. The interpretation of her feat in terms of a true OOB or "remote viewing" experience is, however, problematical. It may well have been due to paraexperimental telepathy from the experimenter.

The Case of Ingo Swann

Similar considerations apply to the pioneering experiments with remote viewing carried out by Russel Targ and Harold Puthoff (1977) at the Stanford Research Institute in California. In this series the subject seeks to project himself into a specific geographic target area selected randomly by the experimenters. The subject, staying in the laboratory, tries to give a verbal or pictorial description of what he sees. At about the same time "outbound" experimenters are sent to scout, and to take pictures of, the target area. While in some of these cases ESP from the scouts could be responsible for the surprising accuracy of subject responses, in other experiments such virtuoso subjects as Ingo Swann or Pat Price gave veridical descriptions without such potential extrasensory or cosensory aids. In such cases precognitive telepathy or clairvoyance focusing on the subsequent verification or protocols of the subject's exploits seems to be the only alternative to the hypothesis of true remote viewing.

However, Ingo Swann is more than just another subject reporting recurrent OOB experiences. He took an active part in the planning and design of the Targ-Puthoff experiments. He is a thoughtful and original student of the field in his own right. A gifted surrealistic painter with an IQ of 147, a bachelor in his early forties, he is a typical extrovert, with an unconventional life style but no history or present evidence of neurosis. One of his extraordinary feats as a psychic is his ability to raise or lower, at a distance, the temperature of a sensitive thermal recording device (Schmeidler 1973). Equally striking are his exploits with a magnetometer in the Stanford Research Institute laboratory. In a rigidly controlled series reported by Targ and Puthoff, he succeeded in bringing about psychokinetic changes in the graphs produced by a heavily shielded instrument located in the floor below.

Like my first subject, Swann too reports that his first OOB experience occurred in early childhood following a tonsillectomy at two or three years of age. While given the anesthetic he felt he was "rising up in the air." Otherwise, most OOB experiences (which he prefers to describe as "externalizations"), are confined to the waking state. He feels he is being transported out into the open, often to the sight of the starry sky, to many and varied faraway places, including other planets of the solar system. On one occasion he had a *déjà vu* on approaching the coast of Japan. It was the vision of a "cone-shaped volcano" at a distance. On going ashore his vision was confirmed by the actual appearance of the volcano. He attributed such incidents to his previous "Catholic" reincarnations. He said he had gone through many ups and downs in his life but never went through any major emotional disturbances or episodes of depersonalization or derealization. Nor has he ever felt the need for psychotherapy. By contrast to Martin H., he gives the impression of a well-adjusted, easygoing, creative individual who has managed to integrate his psychic abilities and OOB experiences with the rest of his personality. His autobiographical account *To Kiss Earth Good-bye* (1975) is a human document of considerable interest.

The Cases of Robert Monroe and John Lilly

Robert Monroe, author, inventor, and businessman, has written a book describing hundreds of OOB experiences and quoting several witnesses who testify to their authenticity (1971). More recently he has founded a research institute of his own. Charles Tart, professor of psychology at Davis, California, who made a special study of OOB cases, has written an introduction to Monroe's book.

Clinically, Monroe's case differs, however, from both Martin H. and Ingo Swann in several respects. His first OOB experience occurred in adult years and was not associated with a history of physical illness. It was ushered in by what he describes as a severe anxiety attack with the feeling of impending death, a sense of "vibrations," various bizarre changes of the body image, and distortions of the perception of space. Sexual excitement and the hallucinatory experience of a "whiskered man" lying behind him in bed was another feature of the attack. Mr. Monroe was first dismayed by the apparent homosexual implication of this experience, until he realized that the whiskered man was in effect his own unshaven self. The psychoanalytic significance of such an autoscopic hallucination must remain a matter of speculation.

At an informal social meeting with Mr. Monroe, I gained the impression of a poised, relaxed, self-assured man with no hint whatsoever of an existing personality deviation, paranoid, sexual, or otherwise. His general demeanor, his apparently happy family life as husband, paterfamilias, and grandfather, his typical American success story as an engineer and president of two corporations, his exploits as a magazine writer, lecturer, director of a radio station, and one-time glider pilot, all suggest a solid citizen with his feet firmly planted in reality—except when he claims he is off on one of his OOB trips, leaving his physical body behind in his bed, to catch glimpses of faraway places, objects, and people, or ever causing black and blue pinch marks on the bodies of some of the persons (preferably women) on whom he happened to drop in.

Stripped of its paranormal aspects, Monroe's case could be brushed aside as a familiar example of a circumscribed delusional trend in an otherwise well-adjusted and well-integrated personality. But Charles Tart, in the Introduction to Monroe's book, describes several incidents and experimental observations strongly suggestive of psi phenomena. We are told, furthermore, that witnesses have confirmed at least some of

Monroe's reports of his long-distance "fact-finding" exploits. All this is incompatible with the hypothesis of purely hallucinatory manifestations, though it does not by itself afford any evidence of anything like "astral travel." Be that as it may, a purely psychiatric reading cannot reasonably do justice to Monroe's personality.

Nor does his presumed psychodynamics conform to that of the preceding subjects. On the physiological side, Monroe's experience of floating may have been aided by his previous conditioning as a glider pilot. On the other hand, the panic ushering in his OOB states may have been due to his repressed emotional conflicts. Thus, in spite of differences, both his panic and the associated feeling of ego disintegration and fear of death may well have mobilized in him the identical tendency toward denial as his idiosyncratic pattern or "mechanism" of defense.

Similar considerations apply to the noted psychiatrist and psychoanalyst John Lilly, as documented in his autobiography (1972). He has variously been described as a pioneer investigator of the mind of the dolphin and of sensory deprivation or as a cartographer of diverse altered states of consciousness. Sam Keen (1970) interviewing him for *Psychology Today,* even asked the (rhetorical) question, whether he did not consider himself a "first-class schizophrenic"?

Lilly's case is yet another variation on the theme of OOB experiences, although he prefers to describe them in terms of excursions into "inner space." Some occurred in his childhood and during his twenties. Some were associated with physical illnesses or surgical operations. Others occurred during LSD trips. On one occasion, after injecting himself with an antibiotic, he lapsed into a prolonged coma which carried him close to death. "The pounding headaches, the nausea and the vomiting that occurred, forced me to leave my body," he writes. "I became a focused center of consciousness and traveled into other spaces." He felt, "I have no body, I have no need for a body. There is no body. I am just I." That Lilly also came across a "superself," a "superspecies," and diverse supernatural entities on his trips may be mentioned in passing only.

Such an account may strike the reader as rather bizarre, impossible to substantiate and out of character with a noted author, scientist, member of the American Psychiatric Association, and whatnot. But here again, the individual's Promethean struggle to free himself from the encumbrances of the flesh, from the pull of gravitation, from a parochial, earthbound existence, is the dominant theme. And here, again, Lilly's dramatic experiences were opened up to him in part by mind-expanding drugs and in part by emotional conflicts, aided by a circumscribed cerebral lesion. It is this combination of organic and psychological factors which brings his case even closer to the observations discussed on an earlier page.

Thus, on reviewing a few representative samples taken from the broad spectrum of pertinent observations, ranging from frankly pathological cases of depersonalization in organic conditions, in psychotics, and in neurotic patients to nonpatients subject to classical OOB experiences, we see that they all have one thing in common: they exhibit an assorted set of defenses and rationalizations aimed at warding off anxiety originating from the breakdown of the body image, from the threatening split or disorganization of the ego, and, in the last analysis, from the fear of death as a universal human experience. Indeed, Ernest Becker has rightly pointed out that "the idea of death, the fear of it, haunts the human animal like nothing else." It is a fear he tries to overcome "by denying in some way that it is the final destiny of man" (1973, p. ix). Viewed in this light, OOB experiences, stripped of the stigma attached to their pathological variants, are expressions of man's perennial quest for immortality. They are faltering attempts to assert the reality and autonomous existence of the "soul"—a deliberate challenge to the threat of extinction, sometimes amounting to near-suicidal experiments with the process of dying itself.

To sum up, there are few well-substantiated data of OOB experiences which cannot more parsimoniously be interpreted in terms of telepathy "pure and simple," or rather of what is here described as the psi syndrome, as opposed to what some authors prefer to describe in terms of "direct viewing." In some cases OOB experiences are coupled with a dramatic elaboration of a few readily identifiable subliminal or clairvoyant telepathic cues. As in the case of purported possessions, such cues may under suitable conditions be fleshed out, embroidered, dramatized and upgraded to assume lifelike proportions. If they are combined with physical manifestations, they may give rise to fanciful ghost stories and to accounts of apparitions or spectral visitations by the living or the dead. The resulting medley is then made up of a genuine psi ingredient, together with the wish-dreams and fantasises of those involved in the incident, interwoven with diverse mythical and esoteric beliefs current in a given culture. In any case, the evidence in support of "true" OOB travel is still highly controversial.

16

Hitler: Shaman, Schizophrenic,

or Medium?

W<small>HY</small> SHOULD a study of Hitler, of all people, be included in the present volume? The reason is that individuals with psychic traits are not necessarily confined to the parapsychological laboratory, the spiritualistic séance room, or the temples of paranormal healing. The annals of history are replete with reports of extraordinary personalities, religious reformers, mystics and prophets—false or genuine—who have become shakers and movers of their time, leading their followers to greatness or destruction, as the case may be. Messianic figures like Jesus, Muhammad, or Mary Baker Eddy seemed to have been endowed with authentic psychic gifts.

On the other end of the spectrum are the Sabbatai Sewis, the Cagliostros, the Rasputins, and a host of lesser figures who had their share of dubious impact upon world events. Adolf Hitler was among them. There is reason to believe that the study of his personality should provide us with some clues about the leverage his apparent psychic endowment has had upon his stormy career and upon the rise and fall of the Third Reich.

In September 1939, during my wartime exile in England, I had a haircut in a London barber shop. It was a time when Englishmen added a new topic to their small talk about the weather: "What do you think about Hitler?" asked the barber. My English was still more geared to technical than to plain colloquial language. "He may be a paranoid schirophrenic," I said. "Or else a neurotic psychopath with ideas of persecution and grandeur." "You mean to say he is mad," remarked the barber.

I have pondered the question ever since. So have countless historians, psychologists, psychiatrists, and other students of human behavior. The final verdict is not in and presumably never will be. But our standard approach to psychology and psychopathology alone is unlikely to take the whole measure of the man. He may have been a shaman, a schizophrenic, an evil genius, or an artist manqué. But I submit that so long as we fail to make allowance for parapsychological dimensions, the appraisal of his personality remains incomplete.

What, then, is responsible for his spectacular rise from obscurity and his volcanic impact on the historical scene? What gave him the confidence that he had been chosen by Providence to raise the German people to the pinnacle of power and to use them as his launching pad for personal greatness? What gave him the uncanny ability to manipulate, to mesmerize, to seduce his countrymen to surrender their individual selves to his stewardship?

Shaman?

Those who have compared Hitler—the Unknown Soldier of the First World War, the new Pied Piper of Hamelin—with the wizard, shaman, or medicine man capable of inflaming the passions of his tribe and of catching fire in turn from their passions, have already supplied part of the answer.

We know today that the medicine man derives his power from a circular feedback involving his personal myth and the hopes and expectations of those who share it with him. The ensuing "mutual exaltation" was studied by McDougall and by Gustave LeBon many years ago. It is still regarded as one of the key factors in the psychology of masses. It has subsequently been reinterpreted in Freudian terms as the individual's willing surrender to an all-powerful father figure capable of meeting the childish dependency needs still lingering in members of the group. But it should be noted that the Freudian reading likewise implies a specific type of reciprocity between the leader and the led. The circular pattern is equally apparent in the therapist-patient relationship, described in Chapter 25. Here, too, the therapist's motivation to help, and his implicit faith in his ability to do so, is met halfway, as it were, by the patient's confidence in his helper and by his expectation that he will indeed be helped.

Needless to say, such a simple formula cannot sum up the intricacies of the Nazi phenomenon. Still, the mutuality of assorted needs and expectations is certainly one of its prominent features. The circular pattern of feedback between the one and the many is unmistakable. But the myth shared by the Führer and his people, and the passions generated in the process, are worlds apart from the original prototype. Hitler's myth is no longer that of a charismatic healer drawing more strength from those who believe in him, and the emotions aroused are no longer those of mutual trust or even shared belief in the efficacy of his healing magic. The passions are fed on the magician's will to dominate, to exercise power, or to destroy. His avowed determination to wreak violence and destruction on a hitherto unprecedented scale sets Hitler, the twentieth century shaman, apart from minor figures of his profession in other cultures and other historical periods.

The formula needs amplification in at least one more respect. It was the very complicity of Hitler's associates and followers in his crimes which made them mutually indispensable. Hitler, by assuming total responsibility for all decisions that had to be made since his rise to power and particularly since he had plunged his nation into war, relieved the individual German of his guilt. At the same time, Hitler's insatiable lust for power made him eager to play the role of the sole decision maker, the Lord and Master of the Master Race and, by the same token, of the so-called inferior races he had brought under his heel.

In turn, his followers, encouraged by his example, could give free rein to their own sadistic impulses. The difference between them and the reader of the Marquis de Sade or the viewer of a horror movie or a prize fight in our day merely lies in the fact that the average spectator participates in the action vicariously only, while the SS man, the Gestapo officer, or the guard in a concentration camp steps over the boundary line between wish-dream and reality unawares, and gets "in on the act" before realizing what he is up to.

The Führer, on the other hand, felt called upon by Providence to open the floodgates of hatred, cruelty, and mass destruction and to delegate their execution to his underlings. A veritable antichrist, he preached that it is the high, the mighty, the strong, and the reckless who will inherit the earth and gain salvation—through expropriating the Jews, enslaving the Czechs and the Poles, and colonizing the conquered eastern territories. To achieve this end, he was ready to crucify the multitudes and to proclaim: "All this is done in my name and on my behalf. It is in effect my doing."

It is fully consistent with this state of affairs that Himmler, Goering, Speer, and tens of thousands of their henchmen could wash their hands of the blood spilled on the battlefields and in the concentration camps of Europe, since the Führer's inverted self-sacrifice absolved them from their guilt and expiated their sins. More than a quarter of a century after Hitler's own sacrificial death, his power to soothe guilty consciences does not seem to have diminished.

The fact that their willing compliance (and complicity) with Hitler's pseudomessianic complex had served to reinforce further his perseverance in his mission is in good keeping with the formula of circular feedback.

Hitler's unwritten covenant—the "contract *anti*social," as it were—between himself and a vast segment of the German people was certainly one of the indispensable prerequisites of his iron grip over the country. But what are the secret arcana that helped him, the country boy from the Austrian backwoods, the Unknown Soldier of World War I, the down-at-the-heels roomer in a flophouse in Vienna, to come so close to his goal? Countless essays and books have been written to answer this question. They point to the concatenation of such external circumstances as the frustrations engendered by the Versailles Treaty, the downfall of the German middle class, unemployment, and growing inflation in the wake of World War I. Hitler is described as the personification of the hopelessly disillusioned petty bourgeois and would-be intellectual whose plight was shared by a whole generation of equally disillusioned Germans for whom dreams of national revival, revenge, and military glory seemed to be the only antidote for despair and feelings of abject inferiority. All these and related explanations are certainly to the point. But they still do not tell us how the Pied Piper of Hamelin, the conjuror of the Munich Bürgerbräukeller did his tricks.

According to Herman Rauschning (1940), Hitler's early associate and later disenchanted critic and biographer, "it is the Shaman drums that beat around Hitler. Asiatic and African cults and bewitchments are the true elements of his spell, and furious dances to the point of exhaustion." In a phrase which could have been taken from *Mein Kampf*, he noted: "The primitive world has invaded the west." Allen Bullock, author of *Hitler, a Study in Tyranny* (1962), places great emphasis on the shamanistic aspects of Hitler's personality. It was an attribute which had apparently impressed most people—generals and diplomats, newspapermen and heads of state, friends and foes alike. Rauschning reports that sometimes, following a meeting with the Führer, he felt he had to shake off "some sort of hypnosis." The level-headed Admiral Doenitz, commander in chief of the German Navy, confessed: "I purposely went very seldom to his Headquarters, for I had the feeling that this would best preserve my power of initiative, and also because, after several days at Headquarters, I always had the feeling that I had to disengage myself from his power of suggestion (Bullock, p. 409). H. R. Trevor-Roper (1968) attributes part of Hitler's spectacular hold over people to his "hypnotic influence which compelled even his critics to worship and obey." Albert Speer (1970), one of the most articulate among these critics, remarks that "Hitler, and Hitler alone, had kept the German people upon the path which had led to the dreadful ending. The nation was spellbound by him as a people had rarely been in the whole of history."

One of the last of Hitler's visitors in the underground shelter in Berlin, Ritter von Greim, was still drawn into the Führer's "magic circle" and "seduced out of his wits" by his extraordinary personality. "Don't despair," Greim told one of the worried generals over the phone. "Everything will be well. The presence of the Führer, and his confidence, have completely inspired me." The general, obviously finding himself outside the "magic circle," was wondering whether "these people had the sixth sense, and could see things unseen by ordinary mortals" (Speer, p. 215–16).

Otto Strasser (1940), another of Hitler's early associates and victim of one of his subsequent purges, wrote about his abilities as an orator:

> Hitler responds to the vibrations of the human heart with the delicacy of a seismograph, or perhaps of a wireless receiving set, enabling him, with a certainty [with] which no conscious gift could endow him, to act as a loudspeaker proclaiming the most secret desires, the least admissible instincts, the sufferings and personal revolts of a whole nation. . . . Adolf Hitler enters the hall. He sniffs the air. For a minute he gropes, feels his way, senses the atmosphere. Suddenly he bursts forth. His words go like an arrow to their target. He touches each private wound on the raw, liberating the mass unconscious, expressing its innermost aspirations, telling it what it most wants to hear . . . (1940, pp. 74–77).

One of Hitler's major assets as a speaker was his reliance on his personal myth and his conviction of the infallibility of his intuitions. "I go the way Providence dictates, with the assurance of a sleepwalker," he declared. And he went on to say: "However weak an individual may be when compared with the Omnipotence and will of Providence, yet at the moment when he acts as Providence would have him act, he becomes immeasurably strong. Then there streams down upon him a force which has worked all greatness in the world's history" (1943).

Hitler's powers to persuade, to carry away, to overwhelm his audience did not merely derive from the spoken word. Bullock notes that he was a consummate actor, "with the orator's and actor's facility for absorbing himself in a role and convincing himself of the truth of what he was saying." Still, the spectacle witnessed by his audience was obviously based on more than mere role playing. The much-vaunted hypnotic power of his eyes, the foaming of his mouth, the strident quality of his voice were more than mere theatrical props. The hapless President Emil Hácha of Czechoslovakia, exposed to Hitler's bullying and Goering's threats to bomb Prague into submission, is reported to have fainted during the conference and had to be revived by injections. Hitler's impact upon the Austrian chancellor Kurt von Schuschnigg, on the Italian foreign minister Count Galeazzo Ciano, or on some of his own generals had been much the same. Trevor-Roper reports that when General Franz Halder, the chief of the Army General Staff, confronted Hitler with the difficulties in the Russian campaign, "he went off the deep end; he was no longer a rational being; he foamed at the mouth and threatened me with his fists. Any rational discussion was out of the question." Hitler's rages were certainly the most spectacular items in his repertoire. "He appeared to lose all control of himself," wrote Bullock, "his face became mottled and swollen with fury, he screamed at the top of his voice, spitting out a stream of abuse, moving his arms wildly and drumming on the table or the wall with his fists . . ." (1962, p. 376).

Such an unbridled show of emotion recalls the classical description by Bronislaw Malinowski (1954) of the wizard or sorcerer performing his act of black magic with a bone dart. "If the spectator were suddenly transported to some part of Melanesia and could observe the sorcerer at work . . . he might think that he had either to do with a lunatic or else he would guess that here was a man acting under the sway of uncontrolled anger. . . ." Malinowski adds by way of an explantion: "For the sorcerer has, as an essential part of the ritual performance, not only to point the bone dart at his victim, but with an intense expression of fury and hatred he has to thrust it in the air. . . . Thus not only is the act of violence or stabbing reproduced, but the passion of violence has to be enacted . . ." (pp. 73–74).

The proverbial dance of the dervishes is a more subdued example of violence acted out in a ritualistic way with the participation of the whole fraternity. Another example is the rainmaker of primitive Indian tribes who seeks to coax, cajole, and coerce the clouds to release their bounty in response to his entreaties and frantic ceremonial dance. He is, in effect, duplicating the infant's attempts to force his will on the symbiotic parent with the kicking and flailing of his limbs—by what Ferenczi has called the "omnipotence of movements." The same is true for the circular feedback Hitler received from the roaring masses of his followers at his carefully staged appearances at the Munich or Nuremberg rallies of the party.

C. G. Jung (1936) was originally inclined to see in the Führer the Siegfried, the Wotan, or the Dionysus archetype but soon become disenchanted with the Nazi movement and referred to Hitler in the end as a mixture of shaman and charlatan.

Schizophrenic?

There is another aspect of Hitler's personality which has given rise to much debate: his apparent paranoid trend. Needless to say, the evidence upon which such a discussion can be based is rudimentary. For obvious reasons his doctors were tight-lipped about his state of health, mental and physical. Those who were not do not seem to have lived long enough to tell more than whispered bits and pieces of the tale. In 1938, Professor E. Gamper, then chairman of the department of psychiatry and neurology at my alma mater, the German University of Prague, was called to Berchtesgaden for consultation about the Führer's health. On his way back home to Innsbruck his car skidded into the Koenigsee. Professor Gamper and his wife drowned in the lake. The fatal accident touched off the inevitable (and inevitably unconfirmed) rumors of having been staged on highest orders, rumors that the professor had made incautious remarks to Hitler's entourage and therefore had to be silenced once and for all.

Widely circulated stories about Hitler having contracted syphilis in his youth are equally unconfirmed. A parkinsonian tremor and stiffness of his left arm had been described by many observers in his later years, but such observations provide few diagnostic clues as to his mental state.

As far as psychiatric aspects are concerned, we are left with Hitler's actions, speeches, "Table Talks," and biographical writings as our main source material. It is here that he has put down for us his own carefully expurgated "case history." It is supplemented by countless anecdotal accounts afforded by friends, casual acquaintances, and other witnesses interviewed by journalists, historians, and psychoanalysts, often long after the event.

Walter C. Langer (1972), the American psychoanalyst, has compiled an illuminating report on the basis of such information. Commissioned by the U.S. Office of Strategic Services close to the end of World War II, it was intended to serve the purposes of psychological warfare. Even though this must have colored the author's conclusions, his data leave no doubt as to Hitler's severe personal pathology. He emerges from Langer's report as a "neurotic psychopath" given to depressive spells and hysterical outbursts and subject to paranoid reactions. The fanciful picture drawn of his sadomasochistic, coprohagic perversions is largely based on hearsay and psychoanalytic reconstructions. However ingenious they may be, they are not direct evidence. More recently, N. Bromberg (1971) has contributed significant psychoanalytic comments on the effects of Hitler's cryptorchidism upon his castration anxieties and warped personality development.

Among many other psychiatric contributions, the late Gustav Bychowski wrote perhaps the most authoritative clinical study of Hitler's personality (1965). He traces the onset of his delusions of grandeur to his (and Germany's) breakdown after the catastrophic end of World War I. This breakdown, combined with Hitler's deprived childhood and youth, should account for his inordinate need to make up for the deprivations and to seek solace in dreams of ultimate victory and grandeur both for himself and for the German people. Germany had become an extension of his own personality, as France had for General Charles de Gaulle. Hitler's feeling of having been chosen by Providence to lead his nation out of the "Babylonian exile" was apparently fostered by his dabbling in mysticism and the occult in the early postwar years in Munich. Bychowski tends to agree with Rauschning's references to Hitler's mediumistic gifts, but emphasizes that they were soon blended with those of the effective hypnotist and manipulator of the mass mind.

Ideas of grandeur, of having been chosen by Providence as an instrument of messianic mission, were not, however, the only symptoms of Hitler's growing paranoid trend. He felt surrounded by hostile forces trying to bar his—and Germany's—way to greatness and mastery over the world. Gradually the hostile forces became incarnate in one sinister figure, the Jew. The Jew was the archenemy and the leader of the world conspiracy against Hitler himself and, by indirection, against the German people and the "Aryan" race at large.

Hitler's gross overestimation of Jewish power and influence on the world scene, combined with his obsessive insistence on the inferiority of the Jews and their subhuman quality as a race, is one of the glaring inconsistencies in his otherwise tightly reasoned, well-integrated, and resilient system of thought, if not his delusional system. Apart from the anti-Semitism that was in the air Hitler had been breathing during his formative years in Braunau, Linz, and later Vienna, his implacable hatred of the Jew was obviously fed from two inner sources: first, from his utter intolerance of every trace of what he considered weakness in his own makeup and from his gnawing self-doubts regarding his masculinity and the attending distortion and stunting of his sex life; and, second, from his tendency to project all his human frailties and iniquities onto a delusionally distorted and inflated figure—or scapegoat—in the outside world. The scapegoat was the Jew.

Much speculation has been concerned with another possible source of Hitler's hatred of the Jew (Shirer, 1960, and others): with the illegitimate birth of his father, Alois Schicklgruber, who was later adopted by his uncle Johann Nepomuk Huetler. Such speculations are largely gratuitous and have little bearing on our issue. No hereditory deus ex machina is needed to identify Hitler's archenemy as the enemy he carried within himself. It is true that the enemy was sealed off in a separate compartment, but it was nevertheless his own flesh and blood—the repository of all the human frailties which he despised in himself and which he was determined to stamp out, root and branch. This is why he had no compassion with the weak and the downtrodden. "Conscience," he once told Rauschning, "is a Jewish invention. It is a blemish like circumcision." He certainly showed little pity for himself, and, on the brink of political or military defeat, suicide was often on his mind.

He failed to comprehend how Field Marshal Friedrich Paulus, after his last stand at Stalingrad, chose captivity in preference to a soldier's death by his own hand. When Field Marshal Erwin Rommel, of African fame, was implicated in a conspiracy against the Führer, he granted him as a special favor the choice of suicide instead of execution by a firing squad.

Hitler's path was strewn with the suicides or attempted suicides not only of those he feared or hated but also of those he professed to love. His niece Geli Raubal, with whom he had been in love, committed suicide in 1931. In 1932, less than two years after Geli's death, Eva Braun made an attempt at suicide, long before 1945, when she joined Hitler in the mass suicide in the Führerbunker in Berlin. They were joined in turn by Goebbels and his wife, who took their six children with them, as Hitler's favorite dog, Blondie, and her puppies had been taken the day before. Hermann Goering, Heinrich Himmler, and many other lesser figures in the Nazi hierarchy later chose the same fate. It was one of Hitler's ultimate disappointments that the rest of the German people refused to join their leader's last suicidal leap into the abyss. "If the war is lost," he told Speer, his minister of armaments, shortly before the end, "the Nation will also perish. There is no need to consider the basis of . . . even . . . a most primitive existence any longer. On the contrary, it is better to destroy even that, and to destroy it ourselves. The Nation has proved itself weak and the future belongs solely to the stronger, Eastern nations. Besides, those who remain after the battle are of little value, for the good have fallen . . ." (Speer 1970, pp. 774–75).

In reality, it was his own weakness which Hitler could not tolerate. He had failed to pass his own test of victory over those who were unfit to live and to rule, and in the end he was ready to pay with his life for having lost his gamble. If megalomania, fears of persecution, projection, and the tendency to destruction and self-destruction are indicative of a paranoid trend, it was obviously one of Hitler's outstanding personality traits. But it accounts for his failures, for his fateful miscalculations only. It provides no clue to his meteoric rise and his achievements prior to his downfall.

Medium?

It is an intriguing detail in Hitler's vital statistics that he was an older contemporary of Willy and Rudi Schneider, the notorious physical mediums born, like Hitler himself, in Braunau, Austria. There is also an unconfirmed report that he had the same wetnurse as Rudi. Obviously, this is barely more than a queer historic coincidence. Still, the question arises whether there has been more to his exploits as the twentieth century shaman or sorcerer than met the eyes of his startled contemporaries. Rauschning (1940) made repeated references to Hitler's interest in spiritualism and astrology and his dabbling in the occult. Hitler himself believed he had mediumistic faculties and had participated in spiritualistic séances in Munich after World War I. According to Rauschning, he saw in his own "miraculous life" a confirmation of his hidden powers. Some of his contemporaries tended to share this opinion. On one occasion the German industrialist Wilhelm Keppler was so impressed with Hitler's performance at a closed meeting that he declared, "The Führer has an antenna to tune him in directly to the Almighty."

Rauschning remarked that "Hitler's henchmen made more and more play with this quality of his as a supreme magician." They obviously had a vested interest in fostering belief in his infallibility. Goebbels' propaganda machine made it an article of the Nazi faith. In view of Hitler's prophecy of the Thousand-Year Reich, it had indeed become a dogma whose validity was to be questioned only under penalty of death.

Here, again, the pattern of circular feedback between the shaman and his tribe is unmistakable. Hitler himself became increasingly convinced of the veridical quality of his hunches and intuitions. This self-confidence was further enhanced by his unusual flair for handling people and by his undeniable political acumen. His occasional flashes of strategic and military know-how took some of his most skeptical generals by surprise.

Some of these apparent feats of intuition had all the hallmarks of rational inferences, though their accuracy appeared to be incongruous with Hitler's spotty education and poorly disciplined mind. Yet even in his last message to posterity, in the testament written prior to his suicide in the Führerbunker in Berlin, he struck one of his surprisingly accurate prophetic chords: "With the defeat of the Reich and pending the emergence of the Asiatic, the African and perhaps the South American nationalisms, there will remain in the world only two Great Powers capable of confronting each other—the United States and Soviet Russia . . . and it is . . . certain that both these powers will sooner or later find it desirable to seek the support of the sole surviving Great Nation in Europe, the German people." The dateline of this document is spring 1945, shortly before the final curtain rang down on the Götterdämmerung of the Third Reich. Quoting this passage in his book, Bullock feels constrained to give grudging recognition to Hitler's unusual foresight of political developments which were to come to pass some twenty-five years after his death (Bullock 1962, pp. 793–96).

There is another intriguing incident in Hitler's stormy career which is more suggestive of a prophetic or telepathic quality than the passage quoted from his testament. Since Hitler's celebrated putsch in 1923 in Munich, it was his custom to deliver a speech to the Old Guard in the Bürgerbräukeller in Munich. On November 8, 1939, I listened in London to a direct radio transmission of his speech. It contained the usual harangues against the perfidy of the Allies and the usual gloating, this time over his victorious Blitzkrieg in Poland and the newly signed nonaggression pact with the Soviet Union. He pledged to go on with the war, no matter how long it would take, and so on. I remember how, halfway through the speech, his tone of voice lost its strident quality. Changing to a somber, funereal mode of delivery, he paid homage to the comrades who had given their lives in their first bloody test of strength in 1923. These are the relevant passages from the speech in my own translation.

"Every German," he intoned, "should realize that the sacrifices of these men was worth just as much as the sacrifice of every German in the future; he should realize that no one has a right to consider his own future sacrifice to be more exacting. We National Socialists should never forget the insight which dawned on us and the pledge which we made in the wake of the Death March [*Totengang*] on November 9th, of the first sixteen victims in the history of our movement—namely, the insight and the pledge that whatever made their sacrifices worthwhile at that time, imposed on others, too, the duty to be ready to make, if necessary, the same sacrifice." Calling up the memories of those who had died for the Fatherland in the preceding centuries, if not millennia, he cautioned his listeners: "None of us knows whether it is not going to hit him too [*Keiner von uns weiss ob es ihn nicht auch trifft*]."

He closed his speech with the promise that "we shall all be prepared to lay down our lives for the goals of the movement . . ." This, he stated, is "the first and last sentence that is written over every National Socialist whenever, at the conclusion of his tour of duty, he departs from this world."

Hitler himself departed from the Bürgerbräukeller earlier than usual "in order to catch the D train to Berlin in time."

Minutes after his departure, a bomb went off next to the speaker's rostrum. It ripped the hall to pieces, killing eight of his comrades of the Old Guard and injuring sixty-three others. His "prophecy" of their impending deaths had come true much sooner than anyone would have expected.

Goebbels, the number one public relations man and the Führer's propaganda chief, made the most of Hitler's prophetic intuition and miraculous escape from what would have been certain death had he spent another few minutes among his comrades. Bullock relates that Hitler himself "immediately seized on his escape as proof of providential intervention. His eyes blazing with excitement, he announced (to his secretary) 'Now I am content. The fact that I left the Bürgerbräuhaus earlier than usual is a confirmation of Providence's intention to allow me to reach my goal.'" A fortnight later he was still in an exalted mood. He spoke like a man of destiny, drunk with his own sense of greatness. "In all modesty," he declared on November 23, 1939, "I must name my own person: irreplaceable . . . I am convinced of my powers of intellect and decision . . . no one has ever achieved what I have achieved. . . ." And he added, apparently as an afterthought to his escape from the assassination attempt:

> In the last years I have experienced many examples of intuition. Even in the present development I see the prophecy [presumably of the Thousand-Year Reich]. . . . If we come through this struggle victoriously —and we shall—our time will enter into the history of our people. I shall stand or fall in this struggle. I shall never survive the defeat of my people. . . . (Bullock 1962, pp. 567–68)

Hitler's reference to his "many intuitions" in the last years sounds very much like the accounts of similar incidents in the parapsychological literature. It is indeed suggestive of an experience of a precognitive or telepathic type. His mood of exaltation, his whole manner of delivery— including the hints of megalomania in his utterances—bear all the hallmarks of a paranormal experience.

According to rumors circulating after the assassination attempt, it was not an act of conspirators or enemy agents but had been arranged by the Gestapo "as a means of raising the Führer's popularity in the country." A bomb had been planted next to the pillar where he was to speak and made to explode by an electrical device after he had ended his speech. More recent studies have dismissed this hypothesis as unfounded. German historians doubt that Hitler had been told of what was afoot. Max Domarus (1962), the editor and annotator of Hitler's speeches, points to the Führer's notorious fear of "infernal machines" and of real assassination attempts against him. Nor is it likely that even Hitler's most ruthless associates would have seen fit to saddle the "boss" himself with responsibility for the carnage among the audience in the Bräuhaus. They may have been satisfied with furnishing one more positive proof of his providential mission and invulnerability. W. L. Shirer (1960) quotes the testimony of Hans Bernd Gisevius, an official of the Prussian Ministry of the Interior, to the same effect.

Similar considerations apply to another assassination attempt on Hitler's life. It was planned as late as February 1945, by Albert Speer, Hitler's "fellow architect" and erstwhile minister of ammunitions. Hitler had, at that time, virtually entombed himself in his underground bunker in Berlin. It was Speer himself who had designed the bunker, including its vital air-intake vent, concealed behind bushes above ground. Speer's plan was to filter poison gas into the bunker through the vent and to do away with Hitler and his entourage in a last desperate try.

It took him a fortnight to make the necessary preparations and to obtain the poison gas. However, once Speer was ready for action, he discovered to his dismay that Hitler had in the meantime ordered the addition of a twelve-foot-high chimney to the air vent. Once again a last-minute attempt to change the course of history had been thwarted, and once again it appears that Hitler's "uncanny intuition," as Speer put it, had been working.

What appears to be a more persuasive paranormal incident goes back to Hitler's experiences in World War I. While having a bite with his comrades in a trench, he suddenly heard a voice ordering him to get up and "walk over there" (1943). It sounded so much like a military command that he automatically obeyed. He walked some 200 yards to finish his meal. Barely had he turned his back on his comrades when they were all, with no exception, killed by a direct hit from an enemy grenade. It was one of the first occasions when he felt he owed his life to the direct intervention of Providence.

What do these seemingly isolated incidents in Hitler's life history add up to? They suggest that our narrow definition of the personality makeup of psychics, sensitives, or spiritualistic mediums cannot possibly do justice to the infinite varieties of real life. The man Hitler was evidently no "psychic" or "sensitive" bent on amassing high extrachance scores in a series of ESP or PK tests. He did not try to excel in the standard type of laboratory experiments. He was not concerned with domesticated, garden variety psi occurrences. He was no physical medium like the Schneider brothers, like Eusapia Palladino or Uri Geller. On entering the arena of history he no longer tried his hands at table tilting, at causing curtains to billow in a cold breeze wafting through a darkened séance room. Rather, he seemed to have brought to bear his hypnotic—or paranormal—powers on his underlings, transforming them into soulless robots who blindly followed his orders, spoken and unspoken, or acted vicariously in his behalf. This is how his bomber pilots, instead of tossing PK dice from a cup or throwing about pebbles or pieces of furniture like poltergeist children in a haunted house, gutted cities with blockbusters released from their planes. Instead of bending spoons like Uri Geller or moving match boxes on tabletops like Nina Kulagina, Hitler dispatched his panzers, his armored trains, and his troop transports all over the face of the Eurasian continent, wreaking death, destruction, and fire storms in the conquered territories. If he was a psychic or *paragnost*, he did not aim to score direct hits on ESP or PK targets, but on airbases, power plants, and munitions factories.

No doubt, Hitler was possessed of a pathologically inflated ego. It stretched to the outermost reaches of his personality structure—a macabre illustration of my extension hypothesis of psi phenomena outlined in Chapter 19. He swallowed up and "incorporated" the territory of the greater German Reich into his bloated and ballooning self. He identified with his realm as Joan of Arc, Louis XIV, or General de Gaulle had identified with *La Patrie*. But his sense of mystic union with Germany was more than a figure of speech. It extended far beyond the boundaries of his individual personality—it included his faithful paladins; the SA, the SS, the Wehrmacht, the judiciary, the church; the whole panoply of power, past, present, and future, possessed or claimed by the German race. He extended his psychological pseudopodia into the hearts and brains of his subjects. He established control over the media, the means of production, the machine tools of his nation. Germany's arsenals, her army, navy, air force, and rolling stock—they all became ectoplasmic extensions of his quest for mastery, dominance, and control—and, if need be, for acts of reckless savagery and destruction.

Whether and how far there was a demonstrable psi factor involved in all this must remain a matter of speculation. But there can be little doubt that his intellectual outlook, his sensory-motor organization, his volitional functions, his whole mode of existence showed close affinity to psi functions. W. C. Langer (1972) has rightly pointed out that Hitler, instead of dealing with problems on the intellectual level, was wont to turn his attention to other matters until his unconscious provided the answers. In this respect, Langer noted, he showed more of an artists' temperament than a statesman's. To this one could add the qualities of the psychic or sensitive.

The reader acquainted with modern split-brain research will perhaps notice at this point that Hitler's own claims of providential guidance, of infallible intuitions, coupled with what Langer describes as his artistic temperament, are in good keeping with recent findings about the part played by the right hemisphere in personalities of this type. I pointed out elsewhere (1977) that the left hemisphere is geared to perform intellectual and linguistic tasks. It stores, processes, and retrieves information. By contrast, the right hemisphere deals with intuitions, with metaphors, with esthetic values. It puts the stamp of reality, of apodictic certainty, on the individual's experiences. By the same token, lesions in the right side of the brain are conducive to feelings of depersonalization, strangeness, and alienation on the left side of the body. The left hemisphere may have all its information in perfect order, but the information tends to be bloodless and flat, "sicklied o'er with the pale cast of thought." On the other hand, the right hemisphere imparts on the individual the unshakable conviction of the reality of his dreams, hallucinations, and delusions. Clearly, this is the stuff prophets, religious reformers—and paranoid schizophrenics—are made of. (See also Chapter 28.)

In decisive moments Hitler seemed to be wholly under the influence of his *daimonion*—or right hemisphere. This is what gave him the unshakable conviction that he was always right. But this, too, imbued him with an ultimately self-destructive contempt for the demands of reality testing as the ultimate arbiter of human conduct. His psi functions ran counter to the rules of conventional logic; they spurned the canons of morality and the requirements of long-range, pragmatic planning. Ultimately, his apodictic sense of certainty turned out to be fallacious, based on delusions of grandeur or persecution held to the bitter end by a maniac. Their only vindication could have been provided by a favorable outcome of his struggle. Conceivably, such an auspicious turn of events could have amounted to a confirmation of his sanity. His failure proved the absurdity of his claims. It shattered his self-image as a seer, a psychic, a superman. It left suicide as he last remaining option.

Thus, the psi factor in Hitler's case had been far more than a harmless laboratory artifact, a game with critical ratios, chi-squares, and statistical significance. It reverted to its archaic prototype of black magic, witchcraft, and demonology. It was worlds apart from an experimental subject's groping attempts to produce extrachance scores in an ESP experiment, or from the creative artist's inspirations welling up from his unconscious. Hitler's stakes in his game of roulette involved life and death—both his own and that of the whole German Reich. Indeed, the failure of his gambler's throw proved once again the doubtful survival value, at the present stage of our development, of an approach to human affairs—or the affairs of state—guided by hunches, intuitions, or even psi, instead of by reason and common sense.

17

Uri Geller and Matthew Manning:

From Spoon Bending to Mind Bending

THE PSYCHIATRIC STUDY of a gifted sensitive or psychic—even if he be less formidable than Adolf Hitler—is beset by several difficulties. He may not take kindly to such an attempt; he may resent being subjected to psychoanalytic scrutiny. He may regard it as an invasion of his privacy. Even if such hurdles can be overcome, the psychiatrist is obliged to refrain from airing in public what he has learned in the privacy of his office. Nor is he likely to feel free to go on record with clinical judgments that might embarrass or antagonize his subject, offend his sensibilities, and detract from the spontaneity of his responses. Indeed, there is reason to believe that safeguarding the integrity of his role as a psychic is one of the very prerequisites of his self-esteem—if not of his sanity and mental health.

An added difficulty is that such media-made celebrities as Uri Geller are usually surrounded by a circle of concerned friends, intimates, agents, or managers anxious to guard their protégé from curiosity seekers, to protect his public image, and to make sure that only true believers and potential champions of his cause have access to him. With Matthew Manning the situation is different. He is a loner, shuns publicity, disdains commercial exploitation of his psychic gifts, and is anxious to "disassociate" himself from his social environment.

Nevertheless, both Matthew and Uri yielded to the growing interest in their case and have gone on record with their autobiographies. Uri Geller's *My Story* (1975) and Matthew Manning's *The Link* (1974) have provided a rich store of information about their respective authors. Together with impressions gained from their films and television appearances, from Dr. Andrija Puharich's monograph (1974), from the Targ-Puthoff report in *Nature* (1974), from J. Taylor's *Superminds* (1975), from M. Ebon's *The Amazing Uri Geller* (1975), from Panatis (1976) *The Geller Papers*, and from assorted personal communications, it is possible to arrive at an at least tentative psychiatric evaluation of the Uri Geller and Matthew Manning cases.

Unfortunately, such an attempt is made more difficult by the widespread publicity and the carnival atmosphere in Uri's case which has surrounded the solid evidence of his psychic exploits. The difficulties are compounded by some of the bizarre claims made in Puharich's highly colored personal report. It contains fantastic allegations about UFO sightings, purported communication with extraterrestrial intelligences, self-erasing tape recordings, and alleged materialization and dematerialization incidents. Some stories are reminiscent of far-out science fiction— if not of material taken from psychiatric case histories.

To make matters worse, Geller's own account is at times colored by what Captain Edgar Mitchell, one of Uri's original sponsors, has described as his messianic complex. In addition, Uri's record is tarnished by reports that he had occasionally resorted to slights of hand and diverse conjuror's tricks to improve upon his genuine psi exploits (Berendt 1974). Yet on separating the wheat from the chaff, the evidence in favor of genuine psi phenomena is overwhelming. On balance, his record and its relevance to the present inquiry derives not only from his individual accomplishments but also from the apparent ease with which they fit in with the overall picture of the psi syndrome that has emerged in the preceding chapters and with the theory to be presented in Part Four. Whether this is apt to add to the plausibility of the Geller effect or to detract from the merits of the theory will be for the future to decide.

Uri Geller

Uri was born in 1946 in Haifa, Israel. His earliest experiences followed the familiar pattern seen in other gifted psychics. At five or six, he would "guess" whether his mother had been winning or losing at her game of cards. He would tell her the exact amount of money she had won. He recalls that he often anticipated the very word or sentence his mother was about to utter. His parents did not get along. He knew that his father was involved with other women. Uri naturally sided with his mother and had always remained deeply devoted to her. To the extent that telepathy was involved in their relationship, it closely conformed to the symbiotic model described in Chapter 2.

But Uri's ability for symbiotic responses soon went far beyond the early parent-child relationship. He recounts numerous telepathic or clairvoyant incidents, usually triggered by the need to "home in" on his parents in an emergency, to locate his lost dog, or to find his way out of a labyrinth of caverns in which he was trapped. His apparent psychokinetic abilities also made their appearance early in life. At age six, his father gave him a watch as a birthday present. Bored to tears at school, he desperately wanted the bell to ring for the recess and release him from his captivity. This is when, according to Uri, he first noted that the hands of the watch had jumped an hour or two *ahead* of time. From then on, Uri seemed to have developed a growing proficiency in making watches and other inanimate objects do his bidding. He made the delicate machinery of timepieces and other appliances literally *bend* to his will.

More puzzling still are the reports that, besides causing watches to go faster or to run backwards, Uri could make their hands bend or curl up under the glass or make broken watches go again by simply concentrating on them. He also found, to his surprise, that gentle stroking of spoons, forks, keys, or other metallic objects made them respond to his will. As a young adult, he could demonstrate his abilities time and again: first in some 800 public demonstrations in Israel (where he was accused of occasionally adding a conjurer's trick to his genuine "Geller effects"), and later in countless television shows and lecture halls in the United States and elsewhere, as well as under rigidly controlled experimental conditions on both sides of the Atlantic. The authenticity of such feats was attested to by such prestigious institutions as the Stanford Research Institute in California or Kings College and Birkback College of the University of London. They were recorded, if not verified, in numerous tapes, films, and audiovisual recordings. As noted earlier, *Nature* and several other prestigious journals have opened their columns to writings by R. Targ and H. Puthoff (1974) and other scientists confirming the effects. In an as yet unpublished experimental series recorded on film at the Stanford Research Institute, he is said to have scored at the level of about 1 million or even 1 trillion (!) to one against chance. The much quoted Targ-Puthoff experiments involved telepathic drawing tests and clairvoyance under double-blind conditions (see Chapter 21). Yet this class of Uri Geller's exploits is by no means unprecedented. What is novel is the accuracy with which he can pinpoint his PK targets, make constructive use of his PK ability, and bring it to bear on such static metallic objects as a key, a spoon, on slivers of platinum, gold, silver, or steel. Controlled experiments and metallurgical studies have shown that the force exerted in this way may amount to pressure of up to 1,270 pounds! (Franklin 1975).

The poltergeist children discussed in Chapter 13 have apparently been capable of harnessing the same amounts of kinetic energy. But by contrast to Uri Geller, they did so in an erratic, disorganized fashion, without trying to attain control over, or even being aware of, their actions.

On the other hand, Uri has been wide off the mark on many occasions. Instead of the spoon or the watch upon which he focused his attention, other objects nearby, in the experimenter's pocket, or even on the floor above or below would bend to his will. On other occasions the response would be delayed by a short or long time lag.

The same imprecision and tendency to "near misses" is a familiar feature of telepathic or clairvoyant impressions. I have described this pattern as scatter effects due to paraexperimental telepathy or telepathic leakage. In some cases, I noted, the scatter includes delayed or precognitive reactions, that is, displacement in time. This, too, seems to be characteristic of Uri's performances.

An amusing, though in all likelihood a fictitious story, is the case of a Danish lady of seventy-six who had been unable to bend an arthritic knee for two years. Instead of focusing attention on a broken watch (as the audience in the Danish television station was instructed to do), she concentrated on her disabled leg. Shortly after the broadcast, Uri was informed that in this instance it was not a watch, but the old lady's knee that happened to be "repaired."

An even more baffling side effect of Uri Geller's television appearances has been widely reported by the British Press and was investigated by Professor John Taylor (1975) of Kings College in London. It involves a veritable epidemic of key- or spoon-bending children who had watched Uri Geller on the BBC. Dr. Taylor's tests with these "mini-Gellers," ranging from seven years to their teens apparently confirmed that they had picked up some of Uri Geller's PK abilities. To complicate matters, occasionally some of Uri's contagious psi exploits were duplicated by viewers watching an audiovisual replay of his performance. We shall see that it is such incidents which are apt to pull the rug out from under all attempts at attributing the Geller effect to some novel form of energy emanating from him. By the same token, more recent reports trying to expose the

Geller effects as mere showmanship and trickery cannot reasonably account for observations of this order (Weil 1974).

Here again, the contagious pattern of the Geller effect has a familiar ring. It is reminiscent of the contagious quality of diverse emotionally charged behavioral patterns, from laughing and yawning to expressions of fear and panic in group situations. The fits and convulsions produced by the crazed nuns of Loudun or the hysterical children of Salem are graphic illustrations of such a tendency. More recent examples of the same order have been reported in the field of sports and musical abilities. Until Roger Bannister, the four-minute mile was beyond the capacity of long-distance runners. Once Bannister had broken the hitherto unsurmountable barrier, more and more athletes succeeded in duplicating or even surpassing this feat. Violin or piano virtuosos in the past decades have likewise been able to outperform the virtuosity of their predecessors once the ground was broken by artists of the caliber of Paganini, Liszt, or Rubinstein. It appears that ESP and PK are subject to a similar principle of learning, conditioning, imitation, and inspiration by example and precedent.

I hinted that all these instances of the Geller effect may in part be determined by his need for symbiotic closeness with parental figures and in part by his quest for mastery and control over his social and physical environment—for magic omnipotence, if you like. They are essentially need-determined and carry the stamp of purposeful, organized, and deliberate activities.

But this is by no means always the case. Some of Uri's PK manifestations seem to be utterly capricious, purposeless, random events, without apparent rhyme or reason. Suddenly a camera levitates during a transatlantic flight. A piece of metal is thrown about in Dr. Taylor's laboratory and comes crashing down some twenty feet away. Geller claims that during one of his appearances in Scandinavia there was a brown-out in the city (?). On another occasion, he reports, there was a breakdown of electronic machinery in the BBC in London. Such reports are unconfirmed, and cannot be taken at face value. Be that as it may, Uri himself is baffled by such bizarre happenings. He attributes them to some mischievous external force, utterly beyond his control—to a "cosmic clown" playing tricks with him and with his friends, if not with humanity at large. Yet the "cosmic clown" may very well reside in the hidden recesses of Uri's own mind. Indeed, the similarity with "tricks" attributed to mischievous poltergeist children is unmistakable. Although Uri's autobiographical account tends to minimize or gloss over his hidden resentments

and destructive impulses against the grown-up world, there are occa-
tional hints of rebelliousness against his father and other figures in authority. He confesses that his early encounters with such scientists as
Andrija Puharich, Professor Taylor, or the staff of the Stanford Research
Institute held a considerable threat to him. There are also indications of
a highly charged ambivalent relationship to Dr. Puharich, his discoverer,
fatherly friend, and spiritual guide. The fact is that all such authority
figures had their share of occasional bursts of poltergeist-like activity
emanating from Uri.

Yet it is also true to say that some incidents cannot by any stretch of
imagination be interpreted in terms of deliberate rebellious acts. We shall
see in Chapter 21 that they can be described as flaw-determined—that is,
as events due to a "flaw" in the subject's mental or neurophysiological
organization. It is randomly occurring flaws of this order which may be
responsible for the occasional release of indiscriminate, erratic motor
activity of the poletergeist type. Such activity is in effect the motor
counterpart of the random intrusion into an ESP subject's consciousness
of meaningless, biologically or socially indifferent telepathic or clairvoyant impressions.

As in the case of the poltergeist children, the origins of such hypothetical flaws must remain a matter of speculation. Uri reports that as a
child of three, he had a striking experience which, in grown-up language,
would have to be described as a mystical illumination or theophany.
First, there was a ringing in his ears, then stillness. Then there appeared
a "silvery mass of light" so that he asked himself: "What happened to
the sun? . . . Then I was knocked out, I lost consciousness completely"
(p. 96). And he adds: "Deep down I knew something important had
happened." Whether or not it had any bearing on Uri's neurophysiological makeup and upon the subsequent development of his psychic abilities
must remain an open question. It is interesting to note that no lesser
figure than C. G. Jung has gone on record with the account of a similar
"mystical" experience as a little boy.

Unfortunately, some of Uri's wilder claims tend to detract from the
credibility of his more solidly established exploits. A glaring example is a
series of incidents reminiscent of science fiction which are mentioned in
his autobiography and in Puharich's report. Some involve the recording
of "direct voice" communications from "outer space," with the tapes
promptly disappearing or dematerializing (!) after the event. The description of alleged interventions in their daily routine by mysterious
extraterrestrial forces or intellectual agencies is no less embarrassing.
Reports of alleged UFO sightings, including a photograph of three

spaceships supposedly taken by Uri Geller, are wholly unconvincing. Significantly, the phenomena were never corroborated by independent witnesses—to say nothing of their reproduction under controlled conditions.

In these circumstances the question no longer is one of consensual validation or objective fact finding. It is rather one of the psychological origin of some of the more extravagant claims put forward by Uri Geller and concurred in by Dr. Puharich. It should be noted, however, that the extraterrestrial communications, the UFO sightings, and the phenomena of the dematerializing tapes seemed to make their appearance only after Puharich had taken Uri under his wings and that on at least two occasions Puharich had hypnotized Uri to retrieve forgotten memories through age regression in the hypnotic trance.

We know today that the hypnotist-subject, therapist-patient, or teacher-pupil relationship creates ideal conditions for doctrinal compliance or what Robert Rosenthal has described as the Pygmalion effect (1973). Thus, we are left with the conjecture that such effects may have been superimposed on what had originally been authentic and unadulterated Geller phenomena.

On the other hand, the possibility that Puharich may have himself been induced to share some of his disciple's messianic ideas cannot be ruled out of the question. The difference is that some of Uri's "grandiosity" happened to be supported by experimental findings, while his and Dr. Puharich's ventures into the realm of the unproven and unprovable were not. It is to Puharich's lasting credit that he first called the attention of the scientific community to a little-known Israeli vaudeville performer. But what followed has cast considerable doubt on the soundness of his judgment and did not serve well the case of science, of Uri Geller, or of Andrija Puharich himself.

Matthew Manning

Matthew Manning, ten years Uri Geller's junior, is another psychic whose striking feats in psychokinesis and automatic writing and drawing set him apart from the rest of his class. He is the oldest of three siblings, the son of a prominent architect in Cambridge, England. Peter Bander, a psychologist, editor of the journal *Psychical Researcher*, and editor of

Matthew's precocious autobiography, *The Link* (1974), describes him as an introvert who, as a child, "absolutely refused to talk to strangers." When scolded for mischievousness, "he would withdraw into a corner and remain there, sometimes for hours, curled up in total isolation" (p. 2). In later years, the headmaster of his boarding school described him as a "loner and rather lethargic."

When interviewed in New York on television by Betty Furness, Matthew, nineteen, appeared unresponsive, aloof, and self-absorbed, insisting on giving written answers to her questions. Yet Mr. Bander stresses his willing cooperation with all comers, his photographic memory, and his almost pedantic need to give a truthful and unembellished account of his experiences.

Matthew's father emerges as a somewhat obsessive, perfectionist type, a "no-nonsense man," sterling citizen, and paterfamilias. Nevertheless, he had apparently shown utmost patience with Matthew's excentricities. Mrs. Manning is described as a devoted wife, a loving mother, and a friend to her three children. We learn little about the younger siblings, except that early in the course of the poltergeist disturbances which were to plague the family when Matthew reached the age of eleven, all three had been suspected of having a hand in the occurrence.

The poltergeist manifestations conform in most respects to those reported in the literature. They consisted of the familiar noises, bangs, and rappings that could not be traced to any natural source. Small objects and later heavy pieces of furniture were moved in the house. Some reliable witnesses reportedly saw them flying around corners in irregular trajectories. Significantly, the first object involved was father's silver tankard, which was reserved for Mr. Manning's personal use. Soon mother's flower vase, cutlery, ash trays, and sundry other objects followed suit. Surprisingly, none was broken and none of the valuable antiques in the house damaged. At one time, eleven objects were moved during fifteen minutes. On another occasion an eraser, used by Matthew's sister, ascended slowly from behind her settee, rose about five feet, and floated down the staircase to come to rest beside her. "We were terrified," writes Matthew, "and for the first time ran out from the house" (p. 36). Among more spectacular performances, Mr. Bander mentions Matthew having bent one of an "unbendable" pair of steel handcuffs, a feat which left both their manufacturer and the police baffled.

When Matthew was moved to a boarding school in Oakham, matters went from bad to worse. A boot was seen floating through the air. The poltergeist raised havoc in the dormitory, displacing bunks or other heavy furniture. Metal coat hangers were hurled around; cold chills were generated; mysterious luminosities appeared on the wall and made it feel warm to the touch. A would-be exorcist was called in, but his hocus-pocus only aggravated the situation. It was only thanks to the headmaster's and the house-matron's patience and sympathetic understanding, conceivably aided by the proverbial British stiff upper lip of all those concerned, that Matthew escaped being expelled from the school.

The counsel and tactful intervention of Professor George Owen, a noted geneticist and author of the book, *Can We Explain the Poltergeist?* (1964), has undoubtedly contributed to an ultimately favorable outcome. He studied Matthew's case and family situation, first in Cambridge and later in Toronto, Canada, where Owen was appointed director of the Horizon Research Foundation for parapsychology. This is where Dr. Joel Whitton (1974) carried out a series of controlled electromyographic and EEG studies of Matthew, both at rest and when Matthew was preparing to "switch on" his PK powers.

Whitton reports that on such occasions "Matthew's brain-wave pattern, registered each time for twenty seconds, was "entirely new." Described as a "ramp function," because of its shape in a given time frame, the wave showed a peak in the delta or low theta band, "with most energy in the lower EEG frequency." "It does not appear related to . . . resting, eyes open, resting eyes closed, movements of muscles, talking or intense concentration . . . It appears to be a unique physiological correlate of paranormal behavior" (p. 179).

Whitton also notes that the ramp function does not resemble Grey Walter's (1970) CNV, or expectancy wave (personal communication), but conforms to earlier findings of increased theta energy in high-scoring ESP subjects during paranormal behavior.

A second finding was that the source of the ramp function could be traced to archaic, limbic midbrain structures of the central nervous system. This observation is still in need of corroboration from other workers, but it will be seen in Chapter 21, "Psi Phenomena in Search of a Neural Foothold," that it is in good keeping with my own conclusions arrived at independently of Dr. Whitton's study.

There are a few additional significant aspects of the Manning case, as far as his symptomatology, genetics, and psychodynamics are concerned. He undoubtedly started off as an "ordinary" poltergeist child with added autistic features. Although our information about Matthew's personality makeup and his family situation is fragmentary, I noted in Chapter 13 that he was locked in a muted conflict with his "no-nonsense" father. He seemed to defy the pedantic, law-and-order routine of the Manning household, deflected his rebelliousness against Mr. Manning to inanimate objects, and subsequently wrought havoc in the study rooms and dormitories of his prep school—one of the last citidels of unchallenged paternal authority in the British Isles.

Yet the making of mischief was by no means the only purpose of Matthew's poltergeist activities. On one occasion, table mats stacked on a tray in preparation for a family meal were snatched from the tray and spaced out in neat order on the floor of the sitting room. At another time a broom handle would appear delicately balanced on a railing. Another feature of Matthew's performances is their remarkable precision and delicacy: "Though physical forces of the order of 30 or so pounds of weight were applied in lifting pieces of furniture," writes Dr. Owen (p. 192) in an appendix to *The Link*, "these objects were deposited so lightly as to do no damage." One gains the impression that in these performances two countervailing forces were at work: one bent on chaos, disorganization, disruption; the other measured, purposeful, controlled, capable of utmost precision. We shall see in Part Four of this book that here, again, they reflect the basic dichotomy of need-determined versus flaw-determined phenomena seen in Uri Geller's case or in Ted Serios' "thoughtographic" exploits. They are obviously characteristic of psi functions in general.

It may be mentioned only in passing that Matthew Manning was quite proficient in duplicating Uri Geller's spoon- and fork-bending feats. But while he was often able to pinpoint a given PK target with great accuracy, his performance was often subject to the same kind of temporal and spatial scatter seen in Uri's PK. At times the effects occurred after considerable delay, surprising both Matthew and his audience. Indeed, Uri as well as Matthew frequently complained of their inability to exercise control over the "poltergeist"; both considered it a force imposed on them from the outside. Psychoanalytically speaking, they felt it was ego alien, emanating from their unconscious, and tended to disclaim responsibility for its actions. In this respect they were in striking contrast to Nina Kulagina's more deliberate control of PK.

While we know nothing of Kulagina's early childhood, the direct derivation from early poltergeist activities of both the Geller effect and of the later, more subtle manifestations in the Manning case is unmistakable. This becomes abundantly clear from Dr. Owen's analysis of Matthew's exploits. "Poltergeistery," Owen suggests, "is at the roots of later PK abilities. . . . It is perhaps the first stage in the natural evolution of a powerful psychic (p. 146). In keeping with my thesis of parent-child symbiosis as the cradle of ESP, it could be stated that the revolt of the poltergeist child is in effect aimed at breaking a prolonged symbiotic bond which interferes with his need for separation-individuation and emancipation from parental control. The bedlam eleven-year-old Matthew caused in his parental home and later in his boarding school is a graphic illustration of this apparently lawful course of events (Ehrenwald 1974).

But Matthew's case history illustrates yet another intriguing aspect of the process. After a two or three month period of violent disturbances, followed by remission and relapse, the physical phenomena seemed to be laid to rest. At the same time, equally dramatic mental manifestations made their appearance: automatic writing and drawing. At age fifteen to sixteen, Matthew produced scripts written both in English and in several foreign languages, including Arabic, which he could not speak. It is also claimed that the writings included information he could only have acquired in some paranormal way.

Even more unusual phenomena were to follow. Although he did not show any artistic abilities in his ordinary state of mind, Matthew's automatic drawings seemed to be a striking mimicry of Albrecht Dürer's, Leonardo da Vinci's, Pablo Picasso's, or Aubrey Beardsley's works. Even though flawed in some technical detail, their style and execution faithfully mirrored the original model. Matthew himself modestly disclaimed credit for his drawings. He considered them the work of discarnate spiritual entites that were guiding his hand, secondary personalities "possessing" him, or grafted on him by external cues, as described in Chapter 12.

Whoever was responsible for the rich crop of Matthew's artistic output, it seemed to deflect his unruly poltergeist activities into new channels; it provided an outlet for bottled-up psychic energies which had previously been engaged in destructive acting out. Analytically speaking, it opened up new avenues for sublimation and creative activity. It was, in effect, successful art therapy, hit upon by trial and error by Matthew himself. He notes in his autobiography: "If I do no writing or drawing for two weeks or more, I become subject to poltergeist activity" (p. 142). In one of his interviews, he has also stated that he avoids dating girls and sex in general because he feels it would detract from his psychic abilities. At the same time, he hints that his psychic development had saved him from becoming an autistic child, and he suggests that this may also be true for others.

All this is in good keeping with the economic principles of Freudian metapsychology. It is also borne out by Jung's account of his self-treatment following a psychotic break by secluding himself in the tower of his estate in Küssnacht, and producing one mandala drawing after another, for days on end. It is also interesting to note that a similar tendency to substitute psychosomatic symptoms for a neurotic disorder, and vice versa, is well-known occurrence in clinical psychiatry. A patient suffering from spastic or ulcerative colitis may go into a remission from his intestinal disorder. At the same time, symptoms of a latent obsessive-compulsive neurosis may come to the fore.

In a similar vein, the emergence of psi phenomena may have a distinctively restitutive value for an individual teetering on the verge of mental disorder. We have seen that the paranoid schizophrenic may derive benefit from the realization that his delusions may contain a grain of truth, based as they sometimes are on his intuitive insight into or telepathic sensitivity to the unconscious of his fellowmen. The same is true for the ego defenses brought into play in the possession syndrome. In both cases, as I stated, therapy has to aim at reducing the level of the existing pathology and to replace malignant, paranoid patterns of projection with such less pathological mechanisms of defense as hysterical dissociation or diverse forms of conversion hysteria. This type of partial self-healing seems to have indeed occurred in Dr. Bender's Rosenheim case.

Thus, it is no coincidence that automatic writing—and other forms of motor or sensory-motor automatism—have gained wide popularity among both patients and nonpatients dabbling in the occult. Yet at the same time, parapsychologists, psychiatrists, and psychologists alike should be alert to both the risks and the therapeutic opportunities that attend such groping attempts at do-it-yourself therapy. They must try to understand the psychodynamics of such procedures and guide the individual toward constructive utilization of his own restitutive potentials. Failing this, the patient is apt to turn for help to a charlatan or exorcist.

What, then, are the lessons to be learned from the Geller and Manning cases, and from the parapsychiatric aspects of psi phenomena in general? I noted in earlier chapters that a one-sided, purely psychological or psychodynamic approach to the psi syndrome can give only half the answer. Why should only Uri Geller, Matthew Manning, and a few more poltergeist children develop spectacular PK or ESP abilities, while millions of others, coming from similar family backgrounds, motivated by much the same need for mastery, control, or rebellion, settle for more pedestrian forms of neurotic pathology or acting out? Why do some "flip" and go beyond the confines of the time-, space-, and causality-bound reality of everyday life? Why do a few succeed in spectacular psychic feats, while most who also try, do not?

We shall see that the answer must be sought by putting the question the other way around: What is it that prevents man's personality from being flooded by an avalanche of biologically and socially irrelevant or frankly undesirable stimuli, telepathic, clairvoyant, or precognitive, impinging on him *all* the time from *all* over the place? By the same token, we have to ask: What is it that *prevents* man's volitional actions or PK impulses from getting out of hand? What stops them from escalating into a pandemonium of indiscriminate, unbridled motor acting out, leaving no electron unruffled, no stone unturned, no table untilted, no spoon unbent, no matter safe from being "dematerialized" and no safe from being burglarized?

Such a new look at the problem is apt to shift our attention from purely psychological aspects to possible organic or structural factors as the missing link in an otherwise puzzling chain of causal events. In effect, we have already done so in our discussion of OOB experiences, of the possession syndrome, or of the biological aspects of schizophrenia. Uri Geller's history contains an intriguing clue in the same direction. He describes his swooning and mystical experience at the age of three in terms that can conceivably be interpreted as a seizure of organic origin, such as petit mal or an epileptic seizure. Perhaps more significant is Whitton's report that Matthew Manning's mother had suffered a violent electric shock during her pregnancy with Matthew. He has come across accounts of similar traumata in the early histories of several poltergeist children. Such findings, coupled with the history of more tangible organic lesions in OOB subjects and possession patients, suggest that we should be well-advised to extend our search for predisposing factors of the psi syndrome beyond single-tracked, need-determined origins and to supplement it with a methodical inquiry into flaw-determined, genetic, constitutional, or traumatic factors.

It is needless to say that all these considerations still fall far short of unraveling the ultimate mystery of psi. They tell nothing about its modus operandi, about the energies or forces brought into play, about their neural substrate, or about their relationship to known (or supposedly known) forms of energy—physical, neurophysiological, libidinal, or otherwise. Above all, they leave us as baffled as before by their incompatibility with our traditional notions of the laws of nature.

It is this problem to which we shall address ourselves in Part Four.

Part Four

THEORY

New facts burst old rules; then newly
divined conceptions bind old and new
together into a reconciling law.

William James

18

Science and the Seven Dragons:

A Note on Theory Making

THE THEORY of psi phenomena to be presented here has already ben prefigured in the material discussed in the preceding chapters. It has been smuggled—somewhat prematurely—into our presentation of mother-child symbiosis as the "cradle of ESP." It amounts in effect to the formulation of a genetic hypothesis of the origins of psi phenomena. Other intimations of a theory are scattered in the text and have yet to be spelled out in the pages that follow.

Before doing so, we have to clear seven major obstacles out of the way. They can be described, in a somewhat purple language, as the Seven Dragons guarding the entrance to the edifice of contemporary systems of scentific thought.

The first dragon is the challenge of pragmatic fact finding. The data have to be assembled and validated by consensus of workers in the field, while doubtful or spurious evidence has to be ruthlessly weeded out. On the other hand, all the evidence that has stood the test of scientific scrutiny has to be included—regardless of consequences. Indeed, this is what I have tried to do in the first three parts of this book.

The second dragon is the paradox that, although we feel duty bound to apply the principles of the scientific method to our findings, they run counter to some of the basic propositions of traditional science itself. The third dragon stands for the classical Newtonian or Kantian propositions of absolute time and space, a concept which is evidently incompatible with the spatio temporal anomalies involved in thought and action at a distance, as well as with the reversal of the linear, unidirectional flow of time implied by precognition.

The fourth dragon is the twin brother of the third: Kant's a priori, supposedly irreversible, law of cause and effect. It is one of the limiting principles of classical science invoked by a Cambridge philosopher, Professor C. D. Broad (1962).

The fifth dragon guards our conventional doctrine of cerebral localization which assigns, and indeed restricts, consciousness and other mental functions to more or less circumscribed areas of the brain cortex, mine or yours, or to lower echelons of the central nervous system. The sixth dragon is the picture of a walled-in personality structure suspended in splendid isolation in classical Euclidian space, functioning in pre-Einsteinian, prerelativistic time and subject to strictly foreordained causal laws.

There is a seventh dragon that has managed to slip into the inner sanctum of the parapsychologist's laboratory itself. Strangely enough, its presence has passed largely unnoticed by many workers in the field. It is the tendency to what in earlier chapters was described as paraexperimental telepathy, telepathic leakage, or doctrinal compliance. It goes without saying that the very introduction of the psi factor into the parapsychologist's personal equation should make it an everpresent source of potential error in virtually all experimental procedures in the behavioral sciences, but until recently few parapsychologists have made proper allowance for this state of affairs in their experimental design. They tend to gloss over the problem like the purveyors of the contaminated water supply in Henrik Ibsen's *An Enemy of the People*. As a result, the subject may pick the investigator's experimental design as his telepathic or precognitive or psychokinetic target, instead of producing the authentic psi effect which the experimenter has originally set out to explore. This may indeed provide apparent confirmation of his original thesis. But in the absence of proper safeguards, it does so merely in terms of telepathic leakage or doctrinal compliance, which I have cautioned against time and again.

The parallel with Heisenberg's principle of uncertainty may not escape the informed reader. The seventh dragon can in effect be described as the *principle of uncertainty* in psychiatry, psychoanalysis, and parapsychology.

Clearly, coping with the Seven Dragons requires considerable efforts of mind bending and mind stretching. More than that: it requires the unlearning of some of our conventional habits of thinking and tacitly implied theoretical presuppositions. Fortunately, modern relativistic physics, diverse non-Euclidian geometries, the probabilistic approach of quantum mechanics, and Gödel's theorem in mathematics have already done most of the job for us. We have to realize, however, that our current theories of personality—the kingpin of the behavioral sciences—are still lagging some half a century behind the natural sciences. We are still committed to the picture of human personality conceived as an impenetrable fortress, instead of an open-ended, surrealistic montage pervious to psi: "personality without walls."

Yet the early workers in psychical research have gone far to prepare the ground for such an approach. The list is headed by F. W. H. Myers (1903), Sidgwick, and Gurney, who first staked out the "subliminal"— that is, unconscious—self as the habitat of psi phenomena. They were followed by Henri Bergson (1913) with his thesis of the brain as an organ limiting attention and conscious awareness to biologically advantageous experiences and memory traces. Other pioneers of the Society for Psychical Research working in the same direction were G. N. M. Tyrrell (1963), Professor H. H. Price (1949), and C. D. Broad (1962) with their seminal philosophical contributions as well as further elaboration of Bergson's ideas. Freud's thesis of the screening function of the ego and modern inquiries into perceptual defenses have further helped in the formulation of the theory presented here. Due acknowledgement has to be made also to R. H. Thouless and B. P. Wiesner (1946) for their formulation of psi phenomena, including a hypothetical Shin factor mediating volitional and cognitive responses. They have inspired my own emphasis on the basic continuity of mental processes in the autopsychic and heteropsychic spheres, as proposed in the extension hypothesis.

Another important influence has been Professor Gardner Murphy's field theory of personality and interpersonal relationships (1945). It was in part suggested by embryological findings that pointed to the basic biological unity of the maternal and fetal organism. Murphy's (1943) emphasis on the need-fulfilling quality of psi functions likewise served as an important stepping stone, even though it glosses over what I described as flaw-determined psi responses involving emotionally indifferent, forced-choice target materials of the card-calling type.

At least a few comments on more recent theories of psi phenomena may be in order at this point. In a 1968 survey of the field, a German parapsychologist listed some thirty attempts at explanation, ranging from purely physical to biological and essentially psychological theories. One of the early physical theories has been proposed by Hans Berger (1940), the discoverer of electroencephalography. Telepathy, he suggested may be due to the effect of the agent's electrical brain activity. Yet the wave or radiation model runs counter to the principle of the decline of energy with the square of distance from its source. Furthermore, psi signals are not impeded by solid metal shielding, the Faraday cage, or hundreds of feet of water, which are impenetrable to electromagnetic impulses. Nor has any neural structure in the brain or elsewhere in the organism been discovered that could serve as the source of the large amount of energy required for long-distance transmission of signals. Above all, purely physical theories of the traditional type are incompatible with precognition.

Similar considerations apply to such theoretical constructs as "psitrons," "tachyons," "biotronic vibrations," or a fourth "bioplasmic" state of matter, postulated by Czech and Russian investigators. Most of these concepts likewise fail to come to grips with the temporal and causal anomalies inherent in the psi syndrome. Some merely amount to bold and imaginative metaphors whose heuristic value has yet to be proven. Whether or not neutrinos are likely to fill the bill is an open question. More about physical theories can be found in J. R. Smythies' *Science and ESP* (1967). An interesting new departure is M. Ruderfer's neutrino-operated computer model, which tries to bridge the gap between the physical and the nonphysical (1976; see also Whiteman, 1977).

Among other major contributions to the field is Jung and Pauli's (1955) theory of synchronicity. It has received considerable popular attention and is based on the thesis that emotionally charged "numinous" or archetypal events are tied together by a mysterious acausal bond operating outside the categories of space and time. It is a thesis which indeed serves as a convenient framework to accommodate most psi occurrences. It was originally proposed by Arthur Schopenhauer (1851), the nineteenth century German philosopher, and has been one of the premises of my own thinking about psi. But it has not in itself much explanatory value and is plainly inapplicable to flaw-determined micropsychological events of the ESP type: there is nothing to indicate that an experimental subject who scores above chance expectation in a series of card-calling tests does so under the influence of an emotionally charged archetypal complex.

Similar considerations apply to Arthur Koestler's (1972) appealing theory of "confluent" or "meaningful" coincidences. Such an interpretation is tailor made for major psi incidents in crisis situations or for telepathy in the mother-child relationship, between therapist and patient, or in the psychoanalytic situation. Indeed, I have pointed to the meaningful nature or the *psychological significance* of such occurrences as far back as 1954. But here too, the telepathic or clairvoyant percipient's occasional direct "hit" upon a triangle, a cross, or a wavy line can hardly be interpreted in terms of a psychologically meaningful or numinous coincidence.

It is in the face of such difficulties that the British philosopher Spencer Brown (1957) offered the thesis that psi coincidences are artifacts, largely due to statistical resonance between two sets of numerical data: the score sheet of a subject's guesses and published tables of random numbers used in setting up an experiment. Such an intriguing proposition casts doubt not only on the vast body of statistical evidence. It also throws the surviving baby of need-determined spontaneous evidence out with the bath water.

Be that as it may, the three nonphysical approaches to theory making reviewed here are more promising examples of current efforts to solve the mystery of psi phenomena. Yet, despite their ingenuity, they too have a serious shortcoming: each is geared to one type of psi phenomena only. Jung's or Koestler's (1972) theories make allowance for temporal and causal anomalies as well as for the major spontaneous, archetypal, or crisis-oriented range of phenomena but cannot possibly account for trivial psi incidents of the forced choice, card-calling type. In turn, theories exclusively concerned with such material—to say nothing of Spencer Brown's hypothesis of statistical artifacts—tend to ignore spontaneous evidence, which is based on the criterion of psychological significance only. Evidence of this order is therefore considered scientifically unproven and indeed unprovable. Thus, the strict quantifier, who is not prepared to take cognizance of psychic events which are features of a meaningful, teleological series, leaves what is "merely" psychologically significant out of his frame of reference. Similar difficulties are inherent in attempts at viewing the problem in purely abstract mathematical terms. Professor C. W. K. Mundle (1973), in his presidential address to the English Society for Psychical Research, arrived as a similar conclusion.

To sum up, virtually all current theories of the psi syndrome fall short of giving a reasonable account of all its facets. They do justice only to one or another modality of psi. We shall see in the chapters that follow that as a result only one or another aspect of the problem is brought into focus. Above all, what I describe as flaw-determined versus need-determined phenomena are lumped together, thus hindering the formulation of an all-encompassing, global theory of psi.

19

The Extension Hypothesis

THERE ARE five interlacing and mutually supportive hypotheses that go into the making of the theory of psi phenomena proposed here. The genetic hypothesis was already outlined in Chapter 2. The next in line is what is here described as the extension hypothesis. It suggests that psi functions and dysfunctions are linear—but by no means unbroken—continuations of our customary sensory-motor behavior. Extrasensory perception and clairvoyance are an extension of perceptions and subliminal perceptions beyond the ordinary reach of the senses. Indeed, Kreitler and Kreitler (1973), in a series of ingenious laboratory experiments, have demonstrated the close correlation between extrasensory and subliminal perceptions. In a similar vein, PK is an extension of motor behavior usually beyond the reach of the central nervous and skeletomuscular system into the autonomic system, visceral organs, and from there into the outside world. It is an outgrowth of "subliminal intentions," as it were.

The extension hypothesis takes its point of departure from the elementary fact that the reliability and sharpness of my cutaneous perceptions or my sensitiveness to touch is at its best, say, at my fingertips, that it is less at the back of my hand and still less on the surface of my intestinal organs, and that it dwindles to zero on my fingernails, on the enamel of a tooth, or on the lock of hair clipped off by the barber. Psychologically speaking, the lock of my hair, my nail clippings, or my extracted wisdom tooth belong to the nonego. They are no longer part of my body image— or at least only an expendable part of it. This state of affairs is illustrated on the left side of Figure 1.

The same conditions apply to the efficacy of reliability of volitional impulses originating from the executive branch of the ego and channeled into the skeletomuscular system, the smooth muscles, and so on. As illus-

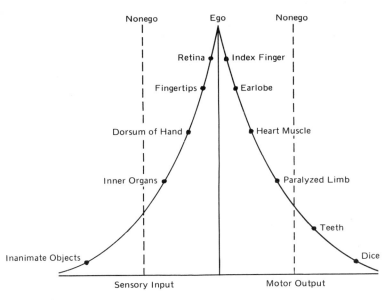

FIGURE 1

The sloping curves diverging from the imaginary point of the ego represent the diminishing return of the efficacy of motor action and the decreasing reliability of sensory perception as we move from the ego to the nonego. Note that the outer reaches of the curves do not touch the base line. They enclose, but do not seal off from the rest of the world, the open model of personality described in this and the next chapter. In effect, Figure 1 is a portrait of the open personality structure proposed here.

trated on the right side of Figure 1, they range from diverse parts of the body image to the nonego or objects in the outside world. Although it is difficult to express such qualitative data in strictly numerical terms, the efficacy of my impulse to move my right index finger comes close to 100 percent. I am ready to take a betting action to that effect. My chances of success are lower when I try to raise my left eyebrow, while no one except a miraculously endowed Yogi can deliberately innervate his heart muscle. Likewise, the efficacy of a hemiplegic's motor impulse is close to zero when he seeks to lift his paralyzed leg. Similarly, there may be astronomical odds against my being successful in inducing a telepathic percipient seated in the room below to do my bidding and to move his right hand in a certain direction. Nevertheless, the celebrated Brugmans–Van Dam (1922) experiments indicate that under favorable circumstances occasional tests along these lines have actually met with success in excess of chance expectation. Nina Kulagina, Uri Geller, and Matthew Manning illustrate the same point in an even more dramatic fashion. In such cases, the subject's efforts have indeed succeeded in reaching out beyond the traditional confines of personality structure; we are confronted with the telepathic or psychokinetic effect extending from what I have described as the autopsychic into the heteropsychic sphere.

Psychoanalytic theory has made allowance for the diminishing return of volitional impulses or sensory stimuli directed toward—or originating from—preconscious or unconscious portions of the ego. It has taken cognizance of the dynamically or biologically determined and over-determined fluctuations of the boundaries of its respective domains—for example, in sleep and wakefulness, in hypnotic trance, or in schizophrenic reactions.

But it should be noted that despite Freud's occasional forays into the occult, psychoanalysis has closed its system of thought to the possibility of direct communicative contact extending from the ego to the nonego—with all its implications.

Viewed in this light, my attempts at functioning as a telepathic percipient or as an agent in PK experiments are simply *less likely* to succeed than my corresponding efforts geared to functioning closer to home—in the autopsychic sphere. Statistically speaking, the difficulties of moving my left eyebrow or of innervating my heart muscle are merely compounded, although admittedly to a high degree, when I address myself to the task of making a table tilt or dice fall in a certain way. In the end, my paranormal abilities to do so may at best be indicated by a slightly extrachance results in statistical mass experiments.

In a similar vein, ESP is far less dependable in keeping me informed about biologically relevant—or not so relevant—stimuli originating from the outside world. Here, too, we have to admit that even with a highly successful subject in ESP experiments, the odds against "guessing" correctly a certain card symbol are far below the efficacy of direct inspection of the same target material. Likewise, the visions of a clairvoyant are rarely "clear," and the readings of the most gifted psychometrist are likely to fall short of the accuracy of firsthand, on-the-spot observation of a given subject. The odds against the occurrence of certain psychophysical events as we move further and further away from the vantage point of the ego merely suggest that human personality is indeed ill-equipped to mobilize, to register, and to control the phenomena under review.

This is why contemporary Western man feels so sure that perceptual or volitional contact with the outside world can only occur with the aid of the usual channels of sensation and neural conduction.

But it may be as well as recall at this point that even under "ordinary" conditions of perception and volitional action, our adaptation to the environment is far from perfect. The psychologist E. Brunswick (1952) has rightly pointed out that the human organism is an imperfect machine—that "perceptual and behavioral functioning is spoiled much in the manner in which stray rays are apt to interfere with perfect focusing." In a similar vein, our communication with the outside world is marred by what communication theory describes as noise originating from our channels of communication. The same holds true for the efficacy of our motor or psychomotor behavior in seeking to effect changes in the environment. Our volition is usually considered the lawful antecedent cause of our actions. This expectation is indeed borne out by the vast number of experiences both in ourselves and in our fellow men. But it should also be recalled that temporary illness or incapacity are significant exceptions to the rule. We must realize that the much-vaunted efficacy of volition is a purely probabilistic statement. Its success ratio falls short of the unfailing dependability of causal law. Jerome S. Bruner, formerly of Harvard University, now at the University of Oxford, has observed that voluntary action is uneven, imperfect, spasmodic, incomplete. "The programs that guide voluntary action do not achieve full control" (1968, p. 178).

The fact is that our organism—and living organisms in general—are operating against considerable odds. We have to cope with an environment full of built-in uncertainties. It has been stated that the statistical approach demanded by modern quantum theory should become the "ultimate norm" in psychology as a whole. This is still more true for the precariously poised hit-or-miss ratio which is the daily fare of the parapsychologist.

There is another aspect of psi phenomena which is in good keeping with the extension hypothesis proposed here. While the fitful, seemingly capricious quality of extrachance results in ESP research tends to confuse the uninitiated, Dr. Rhine's experiments have shown that ESP and PK are subject to characteristic decline or position effects in a given series. Even with the best subjects, scores tend to decline over a period of time. They show a tendency to what would be described as boredom or fatigue under ordinary conditions. It is much the same thing which in common parlance is referred to as the beginner's luck in such games of fortune as roulette, pinball machines, the horse races, or, according to some experts, even the stock market.

In the performances of such physical mediums as Kulagina, or Ted Serios in this country, the decline effect is masked by another feature. They need a period of warmup before going into action. It is accompanied by their characteristic histrionics and display of frantic physical effort, reminiscent of the rainmaker's attempts to wring water from the clouds, leaving them physically exhausted and spent after the event. It is also interesting to note that a similar warm-up period is usually required by the professional dancer, the concert pianist, the psychodramatist, and some aficionados in the ways of lovemaking. Thus, both the position and decline effect in ESP and the need for an initial warm-up in PK tests is in good keeping with the extension hypothesis.

Returning to the diagram in Figure 1, the decline indicated by the two symmetrical curves is another matter. They show a rapidly diminishing return as we move from the ego to the nonego and from there into the outer reaches of the curves—or the world at large. Nevertheless, it will be noted that the two respective curves do not end up touching the base line.

There is one more clue suggesting the gradual merging of the ego with the nonego. It was originally described by Lipps (1897) as *empathy*. Empathy is the imaginative projection of our consciousness into another person or even into an art object or a slice of nature. It is our tendency to extend tentacles of awareness and intuitive understanding to minds and objects outside our ego boundaries. There is, however, another distinctly motor or psychomotor side to the essentially afferent or receptive aspect of empathy which I have termed subliminal intention or *enkinesis*. Paraphrasing the usual definition, one could say: Empathy is projection, guided by perception. By the same token, *enkinesis* is introjected movement, guided by empathy. Here, again, the basic dichotomy of our mental organization in terms of *afferent* versus *efferent* functions is unmistakable.

Yet on making due allowance for their operation in human affairs, we must not forget that there is no sharp demarcation line between these two imaginative extensions of the ego and psi phenomena in a stricter sense. The fact is that the term "empathy"—with a dash of intuition mixed into it—has often been resorted to in order to camouflage such scientifically more objectionable terms as telepathy or clairvoyance. The difference is that empathy—and its psychomotor counterpart, enkinesis— are terms which are usually applied in a metaphorical sense. They lie in the eyes of the beholder, while ESP and PK are based on statistically verifiable objective findings.

One of the less obvious and seemingly more remote implications of the extension hypothesis calls for a brief digression into the field of clinical psychiatry: to the sensory and motor manifestations of conversion hysteria. These disturbances consist, among other things, of glove- or stocking-shaped anesthesias and motor paralyses which run counter to the familiar principles of cerebral localization and neural distribution. They cannot be explained by reference to organic lesions in the central nervous system. This is why neurologists before Charcot, Janet, or Breuer and Freud were at a loss to account for their etiology. It was Charcot, Janet, Freud, and their followers who found the answer to the problem: there was no organic lesion responsible for the symptoms of conversion hysteria. The roots of the trouble did not lie in the nervous tissue at all: it was the patient's *imagination* or *ideas* which caused the deficit in his sensory awareness or motor functioning.

What is the relevance of these findings to the extension hypothesis? It shows a striking correspondence with the basic dichotomy of psi phenomena outlined here. The crucial point is that in conversion hysteria a specific area of the body image is either cut off from conscious perception or becomes inaccessible to deliberate volitional control; it is anesthetic or paralyzed. In either case, the affected limb is dissociated from the self or turned into nonego. By contrast, in telepathy, clairvoyance, and PK, a segment of the outside world, selected and invested through cathexis, is being incorporated into the body image; it becomes temporarily alive, accessible to direct awareness, and amenable to a modicum of volitional control. It is turned into an extended part of the ego or personality structure (Figure 2).

Viewed in this light, the two contrasting situations show a strictly symmetrical relationship—to the "right" and "left" from the vantage point of the ego, as it were. In short, they too are in good keeping with the extension hypothesis. Yet while the once revolutionary proposition that the cause of conversion hysteria has to be sought in the power of imagination—or in unresolved emotional conflicts—has by now largely been accepted, we may still be wary of the proposition that the power of imagination or of emotionally charged ideas may extend beyond the boundary lines of the organism into the heteropsychic sphere—to say nothing of the supposedly lifeless, inorganic, and inanimate domain.

How, then, can we account for such a leap from "mind" to "matter" and from matter to mind, more mysterious still than the one which had once puzzled Freud at his first encounter with the psychodynamics of hysteria? Clearly, the customary references to the power of ideas or to the largely metaphorical formulations offered by the extension hypothesis are not enough. We have to realize that no conventional spatial rep-

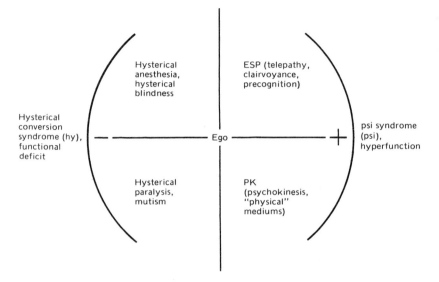

FIGURE 2

The diagram represents the symmetrical relationship of the psi syndrome (Psi), versus manifestations of conversion hysteria (Hy): ESP and PK on top and bottom on the right side; hysterical anesthesia and hysterical paralysis on top and bottom on the left. In ESP and PK the reach of the ego is inflated and extends into the nonego. In conversion hysteria the reach of the ego is diminished: part of the ego is turned into nonego. The two sides are mirror images.

resentation or pictorial image can do justice to the revolutionary implications of psi. The extension hypothesis as outlined here has to be supplemented by a fresh look at human personality, from which all the problems, questions, and concerns of mankind have originated in the first place.

20

Personality: Open or Closed?

An Exercise in Mind Stretching

> We have to have the courage to reexamine
> the structure of human personality and its
> relationship with the universe, and to create
> a new frame of reference capable of adjust-
> ing to the newly emerging facts.
>
> H. H. Price, 1954

MAN'S ACQUAINTANCE with himself—what historians have termed the dawn of consciousness—dates back thousands of years, long before he became familiar with molecules, atoms, or subatomic particles. Yet it is a matter of historical record that man's understanding of himself has always lagged behind his understanding of physical reality. More than half a century after the advent of relativistic physics and quantum mechanics, our theories of personality are still steeped in the classical Judeo-Christian or Aristotelian tradition, brought up to date by Freudian ego psychology or learning theory. Yet even these sophisticated constructs conceive of personality as immersed in Euclidian space, ruled by Newtonian laws of mechanics, and operating in absolute, pre-Einsteinian time.

Now it is readily understood that under "standard operating conditions"—that is, in everyday life, in clinical practice, or in the psychological laboratory—the classical model has abundantly proved its usefulness. Data arrived at from the broad spectrum of individual and statistical observations were found to be consistent and mutually compatible. Predictions based on them were borne out by further observations and validated by repeatable experiments. In short, classical theories of personality, like Euclidian geometry and Newtonian mechanics, have stood the test of pragmatic experience.

Yet recent developments in the natural sciences have shown that under extreme conditions, in the realm of subatomic particles, in the vastness of space, or at speeds approaching the velocity of light, the classical concepts of space, time, and causality are no longer applicable. They had to be replaced by brand-new theoretical propositions, some of them flying in the face of our old established habits of thinking.

If there has been a delay in duplicating such developments in the behavioral sciences and in formulating a new model of personality, it was not for lack of observations. I submit that the relevant observations are those that have come into the purview of the modern parapsychologists. It may well be that it is, in part, because of the absence of a reasonable theoretical frame of reference that they have still remained outside the pale of science.

What are the hallmarks of the traditional Aristotelian, Euclidian, or Freudian models? Virtually all conceive of personality as a self-contained, closed, and isolated system, operating in a universe extended in Euclidian space and prerelativistic time, subject to the traditional laws of cause and effect. It found its classical pictorial representation in Leonardo da Vinci's picture of a male of ideal proportions, safely anchored in the double enclosure of the main standbys of Euclidian geometry, the circle and the

FIGURE 3

Leonardo da Vinci's "Canon of Proportions." It represents the classical, closed model of personality embedded in Euclidian space.

square, setting him apart from the rest of the world. Indeed Renaissance man's personality has been his castle, even more so than the Englishman's home—provided he could afford it. Goethe's pronouncement, "Highest prize of human striving, art thou personality," reflects the same spirit. It is a sentiment echoed, though in the lower key, in Shelley's phrase about the "dark idolatry of the self." It could have been the motto of man of the ancient regime, up to Victorian or Francisco Josephean times. Freud's model of personality, made up of the ego, superego, and id, was conceived along similar lines. It, too, is represented as a closed, self-contained, and isolated system, although Freud did place great emphasis on the notion that the id is basically devoid of spatial and temporal characteristics and exempt from the laws of cause and effect (Fig. 4). More recently Charles Tart (1975) gave a brilliant summary of Western man's rigid, "state-specific" concept of personality.

The American psychiatrist R. M. Bucke extended his focus from the individual to *Cosmic Consciousness* (1964) but had little impact upon the psychiatric profession at large. C. G. Jung's revolutionary proposition of the collective unconscious (1959) was a giant step forward but re-mained anathema to orthodox psychoanalysis. Gordon Allport's (1960) formulation of an open versus a closed system of personality was an im-portant new departure from the traditional position. Yet despite his emphasis on "extensive transactional commerce with the environment," he stopped short of throwing the door open to psi phenomena. Abraham Maslow's (1964) inquiry into peak experiences and their attending sense of communion with one's fellowmen and with the universe at large went one step further toward a broader humanistic, if not transpersonal, psy-

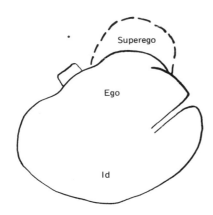

FIGURE 4

The "Mental Apparatus" according to Freud (adapted from Freud).

chology. Similar states have been described by Harold Kelman (1958, 59) in terms of "communing," a condition closely resembling the mystical tradition.

In Europe several idealistic philosophers and such esoteric thinkers as Rudolf Steiner or G. Gurdjieff, followed by some existentialists, also made daring, if largely speculative forays in the same direction.

It was Gardner Murphy's field-theoretical, biosocial approach (1945; 1956), which made the decisive step toward the open, transpersonal model of personality. Following in the footsteps of Frederic Myers and William James, Murphy emphasized that while the constant exchange of matter and energy between the organism and its environment has long been a commonly accepted fact of life, the boundaries of a human being's personality are not sharply defined by the skin in which he is enveloped. The air an organism inhales, the oxygen carried in the red blood cells, is part of both the organism and the environment. So is the food or water which it is about to ingest. So are the end products of its metabolism. "The gradient between man and the world is a gentle one indeed," as Murphy put it (1956, p. 90). "Personality," he stated, does not stand in "solitary grandeur, as we like to perceive it." It is "a node or region of relative concentration in a field of vast and complex interpenetrating forces in which none of us is completely individualized any more than he is completely washed out in a cosmic sink of impersonality" (p. 91).

Yet while the approach to personality as an open system is still a novelty for Western man, it is a familiar experience to the Oriental mind. The Oriental concept of personality is wide open to the rest of the world, fleeting and ill-defined, like ripples passing on the surface of a lake. In Buddhist or Hindu doctrine, the self has but a brief lease on life before it is submerged in the ever recurring cycle of atman, the all-pervading superpersonal cosmic principle. Throughout life, the value of individual existence is belittled and the development of a free and autonomous personality discouraged. Psychologically speaking, the emphasis shifts from the ego to the nonego. Potentially, a man and his fellowmen partake of one all-encompassing cosmic consciousness. It can therefore only be expected that they should share each other's thoughts, feelings, and experiences. This is why in the Oriental world psi phenomena are generally taken for granted. It is in stark contrast to our emphasis on the strict psychological privacy of the self and our doubts and misgivings about paranormal incidents.

Closer to home, the schizophrenic or the taker of various psychedelic drugs may go through the same experience of lost ego boundaries as the mystic, Eastern or Western style. He too may try to convey to us the ineffable feeling of merging with the world mind, of unity with the godhead—and of openness to psi.

We have to realize, however, that there are all shades and gradations between the "open" and the "closed" model of personality, depending upon various situational, interpersonal, and cultural factors or fleeting psychodynamic configurations. In fact, observations of increased sensitivity to telepathy during sleep and in dreams associated with rapid eye movements suggest fluctuations between an open and closed position during the twenty-four-hour cycle of sleep and wakefulness. It would therefore be more appropriate to say that what is here described as the "open" personality structure is in fact one potentially open or closed to psi.

Despite such qualifications, the gulf between the traditional closed model of personality and the open model proposed here goes far beyond mere cultural, religious, or philosophical differences. Trying to bridge the gulf requires a major shift in our habits of thinking, our habits of processing the data of our experience, and our whole outlook on the world. Instructive precedents are attempts made by late nineteenth century and early twentieth century mathematicians and physicists to devise new systems of mathematics, of non-Euclidian geometry and "three-cornered" logic.

A graphic example of mind-stretching exercise along these lines is the French mathematician Henri Poincaré (1905) inviting his readers to visualize non-Euclidian space, that is space of the type postulated by G. F. B. Riemann, J. Bolyai, or N. I. Lobachevski. Poincaré asks us to imagine a world peopled by creatures of no thickness. He suggests that these imaginary creatures "are all in the same plane and cannot get out." He asks furthermore: "What sort of a world would such animals visualize in their world of standard experience?" His answer is: "A world occupying space of two dimensions." And Poincaré goes on to say: "Suppose now these imaginary animals, while remaining without thickness[,] have the form of spherical and not of plane figures and are all in the same sphere without power to get off. What geometry will they construct? They will construct a geometry in which an arc and not a straight line will be the shortest path from one point to another, that is, a geometry totally different from the Euclidian prototype, throwing overboard most of Euclid's original postulates. In short, they will arrive at an anomalous spherical geometry which would be perfectly true and consistent for the imaginary being in such a curved yet two-dimensional world, but it would certainly be most perplexing to beings living in our customary three-dimensional universe" (p. 74).

Poincaré has developed various theoretical constructs to visualize other types of non-Euclidian space, and he arrives at the conclusion that none can, on purely logical grounds, claim to be truer than the other, although for obvious reasons one and only one can stand the test of practical application under terrestrial conditions. An ingenious English schoolmaster, Edwin E. Abbott, wrote an amusing story (1884) to illustrate the difficulties an imaginary species of beings confined to Flatland would encounter in trying to communicate with people living in Cubeland.

The good schoolmaster left Psiland out of his story, but it goes without saying that an even more strenuous exercise of imagination is required when we try to project ourselves onto the psi level of functioning and to learn to understand and to speak its language. As I have noted, one of the necessary steps toward this end is the radical revision of the Aristotelian, Leonardian, or Freudian model of closed personality structure. Yet while Poincaré's or Abbott's models are of a purely abstract nature, it should be noted that "Psiland," as it is conceived here, has proved to be a testable and experimentally established reality.

More recent attempts at formulating 4-, 5-, or n-dimensional spaces were made by the philosophers H. H. Price of Oxford (1949), C. D. Broad (1962) of Cambridge, and John R. Smythies (1965), the neuropsychiatrist of the University of Edinburgh. They went out of their way to replace the old Cartesian dualism of body and mind—of *res extensa* and *res cogitans* —in favor of an all-inclusive cosmology of several intersecting mental or physical spaces or universes. By contrast to the traditional classical models of the mind-body relationship, they are claimed to be compatible with the principles of modern theoretical physics, mathematics, and quantum theory and to have the added advantage of being better suited to accommodate psi phenomena in their overall frame of reference.

All these considerations should go far to suggest that psi phenomena are by no means as bizarre, offbeat, or incompatible with universal human experience as the naive realist would like us to believe. Nor are they wholly inconsistent with some of the current—or at least currently revised—existentialist or neo-Cartesian positions. Indeed, the philosophically inclined reader will perhaps note that the arguments presented here have led, more or less unawares, to an essentially neo-Cartesian concept of the mind-body or, more broadly speaking, of the mind-matter relationship. As we move from the ego to the nonego, from the animate to the inanimate, we are confronted with a gradually diminishing intimacy and declining probability of apparent interaction between the two domains. Yet we have seen that, contrary to still lingering beliefs of the interactionist school of thought, their assumed interaction does not follow the rigid laws of cause and effect. It is merely subject to probabilistic principles. In short, the relationship of mind and matter (or of the psychological and the physical) faithfully retraces the symbiotic gradient described in earlier chapters.

By the same token, the philosophical position proposed here can be described as that of a *psychophysical gradient.* It closely approximates the psychocosmic continuum of Yoga psychology and can be contrasted with the familiar notions of psychophysical parallelism, epiphenomenalism, solipsism, or whatnot. To repeat: on extending the assumed mind-body relationship into the parapsychological sphere, we arrive at a loosely knit symbiotic model, reaching from the ego to the nonego and controlled by probabilistic rather than by immutable causal laws.

What, then, are the basic features of the classical model? One, I stated, is its location in Euclidian space and absolute, pre-Einsteinian time. Another is that communication and interaction between person and person and the universe at large is confined to language, gesture, or written signs propagated through space by sound waves, light, or other physical media. A third proposition takes it for granted that perception, volition, feeling, and memory are everybody's strictly private affair, that remembering involves only the recall of past events, and that no such thing in regard to the future is even remotely possible. A fourth proposition is implied by the tradition of Cartesian dualism: it assigns the soul, the mind, and its diverse attributes to a person's body and, more specifically, to his central nervous system.

Such assumptions have always been considered just as self-evident as Euclid's geometrical theorems—so much so that they were rarely questioned. They have in fact proved their pragmatic value time and again under standard conditions. But they also lead to various logical or spatiotemporal paradoxes where such marginal conditions as birth, death, purported survival or reincarnation, mystic participation—and psi phenomena—are concerned. Before throwing the first stone at the behavioral sciences, however, one should recall that similar limitations apply to some of the basic propositions of classical physics where astronomical

distances, speeds approaching the speed of light, the behavior of subatomic particles, dying stars or cosmic "black holes" are involved.

One of the most perplexing implications of the classical model is the
set of still held views of fixed, anatomically contiguous cerebral localization of motor behavior and consciousness. We have to realize that this too
is one of our ingrained habits of thinking which has to be abandoned at
the outer reaches of the symbiotic gradient illustrated in Figure 1. The
evidence of psi phenomena has forced us to conclude that on rare but
psychodynamically fairly well-defined occasions both volitional impulses
and sensory impressions can be communicated from one person to another
without the benefit of spatially contiguous neural conduction and central
processing of neurophysiological events in what Bertrand Russell (1948)
has called "discrete brain regions." In short, we have to accept the fact
that occasionally an exchange of signals and shared experiences can take
place within a broader network of communication operating under the
control of separate, anatomically noncontiguous brain regions, that is, of
brain regions *scattered* in space but temporarily integrated and acting in
concert to suit the occasion. That the integrative function of such a "de-
centralized" central nervous system should be an ineffectual, rudimentary
effort goes without saying. We shall see in the next chapter that telepathic
messages under such conditions show a close structural resemblance to
the chaotic, disorganized quality of the visual perceptions of brain-injured
patients suffering from optical agnosia due to lesions in the left parieto-
occipital region.

How the awareness of such telepathic or heteropsychic mental content comes about is another question. It may be as well, however, to
recall at this point that in trying to account for the origin of ordinary,
autopsychic awareness, we are faced with the same problem as in the case
of heteropsychic awareness. There admittedly is a mysterious gap between brain event and conscious experience in the ordinary, garden-
variety type of perception. We must not be surprised, therefore, to find
much the same gap in telepathic perceptions, to say nothing of the gap
in our understanding of apparent action at a distance in psychokinesis.
The difference between autopsychic and heteropsychic transactions of
this order lies merely in the fact that in the former case the gap seems
to be small, while in the latter case it is magnified by the more tangible
spatial distances and discontinuities involved in the transaction. Yet here
again, puzzling over the mystery of one while glossing over the mystery
of the other is nothing but a conventional habit of thinking. The apparent

leap from body to mind, and vice versa, within the limited space enclosed in one individual's skull has remained as mysterious as it was when Freud wondered about it half a century ago.

Viewed in this light, ESP is in fact awareness shared by the percipient with the agent's sensory impressions. It is CSP, or *con*sensory, rather than ESP, or *extra*sensory perception. Similarly, PK can be described as TPK, or *trans*personal kinesis, extending in some cases from the interpersonal sphere into the world of objects. Mutatis mutandis, the same is true for clairvoyance.

A third preconception in need of revision and rethinking is the assumed one-to-one correspondence of brain, consciousness, memory, and human communicative behavior in general. The occurrence of psi phenomena compels us to abandon the idea that all psychic functions are necessarily tied to, or imprisoned in, neural substance—that my memory traces can be stored in my neurons or DNA molecules only. The ancient Greeks, who sought to localize mind in the diaphragm or the heart, and Descartes, who looked for the soul in the pineal gland, had their own ideas on this matter. Perhaps they were not much further from the truth than are modern students of brain physiology. Henri Bergson rightly pointed out some seventy years ago that relegating the quality of consciousness exclusively to the gray matter of the cortical centers—that is, to one privileged conglomeration of molecular or atomic particles—should by no means be taken as the final verdict of neurophysiology. C. G. Jung went so far as to suggest that the brain has nothing at all to do with the psyche.

A fourth class of conventional habits of thinking—one of the Seven Dragons of Chapter 18—is concerned with the categories of space and time. Generations of Kantian and neo-Kantian philosophers have held that the human mind is incapable of thinking outside certain fixed, a priori molds of mental functioning. Yet Schopenhauer (1851) suggested more than a hundred years ago that "somnambulistic" phenomena stand outside the three Kantian categories, which pertain merely to the world of appearances. Jung and Pauli's theory of synchronicity and *acausal* correspondences in nature (1955) is largely an elaboration of Schopenhauer's ideas. So is Koestler's principle of "confluent" events (1972).

However, I noted that temporal, spatial, and causal irregularities are by no means confined to psi phenomena. They are characteristic of the perceptual world of the brain-injured patient. No less significant is their striking resemblance to another aspect of mental functioning: to Freud's primary processes. Indeed, structurally and dynamically speaking, psi is hardly distinguishable from the world of the Freudian unconscious. Telepathy is subject to the same principles of symbolic representation, secondary elaboration, reaction formation, and repression as apply to unconscious processes in general. One can say that a would-be telepathic percipient remains unaware of his telepathic impressions for the same reasons that a hysteric remains unaware of his own repressed "complexes." The difference is that in ESP the supposedly repressed or distorted mental content has not previously been part of the percipient's personal experience. It may be part of another person's conscious, preconscious, or even unconscious mental content. All the available evidence indicates that this is equally applicable to psi incidents in the psychoanalytic situation; to occurrences under spontaneous conditions and, to a lesser degree, to experimental observations.

The occurrence of precognition in life and laboratory has remained perhaps even more puzzling than other modalities of psi phenomena. Yet ever since the enormous odds against chance piled up in the Soal-Goldney (1943), the Helmut Schmidt (1969) or the Targ-Puthoff (1976) experiments, we have no option but to swallow the bitter pill. It may be no coincidence that it is a pill whose effects show a striking resemblance to the distortions of space and time that occur under the influence of mescaline or LSD.

Ernst Mach, one of the forerunners of Einstein's theory of relativity, complained nearly a century ago, "You see, physics grows gradually more and more terrible. The physicist will soon have it in his power to play the part of the famous lobster chained to the bottom of the lake . . . [Its] direful mission, if ever liberated, [can be] described as that of a reversal of all the events of the world; the rafters of houses become trees again, cows calves, honey flowers, chickens eggs, and the poet's own poem flows back into his inkstand" (1910, p. 60).

Flanked by Ernst Mach's time reversal, and by Cassandra's even more direful forebodings of times to come, modern theoretical physicists are indeed giving us a terrible time—and space.

21

Psi Phenomena in Search of

a Neural Foothold

IF A SKEPTIC is inclined to dismiss the quest for psi phenomena as a wild-goose chase, he is likely to consider the search for the actual habitat of the rare birds as an even more foolhardy undertaking. Yet there can be no doubt that psi phenomena, regardless of their purported nonphysical, extrasensory, paranormal nature, have a foothold somewhere in our neurophysiological organization. Whether this foothold is confined to my brain or yours, or to some of Bertrand Russell's "discrete brain regions" scattered in space, they must reside in some operational area of the agent's or percipient's central nervous system. Failing this, we would be unable to gather information and exchange ideas on the level of our standard, Euclidian experience about their very occurrence.

But to do so, we have to recall once more the basic sensory-motor dichotomy of ESP versus PK, and we must bear in mind our distinction between micropsychological, forced-choice psi responses of the card-calling or dice-throwing type on the one hand, and the major, macropsychological, spontaneous incidents seen in everyday life and in the psychoanalytic situation on the other. We have to realize, furthermore, that in trying to account for the modus operandi of psi functions, we have tended to ask the wrong questions. We have been in the habit of asking *how* psi incidents come about instead of wondering *what* it is that stops ESP from flooding our perceptual world with the steady influx of trivial, biologically undesirable external stimuli or *what* it is that puts the brake on the outflow of uncontrolled and indiscriminate PK impulses emanating from the motor areas of the brain cortex to wreak havoc in our environment?

The French philosopher Henri Bergson (1913), with his concept of "attention to life" and his theory of the brain acting as a filter to screen out impressions and memories of doubtful biological survival value, has offered at least a tentative answer to the question. He could not foresee that, some sixty years later, the functions of the reticular formation in the brainstem, discovered by H. W. Magoun and his associates, were in good keeping with his thesis. We know today that the ascending and descending tracts of the reticular activating system (RAS) are concerned with facilitating or inhibiting the two-way flow of sensory stimuli to the higher centers, from both inside and outside the organism. They are responsible for regulating arousal, vigilance, sleep, wakefulness, and their fluctuations in the REM state, as well as various aspects of our emotional life.

In a similar vein, it may well be argued that it is the modulating or inhibitory function of the reticular formation which constitutes the first line of the individual's defense against the influx of such biologically indifferent or undesirable perceptual stimuli as ESP, or that puts the brake on the mobilization of such potentially wasteful—or even destructive—motor impulses as PK. The concept of perceptual defenses (Eysenck 1961) proposed by experimental psychologists point in the same direction, as do Norman Dixon's (1971) studies of subceptions, or subliminal perceptions.

According to McLean (1977), J. W. Papez, and other neurophysiologists, a secondary, limbic-midbrain system is likewise concerned with regulatory functions of this order. Dixon suggested that the limbic-midbrain system is particularly involved in the processing of subliminal stimuli. Professor A. R. Luria (1973) of the University of Moscow, Karl Pribram (1973) of Stanford University, and others have noted, furthermore, that the frontal and temporal cortex likewise play an important part in the selective filtering of "afference"—that is, of input from the outside world. So presumably does the corpus callosum.

What, then, is the relevance of these findings to the micropsychological, forced-choice, ESP type of psi incidents? They suggest that the fitful, capricious occurrence of correct hits in a series of card-calling tests may be due to the random occurrence of minor flaws in the screening or inhibitory functions of the reticular formation and higher cortical centers. They result in the intrusion of a few equally capricious bursts of psi incidents—conscious or unconscious—into a subject's scoring pattern. If this is true, psi responses of this order are indeed essentially flaw-determined: they are, as stated in an earlier chapter, due to flaws in the operation of the subject's perceptual defenses, in the screening function of the Bergsonian filter, or of what Freud (1922) described as the *Reizschutz*, protecting the ego from being flooded by stimuli from outside.

I also noted in Chapter 11 that in the extreme case, a schizophrenic patient's ego may be overwhelmed by psi pollution: the ceaseless barrage of both autopsychic and heteropsychic impressions of this order. In turn, the motor counterpart of such a predicament would be the equally indiscriminate unleashing, in all directions, of the individual's uncontrolled motor and psychomotor impulses. It would then be conducive to veritable paroxysms of PK—a contingency that has indeed been taken for granted in folklore, magic, witchcraft, and medieval Christian demonology. By the same token, occasional bursts of capricious physical phenomena are attributed to today's acting-out poltergeist children.

Speculations of this order, however far-fetched, receive some support from the studies of Sir John Eccles (1965), W. G. Walter (1970), José Delgado (1969), and other neurophysiologists. Eccles has pointed out that the firing of a group of brain cells, motor or sensory, or even of one "critically poised" neuron, can be triggered off by a field of extraneous influences or electrical impulses from outside. Such influences may well include a psi factor. Professor C. D. Broad (1962) of Cambridge University, the psychologist Sir Cyril Burt (1968), and John Beloff (1970) of the University of Edinburgh have seriously considered such a possibility. Indeed, it may well be that, in the last analysis, both perception and volition are ultimately based on a process akin to "pure" clairvoyance and psychokinesis (Moncrieff 1951): by the direct effect of "mind" on the brain—and of "matter" on the "mind."

Still, whatever we can learn from these considerations throws light on the neurophysiology of micropsychological, flaw-determined, forced-choice type of psi incidents only. They cannot possibly account for the emergence and central processing of such major, macropsychological, need-determined psi incidents as telepathy in crisis conditions, in the psychoanalytic situation or in experiments with telepathic drawings. They involve mental events of a highly complex nature and cannot be explained in terms of the random firing of a few unruly motor cells in the brain cortex or by reference to a bunch of neurons in the reticular formation caught napping at the job of blocking the entrance to consciousness of some wholly irrelevant ESP or clairvoyant impressions.

Such occurrences clearly require elaborate processing and functional coordination in higher cortical systems, even though we have seen that they, too, are subject to distortion, to telepathic scatter or spatiotemporal displacement before they enter conscious awareness or are otherwise registered by the subject. Typical examples are the older experiments with telepathic drawings published by René Warcollier (1939) in France, those carried out by Mr. and Mrs. Upton Sinclair in this country (1930), the more recent series with telepathic drawings of target pictures used by Ullman, Krippner, and Vaughan (1973) in the Maimonides dream experiments, and the Targ-Puthoff experiments (1974) with Uri Geller at the Stanford Research Institute, and many others.

Some experiments of this order show striking correspondences indeed between the telepathic target and the impressions received by the participant. But I submit that paying proper attention to "near misses" and apparent failures in such tests is far more revealing than confining attention to the few "striking" cases parapsychologists like to refer to in order to bolster their position in the scientific community.

Figure 5 is the telepathic drawing of one of Warcollier's experimental subjects. It shows the distortion and disorganization of the target picture of an airship which the subject failed to recognize. Instead, he sketched part of its oval shape, caught the impression of the propellers, repeated the motif twice, and placed one propeller correctly at the lower part of his drawing.

Figure 6 is a similar example from the Sinclair series. It is this dis-

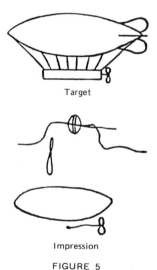

Target

Impression

FIGURE 5

Top: An airship, drawn by the agent. Bottom: Telepathic impression. Note the correct rendering of an oval shape. The propeller motif appears twice. The scribble above the oval is unexplained. Source: *Mind to Mind*, by René Warcollier, 1948.

FIGURE 6

Top: Face, meant to represent a jack-o'-lantern, drawn by agent.
Bottom: Telepathic impression. A moon sickle with "star"
resembling nose in the target drawing. Note that an eye (drawn
and inscribed upside down) was added by the recipient as an afterthought. Source: *Mental Radio*, by Upton Sinclair, 1930.

organization of the telepathic impression which is of particular interest in
the present context. The same is true for some of the less than perfect
responses in the Geller tests (Figure 7).

Comparing the imperfect match of the Warcollier, the Upton Sinclair,
or the Geller experiments with drawings made by patients suffering from
organic lesions in the left hemisphere of the brain reveals a striking similarity between their respective productions.

Figure 8 is a sample of the drawings made by a patient of mine, a
medical student admitted to the neurological department of the University of Vienna (Ehrenwald 1931*b*).

The following is a summary of his case history, as retold in my book
*New Dimensions of Deep Analysis: A Study of Telepathy in Interpersonal
Relationships* (1954, 1975). The patient was hospitalized following a
suicidal attempt with a penetrating gunshot wound in the left parieto-
occipital region. The bullet had been removed by surgery but he was left
with serious damage both to his personality and his intellectual functions.
His speech was awkward; at times he was at a loss in finding the names
of objects or persons; that is, he showed evidence of amnestic aphasia.
His handwriting was impaired, showing slight agraphic disturbances.

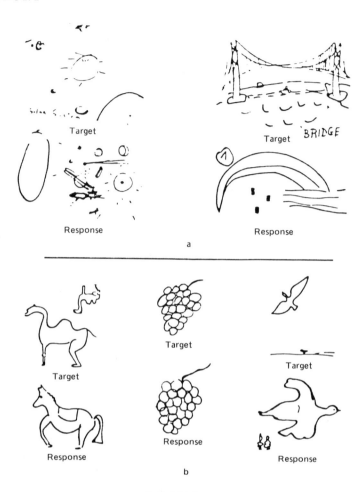

FIGURES 7a and b
Targ-Puthoff telepathic drawing tests with Uri Geller. His drawing
of a bunch of grapes is one of his exceptional "direct hits." Source:
Targ and Puthoff, 1974.

He was unable to perform the simplest calculations—a disturbance known as acalculia. He lost his way in the hospital ward and was confused about spatial relations. His drawing showed the same confusion of up and down, right and left. Figure 8 shows an example of his drawings which he verbally described as follows: (a) a french window in his ward at the Neurologische Klinik in Vienna; (b) a face, *en face;* (c) the window latch; (d) a ship; and (e) a tree drawn upside down with the root at the top, the crown at the bottom, and the trunk in the middle.

The most striking feature in these specimens is the utter disorganiza-

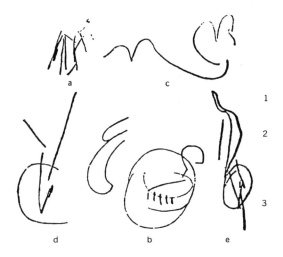

FIGURE 8

Drawings of the patient: (a) a French window; (b) a face, *en face*;
(c) the window latch; (d) a ship; (e) a tree drawn upside down, with
(1) the root, (2) the trunk, and (3) the crown. Reproduced from Jan
Ehrenwald, *Disturbance of Temporal and Spatial Orientation, of
Drawing and Calculation in a Brain-Injured Person*, 1931.

tion of visual perceptions. The material seems to be broken to pieces,
jumbled like meat that has passed through a meat grinder. On a diagram
illustrating the compass, the patient indicated south and west in the
wrong directions. Although his sight was by no means impaired, his visual
world was a jumble of disorganized spatial impressions.

His mistakes in temporal orientation were of the same order. He
could not tell how long he had been in the neurological department, nor
the length of time he had spent waiting to be admitted to a surgical ward.
He constantly confused data referring to his stay in Vienna and to his life
prior to that in a small provincial town in Austria. *Before* and *after* in the
temporal sense had lost their meaning to him, much in the same way as
spatial relationships. There was reason to believe that his acalculia was
likewise due to an inability to organize ideas in a consistent system of
spatiotemporal relationships. In short, he presented the picture of optic
agnosia, combined with other disturbances of his "categorical" behavior.

Professor A. R. Luria, the noted Russian neurologist, has described
similar cases in *The Working Brain* (1973). His patients, too, were suffering from optic agnosia. Figure 9 illustrates samples of their drawings.
The picture on the left represents the patient's jumbled impressions of an
elephant. On the right, equally disorganized impressions of a camel and
of a human figure can be seen. It is interesting to note that such patients,

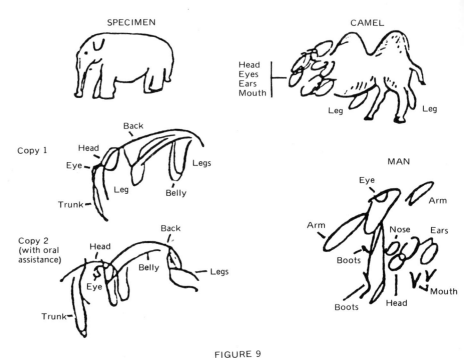

FIGURE 9

Drawings of Professor Luria's patients with optic agnosia. Top left: elephant; below left: two attempts at copying the original. Top right: jumbled drawings of a camel. Below right: figure of a man. Note the disjointed bits and pieces of his anatomy. Reproduced from A. R. Luria, *The Working Brain*, 1973.

in addition to the impairment of their drawing ability, also tend to confuse the meaning of the picture. One of Luria's patients, when shown the line drawing of spectacles, said: "There is a circle . . . and another circle . . . a stick . . . a crossbar . . . Why, it must be a bicycle" (p. 116).

Such responses show both the brain-injured patient's and the telepathic percipient's inability to organize their perceptions into meaningful wholes. The difference between the two lies in the fact that in one case we are dealing with a brain injury, in the other with a normal subject's difficulty in the central processing of his telepathic impressions. The fact is that on a recent occasion, when I was showing drawings of brain-injured patients to a lecture audience of graduate students in psychology, they first mistook them for unconvincing samples of telepathic drawing tests from the Warcollier or Sinclair series.

Reverting to my Vienna case, it will be noted that its description was wholly in keeping with what Luria describes as the "narrow localizationist" tendency current at the time. I, as well as my teacher Otto Poetzl, had paid exclusive attention to the part played by damage to the left hemisphere and the rest of the brain and had ignored the compensatory potential of the right hemisphere and other structures of the central nervous system. The severity of my Vienna subject's spatial disorientation may have been due to an additional massive damage of the corpus callosum connecting the left and right side of the brain.

What, then, is the relevance of the striking similarity between the brain-injured patient's and the telepathic subject's perceptual world? It presents at least circumstantial evidence of the part played by the relatively intact right hemisphere, not only in the rudimentary drawings of patients suffering from optical agnosia, but in the telepathic drawings by "normal" ESP subjects as well.

Such an active role of the "other side" of the brain has been suggested by R. Sperry (1964), M. S. Gazzaniga (1967), J. E. Bogen (1969), R. E. Ornstein (1972), and others in recent years. They have found that the left hemisphere is the logician, the specialist in discursive, analytic thinking, while the right hemisphere is the artist, the poet, the Listener with the Third Ear, as it were. It is concerned with depth perception and facial recognition, and it presides over the intuitive, nonanalytical mode of consciousness. If this is true, we may well assign the central processing of psi impressions to the right rather than to the left side of the brain. This would also account for the conspicuous absence of the coordinates of time and space on the psi level of functioning. By the same token, it is no coincidence that psi phenomena duplicate in many respects the distortions of spatiotemporal relationships seen in my Vienna case or in Professor Luria's cases of optic agnosia.

It should be recalled, furthermore, that telepathy and related phenomena are basically preconceptual and preverbal. Telepathy operates independently of the subject's linguistic skills, localized as they are in the speech centers of the dominant left hemisphere. Luria has emphasized that it is precisely the higher, symbolic, "gnostic" skills of this order which tend to be lateralized or relegated to the dominant side of the brain. This would lend added support to the conjecture that psi phenomena are a function of central structures which have not, or not "as yet," come under the sway of the dominant, culturally favored, hemisphere.

Experimental evidence pointing to the correlations of ESP and the right hemisphere has been afforded by Braud and Braud (1974). R. S. Broughton (1975; 1976) of Edinburgh University has reviewed the latest literature and also developed a promising experimental design of his own.

On the other hand, the latest experimental and clinical findings reviewed by P. Bakan (1976) point to the corpus callosum as a barrier to left hemispheric dominance in the waking state. Defective functioning of this massive brain structure is conducive to dreaming as well as to schizophrenic reactions. By the same token, it can well be assumed that a fully functioning corpus callosum may serve as an added regulatory system blocking or boosting the input and output of ESP.

Similar considerations apply to PK, or the motor counterpart of ESP. PK amounts at best to groping, faltering attempts at coming to grips with objects in the outside world without the aid of tangible effector organs. Even a high-class PK subject's leverage upon dice thrown from a cup, on a compass needle, or on a match box placed on a tabletop is a fitful, capricious, unpredictable affair. The same is true for a brain-injured patient, suffering from motor apraxia, trying to carry out such simple tasks as lighting a cigarette or tying his shoelaces. We know that here, too, a lesion in certain areas of the left hemisphere is at fault. A PK subject, it could be stated, behaves like a patient who has to make do without the left hemisphere presiding over his motor performance. The part played by the prefrontal cortex in activating or inhibiting PK must, of course, remain a matter of speculation for the time being.

Shifting attention from higher cortical levels to lower centers of the brain, we hit upon another analogy between PK and a pathological condition. This is the Parkinsonian patient's slow, laborious efforts at locomotion. Here again, we are dealing with the organism's faltering attempts to cope with a task for which it lacks, or has lost, the necessary equipment.

Another clue to the part played by the right hemisphere in the origin of telepathy, clairvoyance, or psychokinesis is provided by recent EEG findings which suggest an increase of right hemisphere activity associated with psi phenomena.

It is needless to say, however, that even these presumed connections with the right hemisphere fall short of solving the enigma of the ultimate cerebral localization of psi. We may conjecture that it is the right rather than the left side in which the reception and processing of incoming psi messages or the activation of outgoing PK impulses is taking place. But I pointed out as early as 1948 that we cannot tell how, in the last analysis, normal sensory stimuli originating from the outside are turned into conscious awareness: how a certain wave length of light is perceived as "red." Nor do we know how volition, or an ordinary motor impulse originating in my brain cortex, is converted into action. It may as well be controlled by PK. The last step in an extrasensory impression or the first step in a volitional act (or PK) is equally mysterious. All we know is that both take place in the "little black box" of my skull. As noted earlier, the difference between the two lies merely in the fact that in one case the gap in our understanding is small and inconspicuous (and may at best still baffle a few metaphysicians or theologians), while the gap looms woefully large in the case of ESP or PK.

Meanwhile, psychologists and behavioral scientists in general have learned to live comfortably with the gap—or the hiatus—in the auto-psychic sphere, without developing symptoms of an epistemological hernia. It should be only fair to ask for the same privilege for their para-psychological confreres, without pressing for ultimate answers which have so far eluded those engaged in more solidly established fields of scientific inquiry.

In summary, psi phenomena have their neural foothold on two levels of the central nervous system: in the brainstem and in the brain cortex. The emergence of a given incident is predicated on minor irregularities in the operation of the reticular formation in the brainstem. It is coupled with a compensatory function of higher centers. The right hemisphere in particular processes ESP impressions of a higher order, as well as PK impulses which have passed the Bergsonian filter. Indeed there is reason to believe that it is the very preponderance of the left hemisphere, "sicklied o'er with the pale cast of thought," which tends to put a damper on the spontaneity and intuitive functioning of its right counterpart. What in Chapter 24 will be described as the "existential shift" is presumably due to pendulum swings of control from one side of the brain to the other.

22

The Psi Syndrome and Modern

Man Against Psi

P SI PHENOMENA, in common usage, are made up of telepathy, psychokinesis, clairvoyance, and precognition. We have seen that the latter is still considered the black sheep in the family, even though it is usually the Schmeidlerian goats (the skeptics mentioned earlier) who say so. Nevertheless, of all psi phenomena, precognition has remained perhaps the most perplexing. We may be willing to accept the spatial anomalies involved in ESP "pure and simple." We may be ready to fit psychokinesis, or "mind over matter," and clairvoyance, or the direct perception of inanimate objects or configurations, into our picture of the world. But common sense and the scientific mind balk at the idea that a person's behavior or inner experience may be capable of responding to an event which is to take place at some future time. We are repelled by the notion that an effect may precede its cause or that a cause may be found to succeed its effect. Such a proposition threatens to play havoc with our rational way of thinking. It seems incompatible with the very operation of our mind.

Yet the data adduced by parapsychology are not influenced by such attitudes, however well-established they may be. The evidence of precognition in the Soal-Goldney (1943) and particularly the Helmut Schmidt (1969) experiments is as strong as any in the field of parapsychology. Results obtained in the Whately Carington (1947) drawing tests, in which the percipients seemed to "guess" correctly target pictures exhibited nearly 200 miles away the night *before* they were randomly selected, were every bit as good as those of the "straight" telepathic drawing experiments carried out in the 1920s by René Warcollier (1939) and his group, or by Upton Sinclair and his wife (1930). If the evidence of spontaneous cases weighs less heavily on the evidential scale, it is due not to a dearth of precognitive incidents of this order but to the methodological difficulties in corroborating and evaluating the data.

Yet we must face the fact that once we have accepted the evidence in favor of telepathic incidents, spontaneous or experimental, we are heading for epistemological trouble. The very concept of telepathy tacitly implies the simultaneity of the agent's and percipient's mental processes. But such a simultaneity is difficult to ascertain. More often than not we are dealing with situations in which simultaneity, even in the pre-Einsteinian sense, is impossible to establish. We have to make allowance for telepathy "before" or "after" the event—for what I described as telepathic scatter. In some such cases, a subject's clairvoyant perception of the experimenter's physical record of the response may be substituted for direct telepathic interpretation. Or else telepathy may be based on a clairvoyant awareness by the percipient of the agent's brain state. Lastly, as noted by J. B. Rhine, Helmut Schmidt, and others, psychokinesis can be considered as an alternative to precognition. Indeed Rhine questioned the feasibility of proving the reality of unadulterated telepathy "pure and simple."

What do all these mental acrobatics and this juggling with concepts lead up to? They should make us realize that our theoretical distinction between three or four different types of psi phenomena is largely artificial. It may be due to the given experimental design, to experimenter bias, to the subject's personal preferences, or to his idiosyncratic needs. In short, it may well be that, despite occasional successful attempts to isolate telepathy, clairvoyance, precognition, or PK in pure culture, as it were, it is the worker in parapsychology who tries to set apart what nature has originally joined together. The difficulties of making a clear distinction between several modalities of psi phenomena may therefore largely derive from the fact that in real life they "run together." They form what in clinical parlance is described as a *syndrome*: a syndrome of spatial, temporal, and causal anomalies or irregularities which are basically interconnected and mutually interchangeable. Their interdependence can be compared with a delicate three-dimensional latticework made of elastic rubber filaments and cross filaments instead of rigid, unbending wire pieces. In such an elastic, rubbery model, the deformation of one axis automatically leads to deformation of the other two axes.

Yet their interdependence is not merely a matter of purely logical or methodological considerations. We have seen that, apart from an individual subject's personal idiosyncrasies, the predisposing and conditioning factors of precognition are much the same as those involved in the other modalities of psi. A high-class sensitive may claim to have experiences covering the whole spectrum of psi phenomena, from telepathy to clairvoyance, precognition, and unorthodox healing. By the same token, even the statistical criteria used to evaluate precognition in the laboratory are the same as in general extrasensory perception, GESP. By and large, the magnitude of extrachance deviations is the same in virtually all modalities of experimental psi phenomena. We are thus led to the conclusion that one of the major differences between the various types of psi phenomena lies largely in the eyes of the beholder—in our greater reluctance to consider even the possibility of a reversal of the causal chain, of an effect "miraculously" preceding its cause, as is implied by the concept of precognition or prophecy—and not in the nature of precognition itself.

The fact is that to the scientifically less sophisticated observer all manifestations of psi are equally disturbing and intellectually repugnant. They are all incompatible with common sense; they run counter to his everyday experience and provoke well-nigh automatic resistances against them.

Such a defensive reaction is in effect one of the dynamic characteristics of the psi syndrome and has to be contrasted with its four structural or phenomenological modalities. Psi is persistently rejected or repressed by the closed Euclidian mind of modern man. To the extent to which it happens to break through the barriers or the protective screen set up against it, it is subject to displacement or scatter effects, to denial, distortion, symbolic representation, or reaction formation in the Freudian sense. Psi has to pass through a strict censorship by the ego and may be intercepted in the process.

What is the nature of these elaborate defenses and what is their purpose? Their first apparent purpose must be sought in the domain of physiological brain functions, though their specific modus operandi is still a matter of conjecture. They are of the same order as the diverse defensive and inhibiting functions which are built into the central nervous system in order to protect the organism from the destructive effects of sensory overload in general. This is why on the standard level of adaptation, psi phenomena have poor biological survival value. An unlimited influx of sensory impressions from near and far—in both space and time—would wreak havoc with our ego functions and jeopardize our business of living "here and now." From all we know, all species that have developed under terrestrial conditions are geared to a time-and-space-bound and causally determined mode of existence. As far as *Homo sapiens* is concerned, an open, "non-Euclidian" mind has persistently been discouraged—if not penalized—by both natural selection and cultural pressures. It is as though the evolutionary process itself had kept on rejecting psi as a false start—while man seems to be just as stubbornly bent on going on to experiment with it.

Turning from evolutionary aspects to the individual's personal history, it will be recalled that psi plays a vitally important part at the early symbiotic stage. But with the growth and maturation of the child's ego, psi functions, like fetal circulation at the moment of birth, become redundant. Telepathic communication is "repressed" and replaced by verbal communication. Whether or not this process of repression on the level of personal development is a direct continuation, or a Haeckelian recapitulation, of what has been going on all along in the course of evolution, is a moot question. But it certainly made a major contribution to modern man's uncompromising negative attitude toward psi in all its manifestations.

A third reason for rejection goes beyond the tendency to reject, repudiate, or repress psi phenomena on the organic level. It is an intrinsic aspect of what we described as the Euclidian mind: Western man's commitment to "reason," Euclidian style, as opposed to "unreason," represented by vestiges of a thoroughly discredited heritage of magic. Indeed, the tendency to disown and to penalize obsolete habits of thinking associated with the magic tradition seems to run through the life cycles of both the individual and his culture. I have pointed out in the introductory chapters that, viewed in historical perspective, psi phenomena are a direct continuation of the magic mentality and the magic arts. Once we make allowance for this dubious parentage of parapsychology as a scientific discipline, the resistances which are still pitted against it become thoroughly understandable.

It may be as well to realize, furthermore, that psi phenomena do not occur "out there" in empty psychological space or in a neutral cultural setting. They have no existence of their own independent of a human agent. They are a joint product of man and a slice of the universe with which he chooses to interact. His response may amount to religious awe in the face of a numinous experience. It may evoke a sense of the sinister and the uncanny. Alternatively, his reaction may amount to a tendency to uncompromising denial, rationalization, or reaction formation, comparable to the ego defenses mobilized in the struggle with instinctual drives or directed against the return of the Freudian repressed. But the present volume should go far to show that there is a growing breach in the ranks of the crusaders, the wielders and grinders of medieval, if not Stone Age, axes in the battle against psi. An up and coming generation is taking their place to face the phenomena for what they are. Hopefully, they will do so without raising new war cries—or Stone Age axes of their own to grind.

23

Survival after Death?

THE QUESTION of survival after death could conceivably be made
more specific: "Survival of what? Of personal identity? Of consciousness?
Of an immortal soul?" Left ambiguous as it is, the notion of survival after
death is a dogma to the religious believer, a pious wish to the skeptic, and
a matter of ongoing controversy among parapsychologists. In any case,
close to a century of psychical research has left the matter still unresolved.
Recurrent crops of garden-variety trivial messages from the "beyond" had
to be dismissed offhand as spurious or irrelevant; alternatively, they could
be explained in terms of telepathy, postcognitive or precognitive, coupled
with doctrinal compliance by the medium with the respective sitter's
wishes and expectations. They were at best yet another manifestation
of the psi syndrome.

Still, the evidence of some dramatic and occasionally veridical productions of high-class trance mediums cannot be dismissed. It is compounded by the record of some forty years of painstaking research into
so-called cross-correspondences carried out by prominent members of the
English Society for Psychical Research. They have come up with a puzzling series of communications attributed to a purported "Frederic Myers"
personality, surviving after his death in 1901. Put in a capsule, cross-
correspondences are a crazy quilt of seemingly disconnected bits of information fit together in an ingenious crossword puzzle of cryptic messages,
stream-of-consciousness type allusions, and free associations (Saltmarsh
1938). The overall thrust of the material is then taken as evidence of persistent attempts by the deceased Frederic Myers to communicate with,
and to signal his survival to, his friends and associates. Yet I hinted that
the interpretation of the data in terms of Rhine's "super-psi" (1971) or of
H. H. Price's "this-world ESP" (1976) may be a more parsimonious
alternative.

I submit that here again some order can be brought into the welter of conflicting claims and interpretations by viewing them in the light of the basic dichotomy of flaw-determined versus need-determined psi phenomena. On the face of it, most of the cross-correspondence material is flaw-determined. Despite recurrent learned references to Greek and Roman antiquity befitting the classical scholar Frederic Myers, the material usually consists of banal, fragmentary scraps of quotations, pathetic debris from the ruins of a purported personality floating aimlessly on the surface of a disappointingly shallow pool of "cosmic consciousness." This is, of course, in striking contrast to what one would expect a supposedly surviving Myers personality to be able to reveal about life in the "hereafter."

Yet if the messages involved are indeed flaw-determined, their trivial content and fragmentary quality stand to reason. They are more likely to originate from the living or the dying than from the dead. They are manifestations of the psi syndrome breaking through into the world of the living, here and now, in a capricious, haphazard fashion, with their characteristic tendency to temporal and spatial displacement, precognitive or postcognitive, as the case may be. Whatever organization may be discernible in the material may then derive from one or the other of the participants playing the part of a telepathic orchestra leader.

The predominantly flaw-determined origin of the cross-correspondences is also in good keeping with all we know about the sequence of brain events at the moment of death: the cessation of higher cortical activity, followed by the demise of the lower centers. Death itself, it will be noted, is the culmination of all the flaws and frailties human personality is heir to. It is the Great Shredder rather than the Reaper of man, the granddaddy of all minus functions described on an earlier page.

It should also be noted that, by contrast to the banal, fragmentary nature of material of this order, the familiar type of "phantasms of the dying"—that is, communications originating from persons in mortal crises but still alive—bear all the hallmarks of more highly organized need-determined psi functions. They are true messages "to whom it may concern," spelled out in no uncertain terms or couched in Pythian, symbolic language, yet nevertheless leaving little doubt as to their highly charged emotion-laden content.

If this is true, it bears out once more the hypothesis of the part played by the Bergsonian filter, by the screening function of the Freudian ego, or by a fully operational central nervous system in preventing the breakthrough of more than a trickle of disjointed bits of informaion from extraneous, habitually repressed, or long defunct levels of experience.

Failing this, we would soon be overwhelmed by a ceaseless barrage of inchoate messages, memories, and premonitions impinging on us from the past, the present, and the future. We would be engulfed by a deafening chorus of wailing voices, by the disembodied chatter of trillions of "departed dear ones" going back to the Stone Age—or we would find ourselves face to face with a distant future astir with the babble and baby talk of countless unborn generations to come.

The prospect of such an unlimited Malthusian crowding of our psychic universe is likely to dampen the spirits of all but the most enthusiastic advocates of the survival hypothesis. By the same token, the sorting out of the ceaseless turnover of the earthly habitats of billions of migrating souls is likely to boggle the minds of even the more undaunted reincarnationists. Still, reincarnation is another major argument to support the survival hypothesis.

This is not the place to go into the merits of Ian Stevenson's (1974) Herculean efforts to put the problem on solid scientific foundations. His reports of pertinent observations derived from all over the world and from many cultures, past and present, are gaining increasing recognition and cannot be dismissed lightly. But here, too, a skeptic may invoke telepathic leakage from the investigators and doctrinal compliance by diverse witnesses, informers, and interpreters as a rival interpretation.

A more recent controversy about purported survival was touched upon in Chapter 15, "Out-of-the-Body Experiences and the Denial of Death." Here too we are confronted with the cleavage between the champions of the survival hypothesis, insisting on "remote viewing" by a disembodied entity, living or dead, and advocates of the more pedestrian assumption that the OOB subject merely taps the experimenter's or some other more tangentially involved person's brain.

It will be recalled that, here again, I lean toward the ESP hypothesis. At the same time, I noted that the OOB experiences amount to a valiant attempt at denying the reality of death rather than to an indication of survival. In some cases such attempts come to be veritable experiments with death itself. Their frequent repetition may in turn become an esoteric ritual which meets deep-seated unconscious emotional needs of both experimenter and subject. Occasional veridical elements may add to their dramatic quality.

Modern clinical contributions to thanatology by Elizabeth Kubler-Ross (1969), Raymond Moody (1975), and Osis and Haraldsson (1977), bring into focus yet another aspect of survival research. Reports of this order, scholarly and carefully documented though they are, have one basic flaw: they tend to gloss over the difficulty of establishing and pinpointing the moment, if not the very occurrence, of death. Kubler-Ross touches upon the problem when speaking about "pseudoterminal" patients who were brought back from the verge of death by their physicians to talk about their experiences. We know today that the crucial test of death is the cessation of electrical brain activity. No such data have come to our notice in alleged survival cases of this order. The material is usually based on accounts given by the patients, nurses, or relatives. They often rely on casual remarks by the attending physician that the patient had "just passed away," is "as good as dead," or in any case is "beyond help." Thus, it would perhaps be more accurate to say that despite the disappearance of most vital signs, the actual occurrence of death had not been established in these cases.

Yet Moody's case reports convey the impression that the typical deathbed visions, the "dark tunnel," the "Being of Light" seen, or the buzzing or ringing noises heard by the patients were actually postmortem experiences emerging on their return from the "other world." Unfortunately, such an interpretation, however appealing it may be, is open to a rival explanation: they may be due to diverse metabolic changes, noxious stimuli, anoxia, or fluctuations of the blood supply of certain brain centers. They are more likely to be hallucinatory experiences, *here* and *now*, than disembodied postmortem events. The familiar responses to psychedelic drugs or Wilder Penfield's experiments with electrical stimulation of the brain illustrate the same point.

Similar considerations apply to the OOB experiences Moody (1975) and Osis and Haraldsson (1977) have described in dying patients. Yet, as I pointed out in Chapter 15, they are in effect dramatic illustrations of the universal human need to deny the reality of death. By the same token, the incidence of the identical deathbed observations found by Osis and Haraldsson in such diverse cultures as North American, East Indian, or Icelandic can readily be explained by reference to the identical neurophysiological organization of the human brain, including its vulnerability to anoxia and other afflictions.

There is another feature of deathbed observations that calls for comment in the present context: the feeling of serenity, peace of mind, and even euphoria reported by some patients. These too can more readily be interpreted in "this-worldly" than in "other-worldly" terms. They may be due partly to successful denial of the patient's plight and partly to the relief attending the cessation of pain and suffering once he has passed the point of crisis: "Yes, I have been close to death, but how good it is now to be back and alive again!"

Hallucinatory wish fulfillment may also be responsible for the frequently reported visions of the patients' departed friends or relatives at their bedside. Wish fulfillment is a characteristic feature of dreams, reveries, and hallucinations alike. But the dramatic appearance or apparition of a departed "dear one" is also apt to meet the patient's need to deny the imminence of death—or the reality of death in general: "Lo and behold, he or she has returned from the grave . . . If so, I too may be immune to death and have a new lease on life again. . . ." In some cases it appears that the purportedly dying patient's faith and belief in a life hereafter is reinforced by corresponding attitudes of his friends and relations—including the investigator as a participating observer of the death-bed scene.

If this is true, most claims of apparent survival near death or after resuscitation result from a blend of hallucinatory wish fulfillment and massive denial of illness in terms of familiar defensive maneuvers. They are due to a combination of what neurologists describe as anosognosia, or imperception of organic illness, and typical ego defenses in the Freudian sense. Occasional veridical elements entering the picture may then give rise to reports of "phantasms of the living" or apparitions described by early workers in psychical research.

This is certainly not the last word on the survival hypothesis. We have seen in Chapter 15 that its advocates are still inclined to claim cross-correspondences, reincarnation, or "remote viewing" by OOB subjects to buttress their case. But at the risk of taking the fun out of the process of dying and denying, I submit that, here again, doctrinal compliance, Rhine's "super-psi" (1971), or H. H. Price's "this-world ESP" (1976) are more parsimonious explanatory hypotheses.

Still, last-ditch defenders of the survivalist position may ask at this point whether or not the principle of parsimony or other postulates of the scientific method may be legitimately invoked as the final arbiters at such extremes of the human condition as birth and death—emergence and eclipse of individual consciousness? Such an argument is not without its merits. Our beginning and end cannot apparently be encompassed within the closed, self-sealing system of traditional science. I noted earlier that the same considerations apply to the world encompassed by classical physics and geometry. Newtonian mechanics, Euclidian geometry, and pre-Einsteinian physics cannot possibly do justice to events on the sub-atomic, quantum mechanical scale. The familiar laws of nature break down in the face of cosmic distances, of velocities exceeding the speed of light. The infinitely small and the infinitely large are beyond the comprehension of the Euclidian mind: it throws both our habits of logical thinking and our monitoring devices out of kilter. The problem of individual survival belongs in the same category. It is not subject to "falsifiability." It can neither be conclusively asserted nor conclusively refuted and must therefore be respectfully passed to the attention of the theologian or speculative philosopher.

24

Altered States of Consciousness

and the Existential Shift

In the preceding chapters I put forward four interlocking and mutually supporting hypotheses knit together in a theory of what, in shorthand and with some sacrifice of scientific precision, can be described as the non-Euclidian mind. Yet this still leaves open the question of how the non-Euclidian—or psi—level of experience is related to our standard, Euclidian, Aristotelian, or Newtonian mode of experience.

On trying to answer this question, we have to realize that modern parapsychology, in its transition from nineteenth century psychical research, increasingly lost sight of the psyche and paid more and more attention to ESP, PK, and related "phenomena." Yet it may be well to recall that psi functions—like sensory stimuli and motor responses of the familiar kind—have no existence of their own independent of the human personality from which they sprang and in which they are brought into focus. It is the biological makeup, the psychological orientation, the goals and expectations of human personality which determine what segment of psychic reality is being perceived or acted upon—not aggregates of atoms and molecules, wave patterns, or vortexes of energy impinging on our senses from somewhere "out there."

I pointed out in Chapter 20 that, as a general rule, human personality is geared to functioning on the standard Euclidian, Newtonian, Darwinian, or Freudian level of adaptation. It functions as a system that is open to its time-tested physical and psychosocial environment but stubbornly and consistently closed to psi. External stimuli reach us through the "ordinary" channels of sensation and are conducive to motor, psychomotor, or auto-nomic discharge within the same closed and virtually self-sealing system.

But we have also seen that under more or less well-defined conditions we can shift to an altogether different level of adaptation. It is a shift in which we relinquish part or all of our customary defensive posture toward psi phenomena, while at the same time withdrawing attention from our time-and-space-bound universe. Typical examples are such altered states of consciousness as sleep, dreams, hypnotic trance, ecstasies, transcen-dental meditation, or crisis situations. Yet altered states of consciousness are only a small segment of the existential shift as it is conceived here. It includes abrupt changes in the subject's volitional and behavioral atti-tudes, his motivations and orientation toward the world. Analytically speaking, it may amount to profound ego regression affecting an indi-vidual's interpersonal relationships and thereby recapturing, if only for fleeting moments, his original symbiotic bond with parents, parent surro-gates, or sibling figures, with things animate and inanimate, and ultimately with the universe at large. This is what is here described as the existential shift.

It should also be noted, however, that the existential shift is by no means confined to the field of parapsychology proper. Indeed, it derives its heuristic value from the fact that the tendency to the existential shift is a universal feature of the human mind. It is involved in the switch from magic to science; from myth to method (Ehrenwald 1966), from the logical to the intuitive mode; from prose to poetic diction; from the sacred to the profane, from sleep to wakefulness, from left to right hemispheric dominance, from compulsive intellectual concentration to transcendental meditation. In short, the switch from the standard to the psi level of adap-tation—and the other way round—is but one among many possible changes of roles or modes of existence available in man's total behavioral repertoire.

We know today that magical, prelogical, or paleological patterns of thinking, which were once believed to be distinctive features of "primi-tive" mentality, tend to alternate—or to coexist—with thoroughly prag-matic attitudes in both primitive and modern man. Primitive man is in effect merely a part-time primitive. Nor is modern man his full-time counterpart. Malinowski (1932) has observed that the Trobriand Island-ers, when embarking on a routine fishing expedition, make sure that their canoes, paddles, and fishing gear are in proper working order. But when they are setting out on a more hazardous journey, they also resort to magic spells and incantations to assure their safe return. In a similar vein, the United States Navy, commissioning a new atomic submarine, sees to it that all the available scientific know-how goes into its construction. Yet to make assurance doubly sure, it also observes the time-honored custom of having the Governor's Lady break a bottle of champagne on its bow. The astronaut of our day pins his faith on the computerized miracles of space technology, but he also quotes from Genesis while circling the far side of the moon and bows his head in prayer on returning from a miscarried space mission. In short, both modern man and his primitive forerunners have essentially a dualistic orientation toward the world: one pragmatic, one magical.

This is what the anthropologist Evans-Pritchard has described as the philosophy of dual causality (1937). The same principle can be discerned in the periodic interruptions of our workaday routine for meditation or prayer in places of worship. In many cultures prolonged periods of toil and frugality are followed by traditionally condoned bacchanalia, revels, fiestas, or carnivals. Indeed, existential shifts, theophanies, experiences of self-transcendence, ecstasies, and possessions—divine or demoniacal—are part and parcel of the religious experience. The same dichotomy is involved in the modern town dweller's weekend exodus to the countryside and in the attempts of today's alienated youth to escape from "civilization and its discontents" by way of pot, rock music, and the hippie way of life.

A modern clinical example of an existential shift can be seen in the abrupt transformation of the contemporary psychotherapist donning the mantle of the hypnotist and regressing in the process to the role of the magician possessed of supposedly omnipotent powers. The transformation, incidentally, is a two-way process in which the regressive trend—what psychoanalysts describe as regression in the service of treatment—is shared by both therapist and patient.

Another case in point is recurrent shifts from Freud's secondary process to primary process functioning in dreams, fantasies, and mental disorders. They are part and parcel of the analytic process. In a similar vein, elements of the primary process are interwoven with the activity of the creative artist. So are hunches and intuitions in the work of the scientist.

Perhaps the most impressive example of an existential shift is sleep and the dream state. On the physiological level sleep is associated with such well-defined physiological indicators as changes of the EEG, alterations in body temperature and blood chemistry, enzyme functions and a switch from sympathetic to parasympathetic neural activity. There are changes in the blood flow to the brain, as well as blocking of efferent motor systems and of afferent sensory stimuli through the reticular formation in the brainstem. There are the rapid eye movements associated with dreaming, and there is, above all, a striking change in the dreamer's inner experience—coupled with enhanced telepathic receptiveness, as documented in the parapsychological literature.

In effect, it is the close association between telepathy and dreams, the principal proving ground of Freud's primary process, which suggests the existence of a common denominator between the two: both are predicated on the occurrence of an existential shift. Their close affinity is further borne out by the fact that both dreams and psi phenomena are characterized by a marked disorganization of the categories of space, time, and causality—a disorganization of Broad's (1962) "limiting principles" of the human mind. It should be noted, however, that on the level of the primary process, the causal and spatiotemporal anomalies are only *apparent*. They are

> "... children of an idle dream
> Begot of nothing but vain fantasy. ..."

as the Bard put it. By contrast, psi phenomena, while displaying much the same structural disorganization as their shadowy replicas, do actually live up to some of the wish-fulfilling dreams and "vain fantasies" found in primitive folklore and in the mental life of the child or the neurotic.

Yet our data also indicate that the modus operandi of the existential shift which is conducive to psi is different in every case. It is different for sleep, hypnosis, mediumistic trance, out-of-the-body experiences, Zen meditation, samadhi, or whatnot. Most of us can fall asleep at our habitual bedtime without further ado. But hypnosis can only be elicited by a specific set of psychological paraphernalia; and mediumistic trance or transcendental meditation usually requires a period of ritualistic training, conditioning, and indoctrination. They all may or may not be productive of psi phenomena. As a general rule, the shift to the psi level of functioning is still less amenable to deliberate volition than falling asleep, going into a state of mental dissociation, or having a peak experience. Telepathic or precognitive dreams, clairvoyance, or spectacular levels of ESP scoring almost always come about unexpectedly and cannot as yet be produced to order.

This is why would-be thaumaturges, cultists, occultists, and followers of various esoteric sects have to proceed by trial and error in their quest for the supernormal. From time immemorial they have resorted to a wide variety of spiritual disciplines such as prayer and meditation or to such practices as fasting, ablutions, or frenetic dances to coax or coerce the phenomena into making their appearance.

The forerunners of today's psychedelic drugs supplied another ingredient of the techniques used. But it should be noted that here, too, their use amounted merely to random probing into the unknown by primitive practitioners who had no inkling of the part played by the meeting of faith and chemical agent in bringing about the desired results.

This is a point which even some contemporary advocates of the psychedelic drugs tend to overlook. We know today that in practice the two factors are hard to separate. The chemical agent is inevitably brought to bear within a psychologically meaningful context, and the emotional impact of psychologically meaningful situations is always tied to or accompanied by somatic, neurohumoral, or biochemical changes in the organism. Yet, as I have hinted, the common factor in both psychological and chemical transactions is the existential shift.

The stage managers of the ancient Greek oracles were obviously unaware of this state of affairs. Nevertheless, they tried to make assurance doubly sure by instructing their Pythias to chew laurel leaves or to inhale the legendary vapors of the Delphian cave prior to putting on their performances. On the other hand, the high priests of contemporary psychedelic cults pay just as much attention to the general setting and atmosphere of the drug experience as they do to the drug itself. Although they might frown on such a pedestrian hypothesis, they too reach their goal through a combination of chemical and psychological "final common pathways," as described by the physiologists. Chapter 8 features a typical case history illustrating this point.

The combination of psychological with chemical or neurohumoral factors is less obvious in another example of the existential shift: in the psychoanalytic situation. In this situation a properly timed interpretation may trigger off a striking change in the clinical picture. It occasionally leads to the dramatic removal of a hysteric symptom, described as the Freudian catharsis. Its ancient prototype is the Hippocratic *kairos* or the "favorable moment." *Kairos* was thought to usher in a crisis—or critical change—in an existing illness, mental or physical. It is a moment—or momentum—which may jolt the patient out of his pathological level of adaptation and lead to a temporary adaptation on a new and healthier baseline, or even to an enduring readjustment.

Needless to say, however, deliberate psychoanalytic interventions, "value shocks" or the like, are not the only means by which such changes can be brought about. Hypnotic suggestions, the temple sleep of the ancient Greeks and Egyptians, and the miraculous feats of healing attributed to the shrines at Lourdes, St. Anne of Beaupres, or the Holy Virgin of Guadeloupe, may be conducive to similar psychological or psychosomatic effects. At least some of the cures claimed by contemporary faith healers, psychodramatists, behavioral therapists, encounter groups, or therapeutic marathons are likewise graphic examples of the existential shift. At the other end of the scale are the various modern shock treatments or pharmaceuticals with their ostensibly purely chemical or physical action, while the effects of assorted placebos or otherwise indifferent physical agents are somewhere between the two extremes. It goes without saying that here, too, the existential shift, triggered off by either chemical or psychological factors, is the common denominator.

Thus, the existential shift covers a much wider range of events than the term "altered states of consciousness" introduced by Charles Tart (1969) and his associates. It is not just an individual's private affair. It includes alterations of both conscious and unconscious mental states and behavioral changes. It encompasses motivations and volitional impulses poised for action that remain outside the subject's range of conscious awareness. Yet we know that such subtle shifts in inner attitudes may be possessed of powerful external leverage effects. They may be conducive to psychokinesis or to telepathic agency. They may—or may not—be accompanied by changes of electric brain activity in the direction of alpha or theta waves. They may be accompanied by J. Whitton's (1974) "ramp" function or by Grey Walter's (1970) CNV or expectancy waves in the EEG. Above all, we have seen in an earlier chapter that they may involve a shift from left to right hemispheric dominance.

Thus the concept of the existential shift duplicates the sensory-motor dichotomy of the extension hypothesis. By contrast, the term "altered states of consciousness" makes allowance for only half the story designated by the existential shift.

What, then, is the existential shift, and what is its modus operandi? It consists of an abrupt, global reshuffling and reorganization of a person's psychological and physiological adaptations. In the ideal case, it affects all levels of his spiritual, cognitive, volitional, and perceptual orientation to the world and the whole repertoire of his behavioral responses to the environment. If a chemical agent is responsible for the shift, it is brought to bear on the raw nerve endings, synapses, and central chemoreceptors of the brain. On the other hand, such psychological influences as emotionally charged imagery, symbolic cues, wishes, expectations, or anxieties may "home in" on the identical pharmacological or neurohormonal target areas of the brain, much in the same way as they are affected by a shot of adrenalin, a cortisone injection, or 200 micrograms of LSD. In the last analysis, the "final common pathway" is the same in both instances.

Viewed in this light, the available evidence concerning the factors favoring psi phenomena can be summarized under three headings. They refer, first, to the personality of the sensitive or percipient, second, to the agent, and, third, to the field characteristics of their interpersonal relationship.

(1) The conditions favoring telepathic, clairvoyant, and (presumably) precognitive receptivity are an open mind concerning the very possibility of psi. They are predicated on the positive attitudes of Schmeidlerian "sheep" (see Chapter 1). Beyond that, they are different for need-determined and flaw-determined phenomena. Need-determined incidents require a percipient and an agent reaching out for closeness and intimacy with his social or physical environment. Flaw-determined incidents are favored by a relaxation of tensions, "calm alertness," drowsiness, the REM state of sleep or partial sensory deprivation. As far back as 1947, I described such conditions as "minus functions" whose (need-determined) compensation by either agent or percipient may give rise to psi (Ehrenwald 1948).

On the physical side, the attitude of the percipient is often accompanied by plethysmographic changes or a characteristic pattern of alpha waves as described in Chapter 1. Fewer experimental data are available concerning the physical state of the agent, though I noted that Grey Walter's expectancy waves and Whitton's "ramp functions" in the EEG may provide a cue in that direction. Russian workers observed EEG changes associated with Nina Kulagina's PK experiments.

(2) Observations of telepathic "cross-dreaming" in the psychoanalytic situation indicate that occasionally a sleeping person in the REM state may likewise function as a telepathic agent (Eisenbud 1970). In this case the dreamer's mental content is picked up by another dreamer.

The physical concomitants of persons in distress or of dying patients acting as agents can at best be inferred from the available clinical data. As a general rule, such agents are not aware of their "agency." The same is true for the analyst functioning as a sender in the treatment situation.

What I described as telepathic tracer effects or as doctrinal compliance may be unexpected—or even undesirable—by-products of his primary role as a therapist. On the other hand, I noted that deliberate attempts to get such influences "across" to the patient are usually of no avail.

(3) The third group of factors is concerned with interpersonal relationships and with the existing cultural or subcultural setting: they are field-determined. They usually consist of a circular pattern of feedback involving a properly motivated agent and percipient; or else the experimenter serves as a catalyst in the process. Its original prototype is the symbiotic relationship between parent and child and its extension to the world at large. Other things being equal, it is in this context of dovetailing and interlacing person-to-person or person-to-world relationships that psi phenomena are apt to occur. But they do so only if and when the meeting of the agent's and/or the percipient's mind is triggered by the existential shift.

It will be noted that the psychological conditioning factors of clairvoyance or psychokinesis do not fit in with this simplified scheme. A percipient "guessing" correctly a geometrical design in a sealed envelope or an agent affecting a falling die can apparently "do his own thing" without the aid of a telepathic agent or percipient functioning as a symbiotic partner. To do justice to such a situation, we have to extend the range of parent-child symbiosis—of the symbiotic gradient—far into the symbiotic matrix from which ultimately all creation, including both animate and inanimate nature, has sprung. Such a formulation admittedly throws no light on the modus operandi of telepathic—or rather clairvoyant—receptiveness in the outermost reaches of the symbiotic gradient where the percipient is left to his own resources and has to make do without the aid of a symbiotic or any other external human agency. Like in the familiar Zen story, he must try to hear the clapping of one solitary hand. It is at this point that the existential shift brings us once more face to face with the irreducible epistemological gap discussed in Chapter 20. It is a gap with which we will apparently have to live for some time to come.

Be that as it may, we must realize that the existential shift, as it is described here, is merely the crest of a wave superimposed on the ebb and flow of a person's mental processes. This is true for both experimental and spontaneous evidence, and for observations in the psychoanalytic situation. In the analytic setting it would be wrong to expect the existential shift to take place with an audible click, as it were. My own experiences over many years of practice indicate that in the doctor-patient relationship the shift results from a gradual buildup of the doctor's therapeutic attitude, meeting halfway the patient's hopes and expectations to be helped. If and when the therapist combines such an approach with a genuine openness to psi, the phenomena tend to make their appearance with increasing frequency. As noted in Chapter 6, the therapist's role may alternate between telepathic agency and receptiveness. At times the two roles may blend in a personal union, as it were; while at other times they may merge imperceptibly with his empathic or intuitive approach to both patients and nonpatients, as well as to the world at large.

Apart from my personal experience, these observations are borne out by some of Jung's remarks in *Memories, Dreams, Reflections* (1963) and by the observations and self-observations of Jule Eisenbud, Joost Meerloo, Montague Ullman, and others. Similar considerations apply to the sustained high-level performances of such noted sensitives as Mrs. Garrett, Mrs. Leonard, Mrs. R. Heywood, G. Croiset, Ingo Swann, and a few other gifted individuals. The existential shift, in such cases, is no longer an isolated, capricious event. It is the corollary of a newly acquired and ultimately firmly established existential *position*. It is a position in which the psi level and the standard level of functioning are brought together and coalesce in an integrated, functional whole.

How, then, can the existential shift be captured and made to solidify in the new existential position? How can the crest of a wave be induced to remain suspended in midair in order to pose for a still picture to be painted by a Japanese master? There is admittedly no easy way to do it. It may be the fruit of a lifetime of patient seeking and probing. It may be a process in which success, as in initial runs of ESP tests, is often followed by failure. It apparently may also be amenable to learning, for instance, in experiments with operant control of the alpha rhythm or when feedback techniques are used to improve subject performance.

Whether or not attempts at electronic or chemical shortcuts along these lines will lead to a breakthrough in parapsychology remains to be seen. But there can be little doubt that in the last analysis the decisive factor will always be human personality, the fount and origin of all purpose, planning, and initiative in nature, including chemical, electronic, or other technological expedients. Ultimately, success or failure will hinge on the motivations of man and on his capacity to bring about the existential shift.

Another intriguing question concerns the values attributed to the respective existential positions, or to what Tart called "discrete states of consciousness." At the time of this writing, the standard, Euclidian mode of experience, or Castaneda's (1968) "ordinary" reality, has lost its former status of preeminence. Tart's "consensus rationality" and the associated left hemispheric dominance are being replaced by right hemispheric dominance (intuition, ecstasy, and drug-induced, "higher" states of consciousness). They are hailed as antidotes to alienation, detachment, and all the ills that befall Western man of our day; and the scientist, the psychiatrist, and the social reformer are being told to yield the right of way to the shaman, to the Noble Mystic—the counterpart of the Noble Savage of a past era.

Charles Tart's (1975b) analysis of a broad spectrum of altered states of consciousness—and their attendant "state-specific" sciences—is at pains to avoid such bias. His attitude toward them seems to be strictly egalitarian. It is a position closely akin to the cultural relativism of modern anthropologists or to the hands-off posture of such psychiatric (or antipsychiatric) radicals as Thomas Szasz, R. D. Laing, or John Lilly. But my own reading of Tart's position persuades me that despite his avowed relativism, he is still ready to accept the consensus rationality of the scientific method as the ultimate arbiter—at least so long as he makes due allowance for the exploits and value systems of other state-specific modes of existence.

This is in effect also my own position. We have to keep an open mind to what Tart calls the "hip" way of ordering existential values. But we must also be prepared to see them crumble once the youthful practitioner of the "higher" states comes face to face with the exigencies of a "lower," drugless, and supposedly mind-restricting reality.

We may be hell- or heaven-bent to push our ontological explorations —our metaphysical spacecraft—into the farthest reaches or the deepest recesses of inner space. But in the end both the neophyte and the veteran of psychedelic trips or cosmic flights of fancy has to return to earth again. As of now, it is our only home in the universe, the fixed reference point of our biological adaptations, the operational baseline for our business of living. In the last analysis, our measuring rods, our weighing machines, and our timepieces are geared to this pedestrian, standard mode of existence, and the fact is that, under terrestrial conditions, they continue to give us reliable pointer readings. Indeed, they have served us well in the face of recurrent scientific and psychiatric revolutions in the past century.

There is another stable reference point that comes to our aid at this juncture. What I described as the classical, Euclidian, or Leonardian model of personality makes sure that the same principles should apply to observations in the psychological laboratory, in our transactions in clinic and consulting room, and in human affairs in general. It provides us with a built-in compass telling us what baseline our postulated existential shift is shifting *from* and *where* it is shifting to.

This is particularly relevant in the present context, chiefly concerned as it is with the ultimate merits of the shift to the psi level of consciousness. We have seen that it may range all the way from creative inspiration to the delusions of paranoid schizophrenics. Thus, psi phenomena do not by themselves possess higher or lower spiritual values or biological survival advantages. Viewed in isolation they are neither "normal" nor "abnormal" nor "supernormal." They may be evidence of break*through* as well as break*down*, as J. Silverman (1975) puts it. Their creative potential, their power for good or evil—or the gradations in between—have to be determined in each individual case. We may try to do so by using our favorite system of values—biological, cultural, spiritual, or otherwise —keeping our fingers crossed, and hoping that our judgment will elicit at least a measure of consensus from our peers.

Part Five

USES

25

Varieties of Unorthodox Healing

ATTEMPTS at spiritual healing and "psychic" diagnoses have traditionally been part and parcel of the psi syndrome. They range from the healing miracles of the Bible to the exploits of Edgar Cayce of Virginia Beach or the highly touted and commercialized claims of the Silva Mind Control. Viewed from the present vantage point, they are all varieties of unorthodox healing.

Attempts along these lines are usually separated from scientific medicine by a deep gulf. They are relegated to two disparate, mutually irreconcilable systems of thought which are kept apart by doctrinal, religious, or institutional safeguards or socioeconomic barriers. Only the dire needs of a given primitive minority group living under Western tutelage tend to mitigate the adversary relationship between the two, with an occasional African medicine man or Mexican *curandero* invited to minister to a native patient admitted to the white man's hospital.

Whose ministrations are then to be consigned to the domain of unorthodox healing? The young hospital intern will readily pin such a label on the witch doctor or medicine man. The medicine man, in turn, is not likely to be asked for his opinions. If he is, he will perhaps opine that it is his spells and incantations, his charms, amulets, and herbal concoctions that are the standard operating procedure of his tribe, pitted against the "unorthodox" healing practices of his Western confreres.

Indeed, it could be stated that one man's unorthodox healing is another man's superstition, and that one patient's savior and benefactor may be the American Medical Association's quack or charlatan.

Unorthodox healing is thus a relative term, dependent on the observer's vantage point and system of values. Guided by these considerations, the following varieties of healing fall into our purview: (1) healing magic, as practiced by the supposedly untutored medicine man; (2) faith healing, practiced by devotees of major religions of Western man, such as priests, ministers, or *zaddikim,* or attributed to religious shrines, sacred relics, holy waters, and the like; (3) diverse forms of spiritual healing, uncommitted to any particular institutionalized religious persuasion, as practiced by charismatic personalities; and (4) attempts at paranormal healing specifically geared to the operation of telepathy or psychokinesis emanating from a gifted psychic and brought to bear upon humans or animals under controlled experimental conditions.

It should be recalled at this point that even scientific psychotherapy, psychoanalytic or otherwise, may include a psi element in practice, though not in theory. Tracer effects and doctrinal compliance, as I have stated, are well-nigh ubiquitous features of the treatment situation, even if they are hard to pinpoint in a given case. I also pointed out in earlier chapters that doctrinal compliance, with or without psi, is more than an accidental by-product of the doctor-patient relationship. Few skeptics will deny that a doctor's primary motivation is his emotionally charged therapeutic expectations, his desire to improve the condition of the patient. This is true even if we grant that the purity of his purpose may occasionally be adulterated by self-seeking interests and other personal shortcomings.

The patient, on the other hand, approaches the therapist with the fervent hope that he will be helped. This is how, in the ideal case, he meets halfway, as it were, the practitioner's therapeutic motivations. They are in effect closely interwoven with the patient's doctrinal compliance.

Yet it will be recalled that it is precisely such dovetailing and interlacing attitudes—the warp and woof of the therapeutic encounter—which are also among the foremost predisposing and conditioning factors of psi phenomena. And when they spring from a symbiotic relationship between therapist and patient and, by indirection, from its archaic prototype, symbiosis between parent and child, the patient's doctrinal compliance can be very significant.

Unfortunately, however, all arguments along these lines are merely suggestive. They do not add up to anything like scientific proof of the part played by the psi factor in the treatment process. Most observable transactions between therapist and patient lack the telltale signs of tracer elements or the criterion of uniqueness to clinch the case. Therefore, the role of psi as a therapeutic agent in diverse forms of psychotherapy can at best be inferred by extrapolation.

We shall see that similar considerations apply to most varieties of more strictly "unorthodox healing."

Healing Magic

Healing magic is dominated by a belief in the omnipotence of thought, in the possibility of action at a distance, and in the healer's ability to coerce the forces of nature to do his bidding. Even more than in the case of the paranoid schizophrenic, there is a marked resemblance between the world of the magician and some of the propositions of psychical research. The difference is that the schizophrenic's world is basically evil, ruled by capricious, malignant, demoniacal forces or vengeful parental figures disguised as witches or warlocks, while the world of the magician strikes a more even balance between the good and the bad, between black and white magic.

It is true that viewed in the light of modern science, the magician misinterprets the facts of daily life, does not seem to learn from experience, and allows his judgment to be controlled by wishful thinking. Nevertheless, his outlook on the world has a logic of its own. It embodies a consistent, closed, self-sealing system of thought, not unlike that of the religious believer, the materialistic scientist, or the worker in psychical research. By trial and error, he develops an elaborate set of rituals, spells, and incantations, which happen to meet his fellow tribesmen's needs for an enhanced sense of power and a feeling of security in the face of calamities, existential crises, or death. As in scientific psychotherapy, the pattern of circular feedback between the healer's motivations and the patient's wishes and expectations is unmistakable.

More than that. The paradigm of healing magic in an anthropological setting throws a third ingredient of unorthodox healing, and indeed of the healing approach in general, into sharper perspective. This third ingredient is the tribe's active participation in the medicine man's ministrations. Invariably, he is surrounded and assisted by a group of Schmeidlerian "sheep" (emotionally involved observers) reinforcing the emotional impact on his clients. We know today that it is precisely this threefold interpersonal configuration, enhanced by contagion, suggestion, and a psi factor generated in the process, which is apt to contribute to the efficacy of his approach (Ehrenwald 1976).

It is a matter of historical record that in the presence of this *therapeutic triad* the healer's occasional successes tend to become self-perpetuating and the group's faith in his powers is rarely shaken by his failures. They are attributed to black magic wrought by a rival medicine man who happened to cancel out the effects of white magic.

Faith Healing

Faith healing differs from healing magic in that its belief systems are predicated on the direct intervention of, or cooperation with, the divinity worshipped in the Christian, Jewish, Muslim, Hindu, or Buddhist religions. The healing miracles of the Bible are classical cases in point. It can no longer be doubted that they contain a considerable admixture of magic, giving rise to much theological controversy. The important point is that in faith healing, the supernatural power of the officiating priest, shrine, or ritual is attributed to the divinity and not just to the magic qualities of a charismatic personality. In Christian tradition, the faith healer disclaims such an exalted personal mission. He ascribes his exploits to the grace of God, to the Holy Spirit, to the powers of prayer, and to the believer's faith in divine intervention. Indeed, the seekers of a cure are told over and over again that it can only be expected in the presence of true faith. Thus, here again, the therapeutic triad, made up of the practitioner's belief in his own powers or personal myth, of the patient's corresponding faith in the healer's ministrations, and of the existing cultural climate, is readily discernible. The difference between healing magic, faith healing, and other forms of spiritual healing lies chiefly in their underlying ideological or theological premises.

Yet, on comparing the modus operandi of magic and that of faith healing without reference to church dogma or learned theological disputations, it is readily apparent that both the magician and the faith healer operate in a closed, self-sealing system of beliefs—or in a magic circle—of their own. Both tend to create and to verify their evidence in their own idiosyncratic ways. By the same token, any skeptical outsider trying to break into the magic circle is bound to be rebuffed by those inside. He is rebuffed because his skepticism threatens to destroy one of the major ingredients of the therapeutic triad: the faith in the healer's omnipotence and the religious fervor of the group. In the absence of these ingredients, the process of circular feedback flowing between them is interrupted and healing cannot take place.

Healing Miracles

The healing miracles attributed over the years to the shrine of the Holy Virgin of Lourdes and the massive healing exploits claimed by Mary Baker Eddy's Christian Science are perhaps the most striking examples of this phenomenon in modern times. Claims of the Lourdes miracles are based on findings by a Medical Committee appointed by the Catholic Church. Their criteria of miraculous cures are, among others, a rapid recovery from organic or incurable illness, prompt disappearance of the existing pathology or tissue damage, and persistence of a cure following the visit. Nearly a hundred "miracles" defined by these terms have been recorded since the beginning of the work of the committee. Yet Donald West's (1957) critical review of the claims in the light of rigorous clinical-diagnostic standards has come to a negative conclusion. Even the eleven "best" cases of the series have failed to stand up to closer scrutiny. "Carelessness in presentation," he notes, "which would never be tolerated in a teaching hospital, pervades all the material" (p. 121).

Similar problems arise in connection with the massive claims made by the practitioners of Christian Science; by M. E. Carter and W. A. McGarey (1972), followers of Edgar Cayce; by Kathryn Kuhlman (1962); by Ambrose and Olga Worrall (1965) in this country; or by Harry Edwards and others in the United Kingdom (Rose 1968). Attempts at a clinical evaluation of the German lay healer Dr. Trampler (Strauch 1963) have shown that his cures were best in diverse functional diseases, that they were inversely related to the severity of illness, and that claims of improvement tended to be inversely proportional to the patients' educational level.

Claims of cures are usually supported by glowing testimonials volunteered by patients and their families. They include purported effects of absent healing and intercessionary prayers. In most of these cases the question of bad faith can perhaps be discounted. Indeed, "good faith" is often at the very heart of the matter. We must realize that, in the realm of faith healing and theological doctrine, facts have an altogether different complexion than in the realm of science. They are contingent on validation by the faithful. The determination of evidence depends on the consensus of the patient, the practitioner, and the group. Facts are distilled in the crucible of the therapeutic triad. Yet whatever consensus is achieved in these circumstances has a formidable persuasive power: it both creates and validates its own evidence. Thus, the facts established in the emotional atmosphere of the healer-patient relationship cannot be calibrated against clinical or laboratory findings of science. They cannot be weighed and measured in terms of statistical significance, chi-squares, or critical ratios.

Nevertheless, four tentative conclusions can be derived from the more or less anecdotal accounts in the literature. (1) In spite of differences in the rationale adopted and the technique used by the individual practitioners, their approach is invariably geared to the three ingredients of the therapeutic triad. (2) Therapeutic success is usually contingent on the proper blend of hopes and expectations held by the healer, the patient, and the culture in which they are immersed. (3) Other things being equal, functional, psychosomatic, and organic conditions all tend to respond to the healer's ministrations. (4) Despite claims to the contrary, the response in organic cases (as well as functional conditions) is usually limited by the severity of illness. Faith is more likely to move (or remove) warts than a cancerous growth.

This touches upon the controversial question of cures effected by faith healers in malignant conditions. It is closely linked with the problem of spontaneous remission, described as cure or improvement in the absence of discernible external factors. The surgeons T. C. Everson and W. H. Cole (1966) have reviewed some 700 pertinent publications that appeared since 1900 and found 176 such remissions. Similar observations have since been reported with growing frequency (Booth 1973). The number of such remissions, however, is extremely small compared with the number of sufferers from malignant tumors who have sought help from unorthodox healers during the past six or seven decades. It therefore stands to reason that in such huge populations the random occurrence of spontaneous improvements is virtually inevitable. Still, if they occur during or after the time the patient had been under the care of an unorthodox healer, the improvement will readily be attributed to his ministrations. Indeed, one single case of this order may suffice to establish the healer's reputation. It will serve to substantiate his claims, to bolster his personal myth, and to draw the multitudes to his public appearances.

Yet all these critical considerations must not detract from the indisputable fact that a large number of patients treated by faith healers of all denominations in all historical periods have derived considerable benefit from their ministrations. They show once again the "power of ideas," of imagination, suggestion, or autosuggestion, over bodily processes—to say nothing of the psi factor waiting in the wings to be given credit for its

contribution. The same is true for the remedial effects attributed to autogenic training, biofeedback, or transcendental meditation engaged in by
either the patient or the therapist or both (LeShan 1973).

Whether or not the laying on of hands has a curative effect of its own
is a matter of controversy. Such claims go back to biblical times and
classical antiquity when Roman emperors were using what medieval
Christian tradition later described as the Royal Touch. Paradoxically, we
are told that even such a reluctant healer as the Emperor Vespasian occasionally gave comfort to hapless patients seeking his aid.

Recent reports of Kirlian photography focusing on the laying on of
hands have been invoked to support theories of some new form of energy
emanating from the hands of the healer. Yet critics have rightly pointed
out that the effects of the high-frequency current used in Kirlian photography are themselves apt to generate marked physiological changes on the
interface between the skin and the photographic plate. These effects are
in turn bound to be influenced by the subject's emotional state as well as
by diverse other situational factors. In that respect, Kirlian effects are
comparable to the familiar electrogalvanic skin responses which have
proved to be valuable diagnostic aids. The actual transfer of some unknown form of energy from the hand of the healer is still unproven.

Cultist and Esoteric Practices

Among the esoteric practices of recent times, the work of the so-called
psychic surgeons in the Philippines, Brazil, and Mexico has gained wide
notoriety. A psychic surgeon is supposed to operate on the patient with
his bare hands. He uses no scalpel or other instrument and claims that he
can enter the patient's body without antiseptic precautions, sterilization,
or anesthesia. He claims further that he can remove a tumor or other diseased tissue without leaving a scar or without time needed for tissue
repair. Minutes after the operation, the patient is ready to return to his
normal activities.

A composite picture of the procedure would be as follows: The patient, usually a well-to-do American, Canadian, or European tourist,
contracts with a travel agency and is brought directly to the healer in
Manila or in some remote *barrio* in the back country. He may engage in
some chitchat with the healer, an assistant, or an interpreter, witness a

few operations, and take pictures by himself. Prior to the operation, there may be a prayer meeting conforming to the ritual of the *Espiritista* church. As soon as the surgeon feels he has "the power," he proceeds with the operation. In one of the numerous films brought to the United States, the surgeon's hand can be seen to dig deep into the patient's abdomen. Presently, blood oozes from the site of entry, and the healer may produce a bloody piece of debris, supposedly taken from the abdominal cavity, from an appendix or the uterus. "Bad tissue," or "a blood clot," he would remark. Yet to many observers who watched such procedures at close quarters, the "bad tissue" appeared either as a blood-soaked wad of cotton or some fatty tissue which the surgeon threw into a basket and burned. On one occasion, a specimen of blood was retrieved and subsequently identified to be of animal origin.

Some healers include the giving of "spiritual injections" in their repertoire. The procedure consists of the surgeon's finger aiming at the affected organ without actually touching it.

The American surgeon William Nolen (1974), diplomate of the American Board of Surgery, studied the Filipino surgeons in action for several weeks. His report is a damning exposure of a scenario of primitive mumbo jumbo, fraud, and trickery and is apt to shake the validity of the reports given by perhaps professionally less competent observers of the Philippine, Brazilian, or Mexican scene (Puharich 1974; Sherman 1967; Fuller 1974).

Similar considerations apply to a spate of equally unsubstantiated reports of healings attributed to assorted "spirit guides," discarnate or reincarnated healers, or physicians trying to ply their posthumous trade in spiritualistic séance rooms all over the world.

Eccentric or frankly fraudulent practices of this order have given unorthodox healing a bad name. Whatever beneficial effects may flow from them is derived from the patient's irrepressible "good faith" in a given procedure, even in the face of the dubious quality of the faith of the respective practitioner.

Some contemporary fads involving "psychic" diagnoses and treatment belong in this category. Widely advertised biofeedback techniques offering training to all comers and promising spectacular powers of the mind and cures for all ailments have grown into profitable business ventures. Their courses and seminars are couched in the language of serious research. But their claims are unsupported by proper controls and their diagnostic and therapeutic exploits are at best confirmed by the "graduates" themselves. Rex Stanford (1975), surveying the field in a report to the American Association for the Advancement of Science, gave a highly critical account of one of the most successful groups of this kind and cautions against some undesirable consequences of its activities.

Here, again, it cannot be disputed, however, that some of them do offer temporary relief—if not apparent shortcuts to instant health, well-being, and a sense of personal power.

Meditation and the Relaxation Response

Diverse spiritual disciplines, ancient and modern, aiming at escape from suffering and ill health and at betterment of the human situation, are another matter. Most meditative techniques go back to ancient Vedic times. They have also been practiced by Hebrew sages of old and early Christian mystics. All seek to attain mental and physical relaxation, freedom from disturbing thoughts, "stillness of mind," and altered states of consciousness culminating in the experience of merging with the divinity or the universe at large. Like the various approaches to unorthodox healing, the techniques of meditation use widely divergent external paraphernalia, belief systems, and theological doctrines to attain essentially the same goals.

Transcendental meditation, currently the most popular among them, has developed an intriguing blend of the old and the new as its rationale. The old ingredient is the time-tested Vedic tradition introduced to the West by Maharishi Mahesh Yogi. It is reinforced by the benign, grandfatherly face and flowing white beard of the Yogi presiding over the procedure. Subliminally, such an image cannot fail to evoke childhood memories of similar pictures of God himself in the Western viewer. The new ingredients are the trappings of contemporary science and technology, from the EEG to biofeedback and computerized chemical analysis monitoring the bodily changes that accompany the process.

It seems to be the combination of these ingredients, aided by the leverage effect of suggestion and autosuggestion, which is responsible for the indisputable beneficial effects of TM. Their significance should not be obscured by critics tending to brush them aside as nothing but placebo effects, nor by the fact that other forms of relaxation responses, from Zen to hatha-yoga and kundalini or to Schultz's autogenic training, have been

259

credited with much the same physical, mental, and spiritual responses. Whatever differences exist between them derive from their filtering down to different levels of the central and autonomous nervous system, perhaps because they are geared to different expectations and beliefs cherished by the meditator and his teacher. As a result, these methods are apt to strike different chords in a motley group of followers, catering to skeptics, believers, sophisticates, and gullibles alike.

Nevertheless, it appears that here, too, the "last common pathway" responsible for the existential shift attending the meditation process is the same in all cases. Laboratory findings by G. E. Schwartz (1975); H. Benson, J. F. Beary, and M. P. Carol (1975); and others include marked lowering of metabolism and oxygen consumption, increased skin resistance, shifts to the alpha rhythm in the EEG, and altered levels of blood lactate.

Objective physiological changes of this order have to be viewed apart from the usually inflated claims enthusiasts are inclined to make about their particular brand of meditation. They may irk the critical scientist. But we must realize that belief in such claims is in effect an integral part of the procedure. It provides the cultural or subcultural climate, the spiritual fervor needed for its ultimate success. Whether or not verifiable psi elements are included in the process is an open question. It is a question that was touched upon in our earlier discussion of experimenter bias and doctrinal compliance. It will be taken up again in the next chapter, reviewing modern placebo research.

It should be recalled, however, at this point, that virtually all medical interventions, orthodox and unorthodox, are inextricably blended with their attendant suggestive and placebo effects, based on the practitioner's expectations and the patient's hopes and transference reactions. Here again, we are dealing with what cultural anthropologists have described as the principle of dual causality seen in the Azande or the Trobriand Islanders. More often than not, both the patient and the therapist praise the Lord and keep their powder dry, using both magic and science in their armamentarium. Even the skeptic may consult a faith healer in a pinch. In turn, even the most conservative member of the AMA will concede that the medical man's efforts have to be aided by "Nature's healing powers," or the patient's own regenerative potential.

Unfortunately, until recently, lip service at best has been paid to the need to integrate the two principles. Obviously integration can only be accomplished through a holistic approach to the patient by a well-rounded therapist who can put these principles into practice.

Experimental Contributions

Significantly, serious attempts at affording experimental evidence of paranormal healing have been made by researchers outside the medical fraternity. Foremost among them is the biologist Bernard Grad (1963) in Canada; Grad, Cadoret, and Paul (1961); and the biochemist Sister (Dr.) Justa Smith (1968), in the United States. With the aid of Mr. Oscar Estebany, a Hungarian-born military officer and healer, Dr. Grad studied the effects of "laying on of hands" upon wound healing in mice. Two control groups were used: one was handled by a nonhealer, the other was left to its own resources. Grad's experimental group showed a significantly faster rate of tissue repair and wound healing than the control groups.

Sister Justa Smith obtained changes in the activity of the enzyme trypsin kept in stoppered flasks while held in the hand of Mr. Estebany. Control conditions included exposure to ultraviolet light and to a high-intensity magnetic field. Here, too, effects were in excess of chance expectation, though the magnetic field proved equally effective. Grad found, furthermore, that barley seedlings watered with a 1 percent saline solution which had been held in the hands of the healer were supposed to show an accelerated tendency to growth!

If confirmed, the Grad and Justa Smith experiments would go far to help isolate the part played by the psi factor in the healing approach in pure culture, as it were. They would provide collateral evidence upon which claims of diverse modalities of unorthodox healing are based and help to distinguish psi effects from mere suggestion, autosuggestion, or hypnotic states.

At the time of this writing, these findings are still controversial. But they are straws in the wind indicating that the magic circles of unorthodox healing and scientific medicine are drawing together and can be expected to overlap. Yet we shall see in the next chapter that, unbeknown to the medical practitioner, psi has always played a part in most therapeutic interventions in both orthodox and unorthodox medical settings, ranging from supposedly ineffective herbal concoctions to remedies of the medieval dirt pharmacy, from bloodletting to acupuncture, and from tranquilizers to sugar pills.

26

Psi, Placebo, and the Grin

of the Cheshire Cat

Eᴠᴇʀ sɪɴᴄᴇ the decline and fall of magic and the magic arts, the latter-day magic of psi phenomena has passed into the shadows to eke out a precarious underground existence. Yet primitive magic has by no means become "inoperative" in human affairs. This is particularly true for the healing arts—for man's attempts to lighten the burden of his existence, to allay anxiety, to conquer disease, and, if possible, to defeat death itself.

It is borne out by thousands of years of herbal medicine, of the use of diverse concoctions, potions, and physical procedures, some of them medically active, some inert or even noxious. Nevertheless, they have exerted a powerful and sometimes curative effect upon their users throughout the history of the healing arts. They have since become known as placebos.

What Is a Placebo?

In contemporary usage the term often carries a negative connotation and usually appears with the qualifier "nothing but." Its history goes back to its original place in the liturgical Office for the Dead in which the faithful pledges "I'll please the Lord: *Placebo Domini.*" Yet according to the

Oxford Dictionary, it was the desire to please more worldly masters that gave the term a derogatory slant. It became tantamount to playing the sycophant or the flatterer, to being a parasite. *Sic transit gloria mundi.* In the early nineteenth century, the word "placebo" came closer to its present meaning. It became an epithet given to any medicine adopted more to please than to benefit the patient.

Today "placebo" denotes any substance or therapeutic procedure "that is deliberately and knowingly used for its nonspecific psychological or physiological effect or that is used unknowingly for its presumed or believed specific effect on the patient, symptom, or illness, but which, unknown to the therapist and patient, is without specific activity for the condition being evaluated" (Shapiro 1958).

We shall see that such a wholly negative position carries the imprint of the justifiably skeptical research scientist but is often decidedly unfair to both the dispenser and the beneficiary of the placebo—particularly so when it actually does happen to "please" the patient.

The fact is that modern placebo research takes a dim view of the whole range of drugs, herbs, and other nostrums which were used at the prescientific stage of medicine. In this view, virtually all medications available to physicians of the past era were placebos and nothing but placebos. Such a sweeping statement patently goes too far. The snake root prescribed by ancient Indian folk medicine turned out to be a potent tranquilizer known today by its brand name Serpasil. Quicksilver and the opiate laudanum were successfully applied by Paracelsus, the great Renaissance physician. Even the use of hot dates described in the Old Testament as a cure for boils must have been a useful remedy. It was certainly preferable to the diverse concoctions of the medieval dirt pharmacy such as dried cow dung or preparations made of powdered toads or snakes, urine, or menstrual blood. Indeed such nostrums had been responsible for innumerable cases of lethal infections because they introduced deadly microbes into open wounds, for instance, under battle conditions. The unsuspecting dispensers and recipients of such substances fell victims of placebos whose nefarious side effects far outweighed the pious hopes and expectations of their users.

On the other end of the scale are truly inert chemical agents or procedures which demonstrate the part played by suggestion and autosuggestion, if not of other equally significant but as yet little understood principles in the origin of the placebo effect.

A classical example is the celebrated Weapons Salve of Paracelsus, which was supposed to cure wounds or other lesions when applied to parts other than those affected by the disease, or merely to the weapon which had caused the injury. Even more striking miraculous properties were attributed to what, in the seventeenth century, became known as Sir Kenelm Digby's Powder of Sympathy (1658).

Kenelm Digby was a seafarer, adventurer, and amateur scientist who claimed he had brought his remedy from India. The fact is that there was no need to import it from the "mysterious East." Its main component was copper sulphate, spiked with other inert ingredients and prepared according to secret alchemistic and astrological formulas.

Sir Kenelm demonstrated its most spectacular curative effect in a courtly setting in England when his friend, Mr. James Howell, was wounded while intervening in a duel. The wound bled profusely, though friends tried to stop the bleeding with the wounded man's garter. He survived but wound fever and gangrene set in and the king's court surgeon feared for the patient's life. This is where Digby's Powder of Sympathy came to his rescue. Sir Kenelm asked for Mr. Howell's blood-drenched garter, soaked it in a basin containing the "Powder of Vitrol." Lo and behold, Mr. Howell, standing on the other side of the room, and "not regarding at all" what Sir Kenelm was doing, "started suddenly as if he had found some strange alteration in himself. . . ." His pain was gone; it was like a "wet napkin" spread over his hand "which had taken away the inflammation."

In a second, unintended experiment, Digby took the garter out of the water to let it dry by a "great Coal fire." It was scarcely dry when Mr. Howell's servant came running to report that his master had felt a sudden burning sensation in the affected limb as if it were "betwixt coales of fire." Digby sent the servant back with a reassuring message and put the garter back into the copper solution. He reports that the messenger, on returning to his master, already found the patient free of pain. "To be brief . . . within 5–6 days the wounds were cicatrized and entirely healed. . . ." According to Sir Kenelm Digby, the incident was corroborated by several witnesses and also "registered among the observations of the Great Chancellor Bacon."

Stripped of its superstitious, magical embellishment, it is a typical example of a spectacular placebo effect. Whatever had been its actual therapeutic impact, it was obviously due to the practitioner's fanatic belief in his remedy, to the patient's trust in the practitioner's ministrations, aided by an equally trusting and readily suggestible circle of friends, well-wishers, and bystanders. Indeed, we learn from Mr. Robert Amadou's (1953) story of *La Poudre de Sympathie*, that its effects soon spread far beyond the original group of true believers to a growing number of fans, faddists, and proselytizers. In due course, the powder became a household remedy in England, France, and the rest of the Continent and held its own for the ensuing two or three decades. Yet in the end it apparently could no longer make up for its attendant failures and disappointments. Like innumerable placebos that have come before and after Kenelm Digby's panacea, it lost its initial momentum, its novelty, and its hold over the imagination of its users.

Psi Effect?

But, as I have hinted, the success story of the Powder of Sympathy suggests the presence of an additional feature, one not covered by the generally accepted modus operandi of the placebo. To the extent to which there was an element of truth in Sir Kenelm's account it was due to more than shared belief in sympathetic magic, suggestion, autosuggestion, or even Freudian transference and countertransference. In Digby's second experiment the Powder of Sympathy had apparently served as a vehicle for telepathy from the practitioner to the patient. As such, it is a typical example of countless similar stories of miraculous cures attributed to a wide variety of magic potions, talismans, amulets, or healing rituals from biblical times and classical antiquity down to Mesmer's animal magnetism, to the Baron von Reichenbach's Odic force, to Wilhelm Reich's Orgone Box, and to anecdotal accounts of absent healing by Christian Science practitioners, by Edgar Cayce, and by diverse faith healers and long-distance hypnotists in our days.

Thus, the case of the Powder of Sympathy is paradigmatic of the part played by telepathy—or PK—in what A. K. Shapiro has termed placebogenesis (1958). Yet we must realize that the Powder of Sympathy, whatever be its truth value, is an extreme case. It is the prototype of a placebo from which both actual drug effects and the familiar psychological or psychodynamic factors have been "factored out." It is a purportedly inert substance in which, like the grin of Alice's Cheshire cat, the only active ingredient left is the psi factor.

A companion piece to the Powder of Sympathy are those contemporary forms of psychic healing in which suggestion and autosuggestion have purportedly been reduced to the vanishing point. Intercessionary prayers and alleged healing at a distance are cases in point. They represent a wholly disembodied placebo, as it were. In such a scenario we would have to assume that it is the healer's mental state—particularly his therapeutic motivations dovetailing with the patient's hopes to be cured—which introduces the psi factor into the therapeutic equation. Psi, in such instances, would amount to a psychoactive placebo "without visible means of support."

Such a possibility poses a new challenge to modern placebo research. If there is reason to believe that all the magical, alchemistic, medicinal, and herbalistic concoctions of a bygone time were nothing but vehicles for the undeclared and undetected contraband of suggestion or Freudian transference emanating from the therapist, then there is reason to consider seriously whether or not a similar part is played by ESP or PK among people involved in the modern, supposedly more scientific, approach to drug treatment: psi pollution may become a source of contamination in the pharmacologist's laboratory.

Research Tool?

A brief note for the nonmedical reader on the guiding principles of placebo research may perhaps be in order at this point. There is general consensus that drug effects are invariably due to a combination of chemical and psychological factors. In order to rule out the potential part played by such psychological influences, research scientists have devised ingenious procedures known as single-blind, double-blind, or triple-blind techniques. In the single-blind technique the doctor knows what medication the patient is taking but the patient does not know. It may be an indifferent saline injection, it may be a look-alike, taste-alike tablet, a "perfect copy" of an active substance, made of lactose or some other inert flavoring ingredient, tested against a new drug or a modified version of the old one used as a control.

To exclude potential clues given away by the doctor or his associates who may prefer one agent to another and may thereby let the patient in on the game, the single-blind technique was soon abandoned in favor of the double-blind technique. In this version, the patient, the doctor, and the nursing personnel are kept in the dark as to whether the patient is receiving the drug or the placebo. The drug or the placebo is identified by code numbers, and only the project director is aware of the true state of affairs. In the triple-blind technique, possible sources of bias or attempts at self-serving evaluation of data are still further removed by delegating the process of evaluation and statistical workup to an impartial outside agency or consultant.

The fact is that these sophisticated research techniques and the accompanying statistical methods of evaluation have led to spectacular advances of modern pharmacotherapy. They have resulted in a growing list of "miracle" drugs, from antibiotics to vaccines and tranquilizers, and have given rise to the multibillion-dollar expansion of the industry during recent decades.

Nevertheless, there seems to be an occasional fly in some of the ointments produced by the manufacturers. A few of the miracle drugs proved to be no more than seven-day wonders. They seemed to lose their arcane powers over the years. Preparations which at first were hailed by the industry, the medical profession, and the patients failed to keep their promise. They met with growing criticism and had to be withdrawn by the makers—to be replaced by yet another crop of new, enthusiastically touted products. High-powered research teams have given a great deal of attention to such apparent flaws in research technique, medical application, marketing methods, and advertising campaigns. Their discussion is plainly beyond the competence of the present writer. But to the student of the history of medicine and psychotherapy, such developments have a familiar ring. Countless equally promising new nostrums or new departures in both fields have met with similar setbacks. They led into blind alleys and ultimately fell by the wayside. Like Paracelsus' Weapons Salve or Kenelm Digby's Powder of Sympathy, they proved to be nothing but passing fads. Mesmer's animal magnetism, Gall's Phrenology, or Wilhelm Reich's Orgone Box suffered the same fate. Only a small but precious minority has survived and passed the crucially important test of time.

Some critics of the pharmacological industry assert that even some products that originally passed the scrutiny of the double-blind or triple-blind technique with flying colors have not fared much better. Yet whatever explanations the experts may come up with, there is circumstantial evidence to suggest that one of the flies in the ointment is an effect of parapsychological origin. There is a striking parallel between the vicissitudes of passing fads and fashions in the healing arts on the one hand and patterns of familiar experimental findings in psychical research on the other. For instance, the widely held notion of the beginner's luck is illustrated by the successes of Rhine's and Pratt's card-calling tests with such spectacular subjects as Hubert Pearce or A. J. Linzmayer in the 1930s. However, after initially high extrachance scoring levels, their performances seemed to peter out and declined to below normal. A miniature foreshortened counterpart of such an overall trend toward diminishing returns is the characteristic decline effect in individual runs of Rhine's card-calling experiments. They, too, show the tendency of psi-determined responses to occur in short bursts or spurts of extrachance scoring, to be followed in due course by anticlimactic, lackluster performances.

There is, furthermore, the embarrassing fact that some experimental series which were successful in one laboratory turned out to be failures in another. Parapsychologists have rightly pointed out that, other things being equal, the reasons for such discrepancies have to be sought in the unalloyed attitude of hope and expectancy animating a research team that comes up with positive results, while closed minds and skeptical attitudes prevailing in another group are more likely to be conducive to failure. It will be recalled that such a thesis has been borne out by Gertrude Schmeidler's classical sheep and goat experiments (Schmeidler and McConnell 1958).

Psychoactive Agent?

Once we are prepared to make the quantum jump from experimental parapsychology back to modern placebo research, the similarity between the two widely disparate sets of observations becomes readily apparent. I pointed out in earlier chapters that telepathic leakage, paraexperimental telepathy, or doctrinal compliance due to the operation of an unsuspected psi factor are ever present sources of error in the behavioral sciences. Robert Rosenthal (1973), approaching the problem from the angle of the experimental psychologist, has described the same principle in terms of observer contamination, experimenter bias, or the Pygmalion effect. Such influences are apt to contaminate results both under laboratory conditions and in the teacher-pupil relationship in the classroom. Rosenthal has not committed himself to a telepathic interpretation of such effects. But it goes without saying that psi itself may constitute an ultimately unresolvable source of error in the study of human affairs in general.

Such considerations are particularly relevant to modern placebo research. Evidently, it is not enough to exclude the possibility of suggestion or autosuggestion, of overt or covert observer contamination, or of doctrinal compliance from a given experimental design. Double- or triple-blind techniques have certainly gone a long way toward doing so. But to the extent that a still unsuspected psi factor enters the experimental situation, it may foil the most tightly controlled, antiseptic experimental procedure. There is the team of Schmeidlerian "sheep," rooting for the product to show better results than the placebo. Undetected telepathic leakage from such a team may well tip the scale in favor of a "false positive" outcome in their otherwise well-controlled, bona fide, investigation. Still, it goes without saying that an investigator flushed by the adventure of discovery is apt to become a supersheep, surpassing all other participants in his hopes for a certain outcome.

By the same token, the first wave of high hope and expectancy, and its attending telepathic reverberations, may well sweep across the boundaries of the most tightly controlled double-blind situation. It may spread from the investigator to the nursing personnel, to the medical profession, and finally to patients and the public at large. If so, it may account for some of the striking but elusive and ultimately short-lived effects of a new product or curative procedure, followed by the failure of its attempted replication in other laboratories. In effect, its gradual loss of momentum and decline faithfully reflect the decline effects and difficulties of replication familiar to the student of psi phenomena.

How, then, can the sources of doctrinal compliance, telepathic leakage, or effects of psi-pollution be plugged in modern placebo research? Even though contamination by the psi factor may be only of minor practical importance in routine placebo research, the question is of profound theoretical interest. I noted that psi is a virtually inescapable, built-in problem in the behavioral sciences in general, comparable to Heisenberg's principle of indeterminancy in theoretical physics and quantum theory. Nevertheless, there seems to be at least one criterion which may point the way out from the dilemma of the research chemist, the M.D., and the Ph.D. The last available resort may be the test of time: the survival rate of a given remedy. While countless panaceas and widely acclaimed nostrums were swept to success by little more than their ephemeral placebo effect, the secret arcana of the attending psi factor has apparently not been enough to sustain their curative power over any length of time. This is admittedly a rather pedestrian conclusion; but it is supported by the enduring successes of such unequivocally effective drugs as quinine, aspirin, or digitalis. It is only to be hoped that modern placebo research will be able to offer scientifically more stringent criteria of objective drug actions than their capacity to endure and outlast their rivals.

But we should not allow ourselves to share at this point the research scientist's ingrained distrustful attitude toward the placebo. Clinical practice has afforded a wealth of observations indicating that the placebo, far from being the villain in the play, has indeed always been a potent therapeutic expedient in the hands of dedicated practitioners. By the same token, J. C. Whitehorn (1958), A. P. Goldstein (1962), and others have rightly pointed to the positive placebo response as a favorable prognostic sign in a given patient. In suitable cases it may obviate the need for more elaborate forms of psychotherapy. All this should go far to show that the placebo, in its chemical, physical, or supposedly "disembodied" psychic version, is by no means devoid of specific remedial properties, as implied by the definition quoted earlier. On the contrary, it specifically aims at meeting deep-seated emotional needs of its recipient, and it has amply proven its capacity to alleviate his suffering.

What, then, is the key to a beneficial placebo effect? It is contingent on several, by now familiar, psychodynamic factors. It is contingent on the doctor's authentic therapeutic motivation and on his positive expectations regarding its efficacy, meeting halfway, as it were, the patient's corresponding hopes and expectations concerning the therapist's ministrations. We have seen in the preceding chapter that a similar pattern of mutually reinforcing attitudes is in effect at the roots of every psychotherapeutic approach. It is also one of the basic predisposing and conditioning factors in a successful agent-percipient relationship. On the other hand, any hint of bad faith, of ulterior motive, of attempted deception, or of trying to put something over on the patient is bound to be counterproductive. It is detrimental to the basic trust implied by a wholesome doctor-patient relationship.

Much the same considerations apply to the placebo used in clinical practice. Inevitably, such a use is predicated on the deliberate manipulation, if not misdirection, of the patient's mind. From the patient's point of view, the placebo as a research tool is a ploy—a stratagem of deception. Paradoxically, the clinician may in turn be inclined to scoff at the patient's gullibility in accepting it at its face value. Still, like the smiling Augur of Ancient Rome, he may do so at the expense of his own integrity as a helper and healer. Basically, the placebo is as "good" or as "bad" as its dispensers and user make it. It is active or inert, depending on their interlacing hopes, wishes, and expectations. Potentially, it is a highly effective and specific psychoactive remedy mimicking the effects of proven pharmacological agents.

27

Space, Time, and Picasso

Genius: an error that by chance departs
from the ordinary.

PICASSO

MODERN MAN'S perception of his world is geared to a three-dimensional, parochial universe. For better or for worse, this is his home base and habitat. Yet on trying to advance his domain beyond its built-in limitations, he has devised a stupendous array of technological tools which extend his tentacles of action and perception into the realm of the infinitely large and the infinitesimally small.

The man of genius, if he is a creative artist, follows another path. He experiments with a virtually infinite variety of modes of existence and states of consciousness. By trial and error, if not by design, he may hit upon as yet urealized worlds of form and fantasy. He may plumb depths of meaning and insight undreamt of by his contemporaries. We have Picasso's word for it that his ways may in effect amount to "an error that by chance departs from the ordinary."

How far may he be carried by this departure? We know that Picasso's genius carried him to the farthest frontiers of spatial and temporal disintegration of familiar shapes and imagery. Some of his canvases, sculptures, and abstractions make us literally eyewitnesses to a breakthrough of the barriers of Euclidian space. The random flailings and beatings of his genius against the boundaries of classical Newtonian time are less obvious to the observer. There is no evidence of premonitions or of precognitive or retrocognitive hunches in his opus; at least, so long as we try to measure it by conventional yardsticks or timepieces there is no such evidence. Yet I propose to show that on approaching his lifework on its

271

own terms, both the future and the past are spread out before him like pages of an open book—or telescoped together at each stage of his artistic development.

Pablo Picasso was the son of Don José Ruiz, a painter, curator, and teacher at the Barcelona Academy of Fine Arts. Don José is described as a moody, retiring individual who was suffering from recurrent depressions and anxiety states. He was an accomplished craftsman, painting in the strictly representational, academic manner of the late nineteenth century. He was "a painter of dining room pictures" as·Pablo Picasso put it, "with partridges, pigeons, pheasants, and rabbits." Even in his formative years Pisacco did not conceal his disapproval, if not contempt, for this "mockery of art."

Yet one of his earliest childhood recollections, as told to his friend, secretary, and biographer, Jaime Sabartés (1948), is of one of Don José's paintings of this genre. "An enormous picture, swarming with pigeons. Imagine a cage with a hundred pigeons, with thousands and millions of pigeons. . . ." According to Sabartés, Picasso liked to tell this story "a thousand—no, a million times." He did so "after a period of fifty years and from a distance of 1,000 kilometers over and over again."

Sabarté notes that Don José's canvas was a fair-sized (though by no means "enormous") painting, showing no more than nine pigeons and a dovecote, executed in his characteristic smooth academic manner.

I myself was unable to trace the Ruiz original in the museums of Barcelona, but I found a black and white reproduction of the painting which suggests that, unless there exists another version of the canvas, Sabartés' census of pigeons also was erroneous. There are no more than three birds and a dovecote in the picture. The rest was clearly a product of Picasso's imagination.

What is behind this striking falsification of Pablo's childhood recollection? Is it merely the telling and retelling of a "tall story," exaggerating the accomplishments of a once admired idol? Is it a Freudian screen memory alluding to Don José's superior prowess—sexual, artistic, and otherwise—as it was imprinted on the little boy's mind at an early age? In either case it is an unintended tribute to the older man who had served as teacher and mentor in his formative years and had been the model after whom both Pablo's art and personality had been fashioned.

We learn from Sabartés (1948) that Don José liked to call on the boy of six or seven to help in his work. Dissecting dead pigeons for the painting of still life was part of the procedure. He would pin their severed feet on the drawing board and instruct Pablo to copy them in the required position. Under his father's expert guidance Pablo's drawings soon attained a perfection "almost unbelievable in one so young." He became a child prodigy—as had little Wolfgang Amadeus Mozart under the tutelage of his musician father. In any case, Pablo's drawings and paintings that have come down to us from his years of apprenticeship with Don José show him as a faithful follower in his father's footsteps.

Yet there is another side to the picture. Sabartés gives a few revealing glimpses of Pablo's well-nigh symbiotic relationship with his father in his childhod years.* As a little boy, he literally clung to Don José's coattails. He refused to go to school unless accompanied by his father. He had to be dragged to the schoolhouse, and the moment of parting invariably led to the same "battle scene" between them. Pablo insisted on keeping his father's paintbrush and walking stick, or even one of his pet pigeons, as pawns in order to make sure that Don José would come and fetch him from school at one o'clock. Sabartés describes the child's poor progress in the three R's, his inability to concentrate, his fear his father would fail to come and pick him up, and so on. All this became a veritable obsession to the boy. He was sick and threw up in the morning, or else he feigned illness to avoid the dreaded separation from Don José and from the security of his parental home. In short, Pablo developed unmistakable symptoms of a school phobia—the early childhood counterpart of his father's neurosis.

When Pablo moved into adolescence a radical change in the father-son relationship took place. He became increasingly rebellious against Don José. He rebelled against what by now had become the "stifling atmosphere" of the parental home; he was critical of Don José's set ways, of his philistine outlook, of his old-fashioned artistic standards, and of the classical academic tradition in general. In one of his diary letters to his parents, written at age fifteen, Pablo sketches a gang of young hoodlums engaged in a fight, with knives drawn. A middle-aged gentleman watches the fight in horror. The sketch bears the caption *Todo Revuelto*—All in Revolt.

Three years later, at the age of eighteen, the youth was ready to make the break from his ailing father, his doting mother, a nondescript older sister, and meddling uncle who had tried to interfere with his artistic education. He moved to the bohemian quarters of Barcelona and joined a group of artistic and literary friends, the forerunners of the more

---

* Contrasting patterns of the father-son relationship involving Picasso and Mozart are discussed in *Neurosis in the Family and Patterns of Psychosocial Defense* (Ehrenwald 1963).

recent beatniks, angry young men, or leftist radicals. Shortly thereafter, in defiance of his father's wishes—though perhaps with his mother's tacit approval—he exchanged his "digs" in Barcelona for the glamour of Paris and for the squalor of an unheated and poorly lighted studio in Montmartre.

In keeping with a Spanish custom, his early canvases still show the signature "Pablo Ruiz Picasso," featuring both his father's and mother's surname. But soon he was to drop the name Ruiz altogether and sign his paintings by his mother's name only. Art historians tracing his artistic development date his final break with the academic tradition from the canvas *Les Demoiselles d'Avignon*, painted in Paris in 1907. It may be no coincidence that its title contains a veiled reference to the Rue d'Avignon in Barcelona's red-light district. At the same time it ushers in his Negro or cubistic period and, in effect, stands at the threshold of one of the most revolutionary chapters in the annals of modern art.

Viewed against this background, Pablo Picasso's rebellion against his father, against both the neurotic heritage and the academic tradition he had stood for, may well have been a crucial factor in his personal as well as his artistic development. He was bound to make the break from a compulsive-controlling parent lest he remain saddled for the rest of his life, not only with the neurotic contagion but also with the sterile artistic influence emanating from his senior.

Some of his works from that period are a striking exhibition of undisguised violence and destructiveness, perhaps more so than the art of any of his predecessors, including Goya or Delacroix. Inevitably, the violence is aimed in one of two directions: either at the viewer of the work or at the perpetrator or object which served as the original stimulus for his anger—and its artistic expression. There is the dying horse with its protruding entrails in his *Guernica*. There are the mutilated bodies of human victims and the tortured forms of houses, furniture, trees, and flowers. There is the awful shape of a ferocious cat carrying a lacerated, fluttering bird (Don José's pigeon?) in his mouth. And there are the distorted shapes of a wide variety of monsters—part human, part animal—whose occasional resemblance to one of Picasso's friends or mistresses is only apt to enhance their shock value.

Violence directed against the observer is illustrated by one of his collages from 1926. It represents a guitar and a coarse dishcloth perforated by nails "whose points stick out mercilessly from the picture." According to Penrose (1958), Picasso had originally thought of embedding razor blades at the edge of the canvas so that whoever tried to lift it would cut his hands with it. It is unlikely that such a contraption would have brought him the acclaim of art critics of *Le Monde* or the *New York Times.* But it would certainly have received the approval of a Polynesian practitioner of black magic.

Elsewhere I have tried to trace the origin of Picasso's thinly veiled violent trend to his underlying neurosis, or to what are here described as flaw-determined factors (1963). It too may have been conditioned by his lifelong love and hate affair with his father: by his lingering admiration, combined with his overt rebellion against the painter of "dining room pictures," his "mockery of art," and the whole academic tradition he had stood for. The son's rebellion against the father's well-ordered universe of conventional shapes, colors, and contours, handed down to him on a silver platter, as it were, was perhaps the major source of Picasso's iconoclastic fervor. He literally hacked to pieces Don José's representations of human and animal forms, of animate and inanimate objects. He made mincemeat of them all—including his own sensory impressions. He wrought havoc with the laws of perspective and with space, time, and causality itself.

This radical disorganization of spatial relationships—of Euclidian space itself—is in effect one of the more revolutionary aspects of his genius. Before Picasso's foray into non-Euclidian space the traditional artist was encased in a claustrophobic glass bell, as it were. His world was set apart from all other potential spaces, visual, tactile, or kinesthetic. Pablo Picasso broke the glass and it splintered all around him in a dizzying array of new shapes, crystalline forms, and colors springing to life like new mutations in the geneticist's laboratory.

I hinted that there is another aspect of Picasso's challenge to the three Kantian categories of space, time, and causality: his well-nigh somnambulistic forays both forward and backward in the time dimension.

Such a proposition is illustrated by what amounts to the prophetic self-fulfillment of his story of the "thousands, if not millions of doves" swarming on the "enormous" canvas painted by the "red-bearded giant" of his childhood years. Psychoanalytically speaking, this can well be taken as a screen memory pertaining to the past and expressing his need to identify with his omnipotent father. But it also contains an unmistakable precognitive element: a "memory" pertaining to his own future. Emulating Don José's example, trying to catch up with him and ultimately surpassing the accomplishments of his idol may well have remained Pablo's secret goal. This may account for the fact that drawing, carving, painting, and sculpting doves and pigeons in many and varied forms and media was one of his lifelong foibles. It is as though the seed—or the avian image—planted in the child's mind, was to grow and multiply with the passage of years, hankering for endless self-expression.

The fact is that Picasso has literally attained his goal as far as the imagery of the thousands if not millions of pigeons is concerned. In 1949, some fifty years after the time of the story told to Sabartés, he was asked to design a poster for a peace conference organized by the Communist Party in Paris. It was for that occasion that he prepared a wholly representational lithograph of a white dove. It was subsequently printed in thousands of copies, was posted on the walls and billboards of numerous cities of Europe, and even won a medal sponsored by the Philadelphia Museum of Art. Since then Picasso's doves of peace have flown all over the world. They were reproduced in Christmas cards, in pottery and ceramics and engraved on postage stamps in China and other Communist countries. The dove was hoisted in place of the American eagle atop the Maine Monument in Havana, and in the 1960's a New York City art shop offered a pastel drawing of the bird for $4,000. Since then its price may well have risen tenfold.

Yet while it is true to say that Picasso's childhood memory of the "future" had exerted a profound influence on his subsequent development as an artist in his own right, art historians have called attention to the striking resemblance of some of his sculptures to cycladic and early Minoan figurines, dating back to 2400–2200 B.C. Some of his etchings and drawings could have been lifted from the face of an ancient Etruscan vase. In a similar vein, his celebrated series of *The Minotaur, The Artist in his Studio* are imbued with the spirit of his Mediterranean heritage. It is as though archetypal or mythological themes that had been lying dormant in his unconscious had been reawakened and brought back to life in the work of a twentieth century master. Nothing could serve as a more dramatic illustration of the stratified nature of the human mind than this astonishing spatiotemporal spread and diversity of his creative output. It is in effect a paradigm of multiple spaces and time perspectives superimposed on each other in one vast overarching non-Euclidian montage. It brings into the orbit of a single transcending mind the remote past, the present, and the emerging future. Yet it also suggests that rudimentary vestiges of things long forgotten, as well as prefigurative "memories" of things yet to come, may lie dormant in all of us, even though only a gifted artist or psychic may be able to draw them into the orbit of conscious awareness.

Thus, despite the uniqueness of Pablo Picasso's artistic output—with its intimation of timelessness and self-transcendence—it is paradigmatic of the human situation. His potential for creation and destruction (and for mobilizing psi abilities in the process) is the same as yours or mine, only more so.

It is true that no demonstrable psi factor has ever been discovered in his opus. But if there is some truth in Picasso's claim that he did not imitate Nature but "worked as she does," his chisel and his brush may well have been guided and informed by a principle closely akin to psi. If so, it would be idle to ask whether it was he who used this principle to do his bidding or if it was nature which used his genius—including his psi abilities—for the trials and errors of his artistic creations.

28

What Is It For?

CHAMPIONS of a new movement are wont to overstate their case; peddlers of a new remedy, from snake oil to wonder drugs, tend to oversell their wares. Enthusiasts of "mind over matter" or of the liberation of "untapped resources of your mind" through biofeeedback, control of alpha waves, transcendental meditation, or Kirlian photography are doing their best to discredit the solid achievements of parapsychology in recent decades.

To one who can recall the growing momentum of the early psychoanalytic movement, its breaking up into splinter groups, and Freud's warning against "wild analysis," the new developments in psychical research have a familiar ring. They can be described as "wild parapsychology." It is a fad which increasingly threatens to become the preserve of cranks and charlatans. Psi phenomena, as conceived by the cultist, the faddist, and the devotee, are reminiscent of the *mana* of the Polynesian aborigine, of Mesmer's animal magnetism, of Reichenbach's *Odic* force, and of Reich's Orgone energies. Their scope is supposed to be virtually unlimited. They embrace past, present, and future. They reach to the deepest recesses of inner space and to the farthest corners of the universe. They can penetrate Faraday cages and the stratosphere. They can cure illness and defy death. Psi can pinpoint the seat of an undiagnosed illness or locate a hidden treasure. It can predict earthquakes, the fluctuations of the stock market, or the winner of the Kentucky Derby.

But we have seen that in practice, ESP is subject to spatiotemporal scatter. The accuracy of Mrs. Dixon's or Gerard Croiset's prognostications is in fact severely limited. Telepathic or clairvoyant perceptions rarely score a bull's eye on the target. Faith may be capable of moving mountains, but Rhine's PK tests with dice thrown down a chute have yielded at best fitful scores above chance expectations. ESP as well as PK is subject to what I called the principle of frustrated volition. Like the sorcerers in the fairy tale, even the most successful psychics do not make their fortunes by dint of their paranormal power, and the professionals among them have to sell their services to the general public. Attempts at methodical training of psi abilities through hypnosis, biofeedback, or Tart's *Espatester* (1966), are still controversial and claims of their utilization in casino gambling (Brier and Tyminski 1970) are apparently based more on theoretical projections and *post hoc* analysis of an ingenious sampling technique than on what may be no more than beginner's luck at the game table.

In short, there is still little hard evidence that psi abilities can be mobilized and made use of for the same utilitarian purposes as the standard perceptual, behavioral, or cognitive resources of the individual.

However, in trying to evaluate the uses of psi abilities, a basic distinction has to be made between deliberate attempts to apply them in human affairs, on the one hand, and nature's marshaling of psi phenomena in the workshop of life and in the evolutionary process, on the other. Strictly speaking, we have to distinguish between man's goals and purposes and nature's apparent uses of psi—that is, of information transmission on the psi level—comparable to her "uses" of RNA and DNA in genetics and molecular biology.

A paramount example of nature's apparent use of psi functions is the early symbiotic relationship between mother and child. It is true that the most impressive findings pointing in that direction are observations made under pathological conditions such as a concerned mother seeking to compensate for existing deficiency or "minus function" of her baby—that is, trying to function vicariously, as it were, in his behalf. But we have seen that in a few cases of this order the part played by ESP has been borne out by controlled experiments. The concerted evidence of these observations suggests that the mothers of Ilga K., of Little Bo, or the Cambridge Boy, sought to come to their aid by using diverse means of nonverbal communication—above all, telepathy. If this is true, telepathy in these cases indeed had positive survival value—or at least sociocultural advantage—for both mother and child.

Another group of observations is of neurotic children acting out their parents' repressed hostile-aggressive impulses as though they were responding to a combination of telepathic and other nonverbal cues emanating from them. Such children may be steered to delinquent or otherwise antisocial behavior by remote control, as it were, in a way which is difficult to account for solely by reference to the conventional channels of communications. Alternatively, they may put up a determined resistance to influences of this kind. They may try to ward off both "ordinary" neurotic contagion from their parents and what amounts to psi pollution emanating from them. In such cases, the part played by the psi factor is evidently just as important as in our previous examples, although in the latter it is plainly maladaptive. In the extreme case, it may set the stage for a relentless struggle between a purportedly "schizophrenogenic" mother and her offspring suffering from childhood psychosis of the autistic or symbiotic type.

I noted that at an earlier stage—and under thoroughly normal conditions—mother-child interaction follows the same pattern. Yet it is a stage at which psi is more difficult to detect by reference to clear-cut telepathic tracer effects or other stringent criteria: a telepathic proto-message, command, or injunction has no numerical markings; it is not conceptualized and does not wave a red flag at the observer. Nevertheless, its biological significance seems to be in inverse proportion to its obtrusiveness, or manifest information content. ESP, in the postpartum period, I stated, is a direct continuation of the physiological regulatory functions which safeguard the smooth operation of the maternal and fetal organism during intrauterine life. As such, it helps to bridge the communication gap existing between the two during the period of "postpartum gestation." Hence, it has positive survival value for the child and the human species in general.

Another argument pointing to the biological survival value of ESP was put forward by Ullman, Krippner, and Vaughan (1973) at the Maimonides Dream Laboratory in Brooklyn. They noted that the rapid eye movements (or REM stage) of sleep and such dissociated states as trance, relaxation, distraction, or fantasy tend to create "an area of vulnerability" in the individual. As a result he is less able to cope with demands the external world makes upon him. It is this vulnerability—what I described as *minus function*—and the need for its compensation which call for a novel "constructive or creative solution to make up for the existing deficiency" (Ehrenwald 1948). Ullman, Krippner, and Vaughan suggest that psi is one of the options available to the individual to achieve this end without resorting to neurotic or otherwise maladaptive defenses. Psi may represent a creative thrust in the direction of establishing a new relation with the outside world, and helps to mobilize "new resources of strength from within" (p. 226).

Jule Eisenbud, in the concluding chapter of *Psi and Psychoanalysis*, assigns an even more significant function to psi. "The goals psi serves are primarily not those of the individual at all, but of an ascending hierarchy of interrelated systems" (1970a, p. 337). Metaphorically speaking, Eisenbud sees in psi the equivalent of the vegetative nervous system in nature at large. In a similar vein Alister Hardy (1965), the noted British zoologist, views telepathy as an important factor in the evolutionary process in nature at large. It is responsible for the information carried by the flow of the "Stream of Life," for the manifestation of the group mind in animal societies, and for the purposeful organization of both structure and behavior of living beings in general.

The English biologist J. L. Randall (1971) takes a no less sanguine view of psi. He sees the psi factor as an organizing, patterning principle in nature. It is responsible for communication on the organismic, cellular, and molecular level, superior to man's analytic intellect. It pervades the antientropic, organic enclave in the universe and is capable of infusing meaning, purpose, and information into inanimate matter. In this respect, its organizing effects are comparable with the symbiotic or psychophysical gradient as it is conceived here (Chapter 19).

But I emphasized that on the level of our standard, workaday experience, psi is fallible: its information content is limited and its motor proficiency undependable. I noted that even the best clairvoyant's perceptions are rarely "clear" and that even the most successful healer's exploits are thwarted by incurable illness and death.

Indeed, excessive reliance on psi abilities, on hunches, flairs, or intuitions is often counterproductive. An ominous example is Hitler's self-destructive personal myth and the downfall of the Thousand-Year Reich. The annals of history are strewn with prophecies which failed to come true and with catastrophic events of major proportions which no Tiresias, Nostradamus, or Mrs. Dixon had foreseen. No voice was heard in the fall of 1970 predicting the apocalyptic tidal wave and flooding that struck East Pakistan, wiping out hundreds of thousands of people. On the other hand, prophets foretelling the sinking into the ocean of the shoreline of Adelaide, Australia, or of California failed hopelessly.

By the same token, alleged attempts by the Russians to enlist the aid of sensitives for "paranormal" spying have apparently not come to fruition. Committees of "psychics" have not as yet been able to replace earth-orbiting spy satellites. In a similar vein, all attempts to marshal the gifts of sundry professional clairvoyants to help German military intelligence during World War II proved to be either a hoax or fabrications of Goebbels' propaganda machine. Even Uri Geller takes a dim view of having his formidable PK abilities exploited for the exigencies of warfare. On the positive side, the record of the unusually gifted Dutch clairvoyant Gerard Croiset is spotty at best, as far as unraveling assorted murder cases or locating missing persons is concerned. Those in which he was most successful involved persons who were of special emotionally charged interest to him. Parapsychologists have not as yet evolved a "private eye" endowed with a routinely successful "second sight."

Spotty records of this order do not invalidate such occasional precognitive feats as those recorded by J. W. Dunne (1927), Ian Stevenson (1970), and a few other investigators. They rather indicate that motivations geared to a conventional utilitarian reward-versus-punishment-oriented approach, or to the time-and-space-bound goals and aspirations sanctioned by our culture, simply do not apply to the psi level of functioning. We have to realize that the applications of psi must not be confounded with their *exploitation* by Western man's compulsive pursuit of utilitarian goals and material values. Psi is not one of his natural resources like electricity or atomic energy which can be harnessed at will in order to increase the gross national product or to bolster civic morale. Its value cannot be calibrated against a scale of economic indicators or even the sanitation code. It is an innate potential present in the newborn child pressing for new ways of self-actualization. It is a potential which the adult is able to learn and, hopefully, to integrate with the rest of his personality resources under a set of specific, well-defined conditions only: he can do so in response to compelling needs, psychological exigencies or in the pursuit of novel, self-transcending goals. It is such goals which justify its uses and provide its existential validation.

Yet viewed in the broader evolutionary perspective, psi is more than that. It is a groping attempt to spawn ever new forms of adaptation, comparable to the nonrepresentational artist's quest for unprecedented shapes, spatial configurations, color combinations, and modes of experience. It is a rehearsal of things to come rather than a throwback; it is futuristic rather than archaic. Hence, it has a close connection with creative activity and artistic expression.

It is readily understood that under these circumstances psi abilities—like love, ecstasy, or peak experiences—cannot be "willed" or coaxed into action. Whether or not experiments with biofeedback, with sensory deprivation, or with training in the self-control of a subject's electrical brain activity will bring us closer to mastery over psi only the future will tell.

I pointed out in Chapter 20 that, on the standard level of experience, man is capable of exercising far-reaching control over his sensory input and motor output. He can turn selective attention to a specific segment of his social and physical environment. He can pinpoint his actions toward a chosen target in the outside world. He has, at least subjectively speaking, a considerable measure of freedom to take stock of his options and make his decisions. Yet whenever he tries to shift his attention—or mode of existence—to the psi level, his freedom of action and the dependability of his perceptions diminish by leaps and bounds—perhaps to the vanishing point.

The postulated biological advantages are not, however, the only functions assigned to psi phenomena. At a later stage of the parent-child relationship they are apt to play an increasingly important role in the process of acculturation. A typical example is the six-month-old baby of a demanding mother who seems to "guess" without further ado what he is supposed to do the very first time he is put on the potty. The same is true for a wide variety of do's and don'ts, instructions and prohibitions signaled to a child on both the standard and the psi level of communication at the same time. They include telepathic clues that may be helpful in his acquistion of language, in his seemingly intuitive grasp of syntax and grammar reflecting as they do all the idiomatic nuances of the speech patterns picked up from his parents. The fact is that he can do so even though he has never before been exposed to the same syntactical or grammatical configuration. Professor Noam Chomsky (1975) has attributed this capacity to an inborn quality of the human mind. If so, this innate "linguistic competence" may well receive an added telepathic boost. As a result, subtle parental influences brought to bear on the psi level would help the child to use the right or, for that matter, the "wrong," turn of phrase or grammatical construction, in keeping with their example or their linguistic habits or in response to their unverbalized commands and expectations. Similar considerations apply to the transmission of moral values—the grammar and syntax of ethics, if you like.

While such uses of psi in learning and acculturation are largely a matter of conjecture, the part played by the psi factor in the teacher-pupil relationship has been confirmed by a number of experimental observations reported by American, Dutch, German, and East Indian parapsychologists. Tests carried out under either telepathic or clairvoyant conditions yielded significantly higher scores whenever preliminary inquiry, made under proper safeguards, revealed mutual "liking" between teacher and pupil, as opposed to lower scores or psi-missing in the case of mutual "dislike."

In a similar vein, the influence of teacher expectations on the pupil's classroom performance is an established fact of educational psychology. In the long run such observations may either enhance or stultify the child's intellectual growth and development. The psychologist Robert Rosenthal, in his studies of observer contamination in the classroom or in clinical test situations has made the same point. He described their impact as the "Pygmalion effect" (1973). Here, again, the part played by ESP is diffi-cult to separate from the gamut of subliminal cues, unconscious expres-sive movements, and the like which may serve as either operant rein-forcements or hindering factors.

There is one more aspect of psi phenomena which goes beyond the scope of our conventional notions of communication, verbal or nonverbal, of the transmission on the conceptual or preconceptual plane of messages, or of bits of information from an agent to a percipient. The very occur-rence of psi brings us face to face with a new transpersonal picture of man, connected with his fellowmen and indeed with all living beings, past, present, and future, by what general systems theory would describe as a telepathic feedback loop. Viewed in this light, telepathy could serve as a cybernetic regulatory device designed to maintain a modicum of ecological homeostasis—if not of Confucian harmony—in society at large. It would be possessed of an added, hitherto unsuspected biological sur-vival advantage, extending beyond the early symbiotic stage, after all. It could monitor the vital signs of major human and transhuman ecological systems and help to initiate the necessary regulatory maneuvers char-acteristic of living organisms and social aggregations. "Animal psi" in particular may be involved in the reproduction control of such endan-gered species as the coyote of the western United States and southern Canada. A similar factor, working in the opposite direction, may have a hand in contemporary society's growing permissiveness toward homo-sexuals who refuse to procreate and in the growing proliferation of hip-pies, flower children, or "street people" who refuse to contribute to indus-trial production or population explosion. It may even help to account for the religious doctrines of self-denial and asceticism which generations of sages have been preaching to the teeming masses of the Indian subconti-nent to stem the tide of untrammeled population growth.

Such a vast, indeed unlimited, extension of the potential reach of psi admittedly runs counter to the principle of individuation and the sharp delineation of objects upon which our familiar notions of mental functioning are based. It is predicated on the assumption of a primordial unity of creation from which all things animate and inanimate, from cosmic nebulae, rocks, and protein molecules to plants, animals, and man, have evolved. It is a unity which has been anticipated by the Hindu doctrine of *atman,* by the dictum *tat wam asi* (this art thou too). It has been enunciated by mystics of all ages trying to describe their ineffable experiences of oneness with the universe. It is also a notion which modern theoretical physics, cosmology, and evolutionary theory have spelled out for us in no uncertain terms (LeShan 1973).

Do these considerations imply that psi should forever remain outside the reach of conscious experience and unresponsive to attempts at deliberate control? Viewed in the evolutionary perspective, the slow and laborious development of upright gait by the forerunners of *Homo erectus* may be an auspicious precedent. Initially, this complex motor skill was certainly not "willed" by the hominids descending from the trees of the Pliocene era. Still, one step, evolutionary or otherwise, led to another, until the erect posture and walking on two legs became a smooth, semi-automatic performance, tending toward the same measure of de-automatization and deliberate volition as the skills of a ball player or violinist.

The same may be true for man's present rudimentary control over psi phenomena. The difference is that while the upright gait is possessed of marked biological survival value, it has yet to be proven that psi functions have a comparable survival value once the child is past the symbiotic stage.

But this does not mean that man does not keep trying. We have seen that sustained attention to psi incidents may help the therapist to attain an existential position favorable to their occurrence and facilitate their integration with the rest of his personality. In a similar vein, modern experimental parapsychologists seem to be a step or two ahead of the evolutionary game. Their ratio of success shows at least a slight improvement over their archaic or even 19th century predecessors.

More recent experiments in diverse altered states of consciousness or with sensory deprivation in the *ganzfeld* have taken a major step toward producing an increased yield in ESP or PK scores. Another important advance is Charles Tart's (1976) attempts at improving performance through immediate feedback, informing the subject whether he has hit or missed his target. Tart reports that subjects with a purported innate talent for ESP greatly benefit from such a procedure. While the dreary routine of traditional card-calling tests tends to extinguish whatever abilities a person may have had in the first place, immediate feedback provides a true learning experience and improved performance.

I noted in Chapter One that Tart's results are open to such alternative interpretations as telepathic contagion, cluster effects, or doctrinal compliance. Still, whatever be the merits of his theories, his method does hold the promise of helping to develop a new breed of high-scoring ESP subjects—at least in the laboratory setting. Whether or not it will be able to transfer their ESP abilities from lab to life, from the experimental to the experiential plane, is another question. In Part Three, I reviewed the evidence pertaining to the part played by the right hemisphere in the processing of ESP impressions and in initiating or releasing PK impulses. The right side of the brain, I stated, presides over the individual's hunches and intuitions. It is the poet, the artist, the dreamer, the Listener with the Third Ear, perhaps the principal recipient and originator of psi. In this capacity it functions as the counterpart and junior partner of the left hemisphere, which presides over man's linguistic skills and analytic intelligence. It specializes in reading, writing, and arithmetic and has apparently been conditioned to do so over thousands of years of cultural development. Yet, it seems to be dead set against psi.

But the question is whether the right hemisphere will be able to catch up with its senior partner and match its accomplishments on the psi level of experience? Will Tart's or Honorton's attempts at teaching a crash course in ESP succeed in accomplishing in a lifetime what it had taken *Homo sapiens* millennia to attain? Will their techniques merely manage to breed a new generation of champion card guessers and long-distance spoon benders (whose exploits are eminently suitable for statistical scrutiny in the best tradition of the left hemisphere)—or will the new approach lead to a true breakthrough to an authentic psi experience and its ultimate integration with modern man's scientific outlook and technical know-how? Will he be able to use his new dimension of freedom, his expanded behavioral repertoire, and his increased conscious awareness in the service of greater mastery over his own nature? In short, will it usher in the millennium of a better balanced and enriched existential position of modern man?

Plato's celebrated fable of the Charioteer and his Two Winged Horses comes to mind at this point. The horse on his right represents the noble side of the soul; the horse on the left symbolizes man's savage instinctual drives, his animal nature. It stands for what Freud labeled as the id, while he described the Charioteer and his precarious control over the two horses as the virtually powerless ego. The present context calls for a new reading of both Plato's and Freud's metaphors. The two winged horses stand for the left and the right hemispheres. They are locked in a ceaseless struggle with the raw, untrammeled forces dwelling in man's primitive, phylogenetically oldest neural centers, in what neuranatomists and their popularizers have dubbed the reptilian brain.

Who, then, is the mysterious Charioteer of the Platonian and Freudian troika? Who, in the last analysis, holds the reins and curbs the horses when they are unruly? Who is the ultimate decision maker and asker of questions? Who or what is responsible for the apparent shifting of gears from left hemispheric to right hemispheric dominance and gives the cue for the attending existential shift from our "ordinary" Euclidian to the "nonordinary" non-Euclidian mode of existence? These are questions that we cannot yet attempt to answer.

The psychiatric validation and interpretation of the ESP experience presented in the preceding chapters has thus added one more enigma to a mystery that has been bandied about between churchmen, philosophers, and scientists for thousands of years. But at the same time it has thrown the problem into sharper perspective. It breathes new life into the ancient metaphors of man-made gods, devils, and demiurges intervening in human affairs. Paradoxically, it is also apt to impart a spark of divinity, if not paranoid grandeur, on man himself. Hopefully, the implications of such a broader perception of psi will be taken up in a future volume.

REFERENCES

Abbott, E. A. 1884, 1952. *Flatland.* New York: Dover Publications.

Allport, G. 1960. *Personality and social encounter.* Boston: Beacon Press.

Amadou, R. 1953. *La poudre de sympathie.* Paris: G. Nizet.

Anderson, M., and White, R. 1956. Teacher-pupil attitudes and clairvoyance test results. *J. Parapsychol.* Sept., pp. 141–57.

Arieti, S. 1955. *Interpretation of schizophrenia.* New York: Brunner.

Artemidorus von Daldis. 1965. *Traumbuch,* trans. S. Krauss. Basel: Schwabe and Co.

Auerbach, E. 1966. The Prophets. In *The Jews in their land,* ed. D. Ben Gurion. New York: Doubleday.

Bakan, P. 1976. The right brain is the dreamer. *Psychology Today,* vol. 10, no. 6:66–68.

Balint, M. 1955. Notes on parapsychology and parapsychological healing. *Internat. J. Psychoanal.* 36.

Becker, E. 1973. *The denial of death.* New York: Macmillan.

Beloff, J. 1970. ESP: the search for a physiological index. *J. Soc. Psychic. Res.,* vol. 47, no. 761:403–17.

Bender, H. 1940. Zur Nachuntersuchung des Falles Ilga K. *Zeitschr. f. angewandte Psychologie und Charakterkunde* 58:317–42.

———. 1957. Praecognition im qualitativen Experiment, Zur Methodik der "Platzexperimente" mit dem Sensitiven Gerard Croiset. *Zeitscher. Parapsychol. Grenzgebiete* 6:59–84.

———. 1969. New developments in poltergeist research. *Proc. Parapsychol. Assoc.* 6:81–102.

———. 1974. Modern poltergeist research: a plea for an unprejudiced approach. In *New directions in parapsychology,* ed. J. Beloff. London: Paul Elek.

Benson, H., Beary, J. F., and Carol, M. P. 1975. Meditation and the relaxation response. In *Psychiatry and mysticism,* ed. S. R. Dean. Chicago: Nelson-Hall.

Berendt, H. C. 1974. Uri Geller pro and con. In *The amazing Uri Geller,* ed. M. Ebon. New York: Signet Books, New American Library.

Berger, H. 1940. *Psyche.* Jena: G. Feister Verlag.

Bergson, H. 1913. Presidential address. *Proc. Soc. Psychic. Res.* 27.

Bogen, J. E. 1969. The other side of the brain, I, II, III. *Bulletin,* Los Angeles Neurological Societies, 34:3.

Booth, G. 1973. Psychobiological aspects of "spontaneous" regression of cancer. *J. Amer. Acad. Psychoanal.* vol. 1, no. 3:303–17.

Boyer, P., and Nissenbaum, H. 1974. *Salem possessed: the social origins of witchcraft.* Cambridge, Mass.: Harvard University Press.

Braud, W., and Braud, L. W. 1974. The psi-conducive syndrome: free response GESP performance following evocation of "left-hemispheric versus right-hemispheric" functioning. In *Research in parapsychology,* ed. Roll and Morris. Metuchen, N.J.: Scarecrow Press.

Bridgman, P. N. 1952. *The nature of some of our physical concepts.* New York: Philosophical Library.

References

Brier, R., and Tyminski, W. V. 1970. Psi application. *Parapsychology Today,* ed. J. B. Rhine and Robert Brien. New York: Citadel Press.

Broad, C. D. 1962. *Lectures on psychical research.* New York: Humanities Press.

Bromberg, N. 1971. Hitler's character and its development: further observations. *Amer. Imago* 28:4.

Broughton, R. S. 1975. Psi and the two halves of the brain. *J. Soc. Psychic. Res,.* vol. 48, no. 765:133–47.

————. 1976. Possible brain hemisphere laterality effects on ESP performance. *J. Soc. Psychic. Res., vol.* 48, no. 770:384–99.

Brown, G. S. 1957. *Probability and scientific inference.* London: Longmans, Green.

Brugmans, H. J. F. W. 1922. Une communication sur les expériences telepathic au laboratoire de psychologie à Groningen, etc. In *Le Compte Rendu du Premier Congrès International des Recherches Psychiques,* pp. 396–408. Copenhagen.

Bruner, J. S. 1968. On voluntary acting and its hierarchical structure. *Beyond reductionism,* ed. A. Koestler and J. R. Smythies. Boston: Beacon Press.

Bruner, J. S., and Postman, L. 1949. Studies in perceptual defense. In *Handbook of abnormal psychology,* ed. H. J. Eysenck. 1961, New York: Basic Books.

Brunswick, E. 1952. The conceptual framework of psychology. *International Encyclopedia of Unified Science.* Chicago: University of Chicago Press.

Buber, M. 1963. *Israel and the world.* New York: Shocken Books.

Bucke, R. M. 1964. *Cosmic Consciousness,* 22nd ed. New York: E. P. Dutton.

Bullock, A. 1962. *Hitler, a study in tyranny.* New York: Harper Torch Books.

Burlingham, D. 1935. Child analysis and the mother. *Psychoanal. Quart.* 4:69–92.

Burr, G. L. 1914. *Narratives of the witchcraft cases, 1648–1706.* New York: Scribners.

Burt, C. 1968. *Psychology and psychical research, the seventh Frederick Myers memorial lecture.* London: Society for Psychical Research.

Bychowski, G. 1956. The ego and the introjects. *Psychoanal. Quart.* 25:11–36.

————. 1965. *Diktatoren.* Munich: Szezeny Verlag.

Carington, W. 1947. *Telepathy, an outline of its facts, theory, and implications.* London: Methuen and Co.

Carrington, H. 1909. *Eusapia Palladino and her phenomena.* New York: B. W. Dodge and Co.

Carter, M. E., and McGarey, W. A. 1972. *Edgar Cayce on healing.* New York: Paperback Library.

Castaneda, C. 1968. *The teachings of Don Juan: a Yaqui way of knowledge.* Berkeley: University of California Press.

Chomsky, N. 1975. *Reflections on language.* New York: Pantheon Books.

Cox, W. E. 1965. The effect of PK on electromechanical systems. *J. Parapsychol.* 29.

Crookall, R. 1961. *The study and practice of astral projection.* London: Aquarian Press.

Dale, L. A., White, R., and Murphy, G. A. 1962. A selection of cases from a recent survey of spontaneous ESP phenomena. *J. Amer. Soc. Psychic. Res.* 56:3–47.

Dean, E. D. 1962. The plethysmograph as an indication of ESP. *J. Soc. Psychic Res.* 41.

Dean, S. R. 1975. *Psychiatry and mysticism.* Chicago: Nelson-Hall.

Delgado, J. 1969. Radio-controlled behavior. *N.Y. State Journal of Medicine,* Feb. 1, 1969, pp. 413–17.

Demos, J. 1970. Underlying themes in the witchcraft of seventeenth century New England. *Amer. Hist. Rev.* 1:35.

Devereux, G., ed. 1953. *Psychoanalysis and the occult.* New York: International Universities Press.

Digby, K. 1658. *A late discourse,* trans. R. White. address to the University of Montpellier, London.

Dingwall, E. J., ed. 1968. *Abnormal hypnotic phenomena, a survey of nineteenth century cases,* vols. 1–4. London: J. and A. Churchill.

Dixon, N. 1971. *Subliminal perception, the nature of a controversy.* New York: McGraw-Hill.

Dodds, E. R. 1964. *The Greeks and the irrational.* Berkeley: University of California Press.

Domarus, M. 1962. *Hitler's Reden,* vol. 2. Neustadt an der Aisch.

Drake, R. M. 1938. An unusual case of ESP. *J. Parapsychol.* 2.

Dunne, J. W. 1927. *An experiment with time.* London: Faber and Faber.

Eastman, M. 1962. Out-of-the-body experiences. *Proc. Soc. Psychic. Res.* 53:287–309.

Ebon, M., ed. 1975. *The amazing Uri Geller.* New York: New American Library, Signet Books.

Eccles, J. 1965. *The brain and the unity of conscious experience.* New York: Cambridge University Press.

Ehrenwald, J. 1931a. Anosognosie und Depersonalisation. *Nervenarzt* 13:681–87.

———. 1931b. Störung der Zeitlichen und Räumlichen Orientierung, etc. *Zeitschr. f. d. Ges. Neurologie u. Psychiatrie* 132:525.

———. 1948. *Telepathy and medical psychology.* New York: W. W. Norton.

———. 1951. Precognition in dreams? *Psychoanal. Rev.,* vol. 38, no. 1:726–43.

———. 1954. *New dimensions of deep analysis.* New York: Grune and Stratton. Second edition: New York: Arno Press, 1975.

———. 1955. Principes et premiers enseignemants de l'approche psychoanalytique. In: *La science et le paranormal,* R. Amadou, ed., Paris. I.M.I. 1 place Wagram.

———. 1963. *Neurosis in the family and patterns of psychosocial defense: a study of psychiatric epidemiology.* New York: Hoebner Division, Harper and Row.

———. 1966. *Psychotherapy: myth and method.* New York: Grune and Stratton.

———. 1974. Family dynamics and the transgenerational treatment effect. In *Group therapy,* ed. L. R. Wolberg and M. L. Aronson. New York: Stratton International.

———. 1976. *The history of psychotherapy: from healing magic to encounter.* New York: Jason Aronson.

———. 1977. Psi phenomena, hemispheric dominance, and the existential shift. Paper read to the annual meeting of the Parapsychology Association in Paris.

Eisenbud, J. 1970. *Psi and psychoanalysis.* New York: Grune and Stratton.

———. 1967. *The world of Ted Serios.* New York: William Morrow.

———. 1973. Transatlantic experiments in precognition with Gerald Croiset. *J. Amer. Soc. Psychic. Res.* 67:1–25.

Eliade, M. 1964. *Shamanism.* Bollingen series. New York: Pantheon Books, Random House.

Erikson, E. 1950. *Childhood and society.* New York: W. W. Norton.

Evans-Pritchard, E. E. 1937. *Witchcraft, oracles, and magic among the Azande.* Oxford: Clarendon Press.

Everson, T. C., and Cole, W. H. 1966. *Spontaneous regression in cancer.* Philadelphia: Saunders.

Eysenck, H. J., ed. 1961. *Handbook of abnormal psychology.* New York: Basic Books.

Fenichel, O. 1945. *The psychoanalytic theory of neuroses.* New York: W. W. Norton.

Ferenczi, S. 1950. Stages in the development of the sense of reality. In *Sex and psychoanalysis.* New York: Basic Books.

Fischer, O. 1924. *Experiments with Raffael Scherman.* Prague.

Fitzherbert, J. 1960. The role of extrasensory perception in early childhood. *J. Med. Sci.* 106.

References

Fodor, N. 1947. Telepathy in analysis. In Devereux (1953).

————. 1959. *On the trail of the poltergeist*. London: Arco.

Fox, G. S. 1968. *Science and justice: the Massachusetts Witchcraft trials*. Baltimore: Johns Hopkins Press.

Franklin, W. 1975. Fracture surface physics indicating teleneural interaction. *New Horizons*, vol. 2, no. 1:8–13.

Freud, A. 1966. *Normality and pathology in childhood*. London: Hogarth Press.

————. 1922. *Beyond the pleasure principle*. International Psychoanalytic Library No. 4. New York: Boni and Liveright.

Freud, S. 1932. Eine Teufelsneurose im siebzehnten Jahrhundert. *Collected Paper*, vol. 10. Lepzig, Vienna: Intern. Psychoanalyt. Verlag.

————. 1959. Psychoanalytic notes upon an autobiographical account of a case of paranoia. *Collected Papers*, vol. 3. New York: Basic Books.

Fromm-Reichmann, F. 1950. *Principles of intensive psychotherapy*. Chicago: University of Chicago Press.

Fuller, J. G. 1974. *Arigo: surgeon of the rusty knife*. New York: Crowell.

Gazzaniga, M. S. 1967. The split brain in man. *Scientific American* 508, August 1967, pp. 24–29.

Geller, Uri. 1975. *My story*. New York: Praeger.

Gilot, E., and Kale, C. 1964. *Life with Picasso*. New York: Signet Books, New American Library.

Girden, E. et al. 1964. A review of psychokinesis (PK). *Internat. J. Parapsychol.* vol. 6, no. 1:26–137.

Goldstein, A. P. 1962. *Therapist-patient expectations in psychotherapy*. New York: Pergamon Press.

Grad, B. 1963. A telekinetic effect on plant growth. *Internat. J. Parapsychol.* 5:117–33.

Grad, B., Cadoret, R., and Paul, G. I. 1961. The influence of an unorthodox method of treatment on wound healing in mice. *Internat. J. Parapsychol.*, vol. 3, no. 2, pp. 5–24.

Green, Celia, 1976. Exsomatic experiences and related phenomena. *J. Soc. Psychic. Res.* 44:111–130.

Grof, S. 1975. *Varieties of transpersonal experiences: observations from LSD psychotherapy, psychiatry, and metapsychiatry*, ed. S. Dean. Chicago: Nelson-Hall.

Grosso, M. 1975. *Plato and out-of-the-body experiences. J. Amer. Soc. Psychic. Res.* vol. 69, no. 1, pp. 61–74.

Guarino, S. 1975. *Thermodynamic radiation*. Naples, Italy: Bellavista.

Hansen, C. 1969. *Witchcraft in Salem*. New York: Braziller.

Hardy, A. 1965. *The living stream*. New York: Harper and Row.

Hart, H. 1954. ESP projection: spontaneous cases and the experimental method. *J. Amer. Soc. Psychic. Res.* 48:121–46.

Hart, H. et al. 1956. Six theories about apparitions. *Proc. Soc. Psychic. Res.* 50:153–239.

Hitler, A. 1943. *Mein Kampf*. Boston: Houghton Mifflin.

Honorton, C. 1969. Relationship between EEG alpha activity and ESP card-guessing performance. *J. Amer. Soc. Psychic. Res.*, vol. 63, no. 4, pp. 365–74.

Honorton, C., and Harper, S. 1974. Psi-mediated imagery and ideation in an experimental procedure for regulating perceptual input. *J. Amer. Soc. Psychic. Res.* 68:158–68.

Honorton, C., and Krippner, S. 1969. Hypnosis and ESP: a review of the experimental literature. *J. Amer. Soc. Psychic. Res.* 63:214–53.

Jaffé, A. 1971. *From the life and work of C. G. Jung*. New York: Harper Colophon Books.

Janet, P. 1894. Un cas de possession et l'exorcisme moderne. *Bull. de l'univ. de Lyon* 8:41–51.

Johnson, A., and Szurek, S. 1952. The genesis of antisocial acting out in children and adults. *Psychoanal. Quart.* 21.

Joins, W. 1975. Symposium: energy focusing and lingering effects in poltergeist cases and experimental studies. *Research in parapsychology.* Metuchen, N.J.: Scarecrow Press.

Jung, C. G. 1902. On the problems and pathology of so-called occult phenomena, vol. 1. *Collected works of C. G. Jung.* Bollingen Series, Princeton University Press.

———. 1936. Wotan. *Neue Schweizer Rundschau.* New series 3, March. Reprinted in *Aufsatze zur Zeitgeschichte,* Zurich: Rascher Verlag, 1946.

———. 1953–76. *Collected works.* Bollingen Series, 20. New York: Pantheon Books.

———. 1959. *The Archetypes and the collective unconscious. Collected works of C. G. Jung,* vol. 9.

———. 1963. *Memories, dreams, reflections,* ed. Aniela Jaffé, trans. R. and C. Winston. New York: Pantheon Books.

Jung, C. G., and Pauli, W. 1955. *The interpretation of nature and the psyche: synchronicity and the influence of archetypal ideas on the scientific theories of Kepler.* New York: Pantheon.

Kamiya, J. 1969. Operant control of the EEG alpha rhythm and some of its reported effects on consciousness. In *Altered states of consciousness,* ed. C. T. Tart. New York: Wiley.

Karger, F., and Zicha, G. 1967. Physical investigations of psychokinetic phenomena in Rosenheim, Germany. *Proc. Parapsychol. Assoc.* 5:33–35.

Keen, S. 1970. A conversation with John Lilly. *Psychology Today.* Reprint No. P-124, Ziff Davis Publishing Co., New York.

Keil, H. J., Herbert, B., Ullman, M., and Pratt, J. G. 1976. Directly observable PK effects. *Proc. Soc. Psychic. Res.* vol. 56, no. 210, pp. 197–235.

Kelman, H. 1958–59. Communing and relating, Parts 1–4. *Amer. J. Psychoanal.* vol. 18, nos. 1 and 2.

Khan, M. 1969. On symbiotic omnipotence. *The psychoanalytic forum,* ed. J. A. Lindon. New York: Science Books.

Klein, M. 1948. *Contributions to psychoanalysis, 1921–1945.* London: Hogarth Press.

Koestler, A. 1972. *The roots of coincidence.* New York: Random House.

Kondo, A. 1977. Folklore Psychotherapy in Japan. In *New Dimensions in Psychiatry,* S. Arieti and G. Chrzanowsi, eds., New York: Wiley.

Kreitler, H., and Kreitler, S. 1973. Subliminal perceptions and extrasensory perceptions. *J. Parapsychol.* 37:163–88.

Krippner, S. 1973. A conversation with Stanley Krippner, by Paul Chance, "Parapsychology is an idea whose time has come," *Psychology Today. Reprint* No. 1–P, Ziff-Davis Publishing Co., New York.

Krippner, S., and Davidson, R. 1974. Paranormal events occurring during chemically induced psychedelic experiences and their implications for religion. *Journal of Altered States of Consciousness* 1:175–84.

Krishna, G. 1971. *Kundalini, the evolutionary energy in man.* Berkeley, Calif.: Shambala.

Kubler-Ross, E. 1969. *On death and dying.* New York: Macmillan.

Kuhlman, K. 1962. *I believe in miracles.* Englewood Cliffs, N.J.: Prentice-Hall.

Laing, R. D. 1965. *The divided self.* Baltimore: Penguin Books.

Langer, W. C. 1972. *The mind of Adolf Hitler.* New York: Basic Books.

LeShan, L. 1973. *The medium, the mystic, and the physicist.* New York: Viking.

Lévi-Strauss, C. 1966. *The savage mind.* Chicago: University of Chicago Press.

References

Lilly, C. J. 1972. *The center of the cyclone: an autobiography of inner space.* New York: Julian Press.

Lipps, Th. 1897. *Raumaesthetik und geometrisch optische Taeuschungen.*

Lodge, O. 1916. *Raymond; or life and death.* New York: G. H. Doran.

Luria, A. R. 1973. *The working brain.* New York: Basic Books.

MacLean, P. D. 1977. On the evolution of three mentalities In *New Dimensions of Psychiatry.* S. Arieti and G. Chrzanowski, eds. New York: Wiley.

Mach, E. 1910. *Popular scientific lectures,* 4th ed., trans. I. J. MacCormack. Chicago.

Mahler, M. 1968. *On human symbiosis and the vicissitudes of individuation.* New York: International Universities Press.

Maimonides, M. 1956. *The guide for the perplexed,* trans. M. Friedlander. New York: Dover Publications.

Malinowski, B. 1932. *The argonauts of the Western Pacific.* New York: Dutton.

————. 1954. *Magic, science and religion.* New York: Doubleday Anchor Books.

Manning, M. 1974. *The link.* New York: Holt, Rinehart, and Winston.

Maslow, A. 1964. *Religion, values, and peak experiences.* Columbus: Ohio State University Press.

Masters, R. E. L., and Houston, J. 1966. *The varieties of psychedelic experience.* New York: Holt, Rinehart, and Winston.

Mischo, J. 1967. Personality structure of psychokinetic mediums. *Proc. Parapsychol. Assoc.* 5:35–37.

Moncrieff, M. M. 1951. *The clairvoyant theory of perception.* London: Faber and Faber.

Monroe, R. A. 1971. *Journeys out of the body.* New York: Doubleday.

Moody, R. A. 1975. *Life after life.* Atlanta: Mockingbird Books.

Morris, L. R. 1973. OOB experiments with animals as detectors, In *Research in Parapsychology, 1976,* J. D. Morris, W. G. Roll and R. L. Morris, eds. Metuchen, N.J.: The Scarecrow Press, 1975.

Moss, H., and Gengerelli, J. A. 1967. Telepathy and emotional stimuli: a controlled experiment. *J. Abn. Psychol.* 7:341.

Mundle, C. W. K. 1973. Strange facts in search of a theory. *Soc Psychic. Res.* 56:1–19.

Murphy, G. 1943. Psychical phenomena and human needs. *J. Amer. Soc. Psychic. Res.,* vol. 37, no. 4, pp. 163–91.

————. 1945. Field theory and survival. *J. Amer. Soc. Psychic. Res.* 39:181–209.

————. 1956. The boundaries between the person and the world. *Brit. J. Psychol.* 47:88–94.

Murray, G. 1915. Presidential address. *Proc. Soc. Psychic. Res.* 49:155–69.

Myers, F. W. H. 1903. *Human personality and its survival or bodily death.* London and New York: Longmans Green.

Neureiter, F. von. 1935. *Wissen um Fremdes Wissen auf Unbekanntem Wege erworben.* Gotha.

Nolen, W. 1974. *A doctor in search of miracles.* New York: Random House.

Oesterreich, T. K. 1921. *Possessions.* New Hyde Park, N.Y.: University Books, 1966. (First published in German, 1921.)

Ornstein, E. R. (1972. *The psychology of consciousness.* New York: Viking.

Osis, K. and Mitchell, J. L. 1977, Physiological correlates of out of the body experiences, *J. Soc. Psych. Res.* vol. 49, no. 722 pp. 525–536.

Osis, K. and Haraldsson, E. 1977. *At the hour of death.* New York: Avon.

Osis, K. 1961. *Deathbed observations by physicians and nurses.* Monograph No. 3, Paraphychological Foundation, New York.

————. 1975. Perceptual experiments on out-of-the-body experiences. *Research in*

Parapsychology, 1974, ed. J. D. Morris and W. G. Roll. Metuchen, N.J.: Scarecrow Press.

Ostrander, S., and Schroeder, L. 1970. *Psychic discoveries behind the iron curtain.* Englewood Cliffs, N.J.: Prentice-Hall.

Owen, G. 1964. *Can we explain the poltergeist?* New York: Garrett Publications.

Pahnke, W. and Richards, A. 1973. Religion and mind-expanding drugs, in J. J. Heany, ed. *Psyche and Spirit,* Paulist Press, New York p. 109–118.

Palmer, J., and Vassar, C. 1974. ESP and out-of-the-body experienecs: an exploratory study. *J. Amer. Soc. Psychic Res.* 68:257–80.

Panati, Charles, ed. 1976. *The Geller papers: scientific observations on the paranormal powers of Uri Geller.* Boston: Houghton Mifflin.

Payne, R. W. 1961. Cognitive abnormalities. In *Handbook of Abnormal Psychology,* H. J. Eysenck, ed. New York: Basic Books.

Penrose, R. 1958. *Picasso: his life and work.* New York: Harper.

Pike, J. A. 1967. *If this be heresy.* New York: Harper and Row.

Poincaré, H. 1905. *Science and hypothesis,* ch. 3 and 5. New York: Science Press.

Pratt, J. G., and Rhine, J. B. et al. 1940 and 1966. *Extrasensory Perception after Sixty Years.* Somerville, Mass.: B. Hune.

Pratt, J. G. 1964. *Parapsychology: an insider's view of ESP.* Garden City, N.Y.: Doubleday.

Pratt, J. G., and Roll, W. G. 1958. *The Seaford disturbances. J. Parapsychol.* 22:399–410.

Pribram, K. 1973. *Psychology of the frontal lobe.* London: Academic Press.

Price, H. H. 1949. Psychical research and human personality. *Hibbert Journal* 47:105–13.

Price, H. H. 1976. *Mediumship and human survival.* In *Philosophical Dimensions of Parapsychology,* J. M. O. Wheatley and H. L. Edge, eds., Springfield, Ill.: Charles C Thomas.

Prince, M. 1906. *The dissociation of personality.* New York: Longmans Green.

Progoff, I. 1964. *A report on research with the mediumship of Eileen Garrett.* New York: Helix Press.

Puharich, A. 1974. *Uri: A journal of the mystery of Uri Geller.* New York: Bantam Books.

Randall, J. L. 1971. Psi phenomena and biological theory. *J. Soc. Psychic. Res.,* vol. 46, no 749:151–65.

Rao, K. R. 1966. *Experimental parapsychology.* Springfield, Ill.: Charles C Thomas.

Rauschning, H. 1940. *Gespraeche mit Hitler.* Zurich.

Recordon, E. G., Stratton, L., and Peters, J. 1968. Some trials in a case of alleged telepathy. *J. Amer. Soc. Psychic. Res.,* vol. 44, no. 738:390–99.

Rheingold, J. C. 1967. *The mother, anxiety, and death.* Boston: Little, Brown.

Rhine, J. B. 1937. *New frontiers of the mind.* New York: Farrar and Rhinehart.

———. 1947. *The reach of the mind.* New York: William Sloane Associates.

———. 1952. The problem of psi missing. *J. Parapsychol.* 16:90–129.

———. 1971. News and comments: fruitless research on unsolvable problems. *J. Parapsychol.,* vol. 35, no. 4:5–9.

Rhine, L. 1961. *Hidden channels of the mind.* New York: William Sloane Associates.

Richet, C. 1884. La suggestion mental et la calcule des probabilités. *Rev. Philosoph. de la France et de L'Etrangère* 18:609–74.

Rogo, S. D. 1974. Psychotherapy and the poltergeist. *J. Amer. Soc. Psychic. Res.,* vol. 47, no. 761, pp. 433–46.

———. 1975. Psi and psychosis: a review of the experiential evidence. *J. Parapsychol.,* vol. 39, no. 2:120–28.

References

————. 1976. Aspects of out-of-the-body experience. *J. Soc. Psychic. Res.*, vol. 48, no. 768:329–35.

Roll, W. G. 1966. The Newark disturbances. *J. Amer. Soc. Psychic. Res.* 63:123–74.

————. 1968. Some physical and psychological aspects of a series of poltergeist phenomena. *J. Amer. Soc. Psychic. Res.* 62:263–308.

Roll, W. G., and Pratt, J. G. 1971. The Miami disturbances. *J. Amer. Soc. Psychic. Res.*, vol. 654, pp. 409–59.

————. 1972. *Poltergeist.* New York: Signet Books, New American Library.

Rose, L. 1968. *Faith healing.* London: V. Gollancz.

Rosen, J. 1962. *Direct psychoanalytic psychiatry.* New York: Grune and Stratton.

Rosenthal, R. 1966. *Experimenter effects in behavior research.* New York: Appleton Century Crofts.

————. 1973. The Pygmalion effect lives. *Psychology Today*, vol. 7, no. 4, Sept. 1973:51–59.

Roth, C. 1965. *History of the Jews.* New York: Shocken Books.

Ruderfer, M. 1976. Heuristic models for nonphysical processes. Paper read to the Institute of Parasciences Conference, London, August 28, 1976.

Russell, B. 1948. *Human knowledge.* New York: Simon and Schuster.

Ryzl, M. 1962. Training the psi-faculty by hypnosis. *J. Amer. Soc. Psychic. Res.* 41:234–52.

Ryzl, M., and Pratt, J. G. 1963. The focusing of ESP upon particular targets. *J. Parapsychol.* 27: 227–41.

Sabartés, J. 1948. *Picasso, an intimate portrait.* Englewood Cliffs, N.J.: Prentice-Hall.

Saltmarsh, H. F. 1938. *Evidence of personal survival from cross-correspondences.* New York: Arno Press.

Schilder, P. 1923. *Das Körperschema,* Berlin: Springer.

Schmeidler, G. 1969. *Extrasensory perception.* New York: Atherton Press.

————. 1973. PK effects upon continuously recorded temperature. *J. Amer. Soc. Psychic. Res.* 67:325–40.

————. 1970. High ESP scores after a Swami's brief instruction. *J. Amer. Soc. Psychic. Res.*, vol. 64, no. 1:100–103.

Schmeidler, G. R., and McConnell, R. A. 1958. *ESP and personality patterns.* New Haven, Conn.: Yale University Press.

Schmidt, H. 1969. Precognition of a quantum process. *J. Parapsychol.* 33, June, pp. 99–108.

————. 1974. Instrumentation in the parapsychological laboratory. *New Directions in Parapsychology,* ed. J. Beloff. London: Paul Elek.

Schopenhauer, A. 1851. *Parerga und Paralipomena,* vol. 1: *Versuch über das Geistersehen und was damit zusammenhangt.* Berlin: A. W. Hayn.

Schwarz, B. E. 1968. *The Jack Romano story.* New York: University Books.

————. 1971. Parent-child telepathy. New York: Garrett Publications.

Schwarz, C. E. 1975. Positive and negative aspects of meditation. In *Psychiatry and healing,* ed. S. Dean. Chicago: Nelson-Hall.

Servadio, E. 1935. Psychoanalysis and telepathy. In Devereux (1953).

————. 1976. On the psychology of mediumistic states. *Parapsychology Review*, vol. 7, no. 1:26–28.

Servadio, E., and Cavanna, R. 1964. *ESP experiments with LSD 25 and Psilocybin, a methodical approach.* Parapsychological Monographs, Parapsychology Foundation, no. 5, New York.

Shapiro, A. K. 1958. The placebo response. *Practice of medicine,* ed. F. Tice, vol. 10, no. 32:49–57. New York: Harper and Row.

Sherman, H. 1967. *"Wunder" healers of the Philippines*. London: Psychic Press.

Shirer, W. L. 1960. *The rise and fall of the Third Reich*. New York: Simon and Schuster.

Silverman, J. 1975. On the sensory bases of transcendental states of consciousness. *Psychiatry and mysticism*, ed. S. Dean. Chicago: Nelson-Hall.

Sinclair, U. 1930, 1962. *Mental radio*. Springfield, Ill.: Charles C Thomas.

Smith, J. 1968. Paranormal effects on enzyme activity. *Proc. Parapsychol. Assoc.* 5:15–16.

Smith, M. 1973. *The secret gospel*. New York: Harper and Row.

Smythies, J. R. 1965. The representative theory of perception. In *Brain and mind: modern concepts of the nature of mind*, ed. J. R. Smythies. London: Routledge and Kegan Paul; New York: Humanities Press.

Smythies, J. R., ed. 1967. *Science and ESP*. London: Routledge and Kegan Paul.

Spinelli, E. 1976. Paper read to the annual Convention of the Parapsychological Assoc.

Soal, S. G., and Bateman, F. 1954. *Modern experiments in telepathy*. New Haven, Conn.: Yale University Press.

Soal, S. G., and Goldney, K. M. 1943. Experiments in precognitive telepathy. *Proc. Soc. Psychic. Res.* 47:21–150.

Speer, A. 1970. *Inside the Third Reich*. New York: Macmillan.

Sperling, M. 1954. The neurotic child and his mother: a psychoanalytic study. *Amer. J. Orthopsychiatry* 21:351–64.

Sperry, R. W. 1964. The great cerebral comissure. *Scientific American*, January 1964, pp. 42–52.

Stanford, R. 1957. Scientific, ethical, and clinical problems in the training of psi ability. AAAS Annual Meeting, January 26–31, New York.

———. 1977. The question is: good experimentation or not? *J. Amer. Soc. Psychic. Res.*, vol. 71, no. 2:191–200.

Stanford, R., and Stanford, B. E. 1969. Shifts in EEG alpha rhythm as related to calling patterns and ESP run score variance. *J. Parapsychol.*, vol. 33, March, pp. 39–47.

Stanford, R. 1974. An experimentally testable model for spontaneous psi events: I. Extrasensory events. *Journ. Amer. Soc. Psychical Research*, 58:34–57, and ibid. 1974, 68:321–356

Starkey, M. 1969. *The devil in Massachusetts*. New York: Anchor Books, Doubleday.

Stevenson, I. 1966. Twenty cases suggestive of reincarnation. *Proceedings*, Amer. Soc. Psychic. Res., New York.

———. 1970. *Telepathic impressions*. Charlottesville: University of Virginia Press.

———. 1974. *Xenoglossia*. Charlottesville: University of Virginia Press.

Strasser, O. 1940. *Hitler and I*. London: Jonathan Cape.

Strauch, I. 1963. Medical aspects of "mental" healing. *Internat. J. Parapsychol.*, vol. 5, no. 2, pp. 135–65.

———. 1977. The case for telepathy as revealed in sleep research. Paper read to the 26th Internat. Conference of the Parapsychology Foundation, Paris.

Swann, I. 1975. *To kiss earth good-bye*. New York: Hawthorne Books.

Targ, R., and Puthoff, H. 1974. Information transmission under conditions of sensory shielding. *Nature*, vol. 25, no. 1, pp. 602–607.

———. 1976. *Mind-reach*. New York: Delacorte Press.

Tart, C. T. 1966. ESPATESTER: an automatic testing device for parapsychological research. *J. Amer. Soc. Psychic. Res.* 60:256–69.

———. 1968. A psychological study of out-of-the-body experiences in a selected subject. *J. Amer. Soc. Psychic. Res.* 62:3–27.

References

Tart, C. T., ed. 1969. *Altered states of consciousness*. New York: Wiley.

Tart, C. T. 1971. *On being stoned: a psychological study of marijuana intoxication*. Palo Alto, Calif.: Science Behavior Books.

————. 1975*a*. *States of consciousness*. New York: E. P. Dutton.

————. 1975 *b*. *Transpersonal psychologies*. New York: Harper and Row.

————. 1976. *Learning to use extrasensory perception*. Chicago: University of Chicago Press.

————. 1977. Drug-induced states of consciousness. *Handbook of parapsychology*, ed. B. Wolman. New York: Van Nostrand.

Taylor, J. 1975. *Superminds*. New York: Viking.

Tenhaeff, W. H. C. 1962. *Hellsehen und Telepathie*. Gütersloh: Bextelsmann.

Thouless, R. H., and Wiesner, B. P. 1946. On the nature of psi phenomena. *J. Parapsychol.* 10:107–19.

Tizané, E. 1951. *Sur la piste de l'homme inconnu, les phénomène de hontise et de possession*. Paris.

Trevor-Roper, H. R. 1968. *The last days of Hitler*. New York: Collier Books.

Tyrrell, G. N. M. 1963. *The personality of man*. Baltimore: Penguin Books.

Ullman, M. 1949. On the nature of psi processes. *J. Parapsychol.* 13:59–62.

————. 1969. Dreaming as metaphorical motion. *Arch. Gen. Psychiat.* 216:696–703.

————. 1975. Parapsychology and psychiatry. In A. M. Freedman, H. E. Kaplan, and B. J. Sadock, eds., *Comprehensive textbook of psychiatry*. Baltimore: Williams and Wilkins.

Ullman, M., Krippner, S., and Vaughan, A. 1973. *Dream telepathy*. New York: Macmillan.

Upham, C. W. 1867. *Salem witchcraft*. Boston: Wiggins and Lunt.

Van Busschbach, J. G. 1953. An investigation of extrasensory perception in school children. *J. Parapsychol.* 17:210–14.

Van de Castle, R. L. 1964. Facilitation of ESP through hypnosis. *Amer. J. Clin. Hypnosis,* vol. 12, no. 1:37–56.

Vasiliev, L. L. 1963. *Experiments in mental suggestion*. Church Crookham, Hampshire, England: ISMI Publications.

Walter, W. G. 1970. The contingent negative variation and its significance for psi research. *Psi favorable states of consciousness,* ed. R. Cavanna, pp. 212–26. New York: Parapsychology Foundation.

Warcollier, R. 1921. *La Télépathie*. Paris: Librairie, Felix Alcan.

————. 1939. *Experiments in telepathy*. London: Allen and Unwin.

Weber, M. 1964. *The sociology of religion*. Boston: Beacon Press.

Weil, A. 1974. Andrew Weil's search for the true Geller. Reprint No. P–183, *Psychology Today*, Ziff-Davis Publishing Co., New York.

Weininger, O. 1903. *Geschlecht und Charakter*. Vienna: Braumuller.

West, D. J. 1957. *Eleven Lourdes miracles*. London: G. Duckworth.

Whitehorn, J. C. 1958. Psychiatric implications of the placebo effect. *Amer. J. Psychiatry* 114:662–64.

Whiteman, J. H. M. 1977. Parapsychology and physics. In *Handbook of parapsychology*. ed. B. Wolman. New York: Van Nostrand Reinhold.

Whitton, J. 1974. Ramp functions in EEG power spectra during actual or attempted paranormal events. *New Horizon,* vol. 1, no. 4:174-83.

Wieman, H. N. 1945. *An encyclopedia of religion,* ed. V. Ferm. New York: Philosophical Library.

Worrall, A., and Worrall, O. 1965. *The gift of healing,* New York: Harper and Row.

Yap, P. M. 1951. Mental disease peculiar to certain cultures: a survey of comparative psychiatry. *J. Ment. Sci.* 97:313.

INDEX

Index

Bruner, Jerome S., 63, 201
Brunswick, E., 200–1
Buber, Martin, 97
Bucke, R. M., 207
Bullock, Allen, 165–67, 172–74
Burlingham, Dorothy, 17
Burr, G. L., 144
Burroughs, George, 122, 143, 147–48
Burt, Sir Cyril, 217
Busschbach, J. G. van, 6
Bychowski, Gustav, 116, 123, 169

Croesus, King of Lydia, 95
Carington, Whately, 5, 36, 226
Carol, M. P., 260
Carter, M. E., 255
Cassandra, 93, 98, 214
Castaneda, Carlos, 246
Catherine J., case of, 108–9
Catholic Jerusalem Bible, 99, 100
Catholic Church, 100, 255
Cause and effect, law of, 194
Cavanna, Roberto, 75
Cayce, Edgar, 251, 255, 265
Celia, case of, 154
Cerebral localization, 194, 212
Charcot, Jean-Martin, 30, 35, 59, 203
Charlotte G., case of, 89–90
Chinese folklore, 119
Chinese Red Guards, 150
Chomsky, Noam, 283
Christ: prophecies of coming of, 91, 99–101; resurrection of, 152
Christian Science, 255, 265
Christian tradition, prophecy in, 99–100
Ciano, Count Galeazzo, 167
Cicero, 95
Closed model of personality, 205–14
Clustering, 72, 75
Cole, W. H., 256
Collective unconscious, 207
Communing, 208
Complementarity, principle of, 61
Compliance, *see* Doctrinal compliance
Conditioning factors, 66–73; doctrinal compliance as, 60
"Confluent" coincidences, 196, 213
Consensory perception, 213
Consensus rationality, 246
Contagion, telepathic, 72
Conversion hysteria, 203

Corey, Giles, 143
Corpus callosum, 224
Cory, Martin, 145–46, 149
Countertransference, 54
Croiset, Gerard, 32, 68, 69, 89, 245, 278, 282
Crookall, R., 151
Cross-correspondences, 231–32
Cultist healing practices, 257–59

D., Mrs., case of, 52–54, 66
Da Vinci, Leonardo, 188, 205
Dale, L. A., 11
Danny J., case of, 46
Davidson, R., 76, 82
De Gaulle, Charles, 169, 176
Dean, Douglas, 11
Dean, Stanley R., *ix*
Death: denial of, 151–61; survival after, 231–36
Death March, Hitler's, 173
Delacroix, Eugene, 274
Delgado, José, 217
Delphic oracles, 93, 95
Democritus, 95
Demonical possession, 118–29
Demos, John, 143
Depersonalization, 153–55
Descartes, René, 213
Devereux, G., 51, 89
Dick C., case of, 45–46
Digby, Sir Kenelm, 264–65, 267
Dingwall, E. J., 10
Dionysus, 93
Discrete states of consciousness, 245–46
Divination, 92–94
Dixon, Norman, 216
Doctrinal compliance: in ancient Greek prophecy, 94; drugs and, 74; in experiments, 68; healing and, 252; mediums and, 31; parent-child symbiosis and, 16; in placebo research, 269; in psychoanalytic situation, 56, 59–62; principle of uncertainty and, 194; survival after death and, 233
Dodds, E. R., 92, 93
Dodona, oracles of, 93
Doenitz, Admiral, 166
Domarus, Max, 174
Double-bind technique, 266
Drake, R. M., 18

Index

Index

Mediums, 30–37
Meerloo, Joost, 59, 245
Mesmer, Franz Anton, 10, 29–30, 35, 47, 59, 265, 267, 278
Metapsychiatry, *ix*
Miami disturbances, 134, 138
Minnesota Multiphasic Personality Inventory, 133
Minus-functions of ego, 107
Miracles, healing, 255–56
Mischo, John, 135
Mitchell, Edgar, 179
Mitchell, J. L., 152
Moirai, 93
Moncrieff, M. M., 217
Monroe, Robert, 159–60
Moody, Raymond, 233, 234
Mopsus, 92
Morgenstern, Christian, 4, 53
Morris, R. L., 152
Moses, 97, 101
Moss, Thelma, 8, 13
Mothers: neurotic, 39–48; *see also* Parent-child symbiosis
Mozart, Wolfgang Amadeus, 273
Muhammad, 163
Mundel, C. W. K., 197
Murphy, Gardner, 11, 55, 66, 195, 208
Murray, Gilbert, 5
Muslim tradition, 152
Myers, F. W. H., 5, 31, 33, 34, 195, 208, 231–32
Myths, 91–102; antimyths and, 100–2; "effective," 98–100

Narcissus, 92
Naumov, E. K., 9
Nazis, 150, 164, 168, 171, 173
Need-determined phenomena, 13, 66–71; cross-correspondences and, 232; drugs and, 83; neural basis of, 217; theory and, 197
Neoteny, 24
Neural basis of psi phenomena, 215–25
Neureiter, Ferdinand von, 18
Neurotic acting out: parent-child symbiosis and, 88, 279–80; *see also* Poltergeists
Neurotic mothers, 39–48
Neutrinos, 196
New Jersey Board of Child Welfare, 134
New Testament, 91

Newark disturbances, 132–34, 138
Newtonian thought, 4, 193, 205–6, 237
Nissenbaum, S., 142
Nolen, William, 258
North American shamans, 152
Nurse, Rebecca, 146, 149

Odic force, 265, 278
Odyssey, 92
Oedipus, 92, 93
Oesterreich, T. K., 119
Office of Strategic Service, U.S., 169
Old Testament, 91, 96, 100, 263
Oliver M., case of, 46
Omnipotence, infantile feelings of, 21–22
Open model of personality, 205–14
Optical agnosia, 221, 223
Organic repression, 115
Orgone energy, 265, 267, 278
Ornstein, R. E., 223
Osis, K., 152, 233
Ostrander, S., 8
Out-of-body experiences: denial of death and, 151–61; drugs and, 76; organic lesions and, 190; survival after death and, 233–34
Owen, A. R. G., 137
Owen, George, 136, 186, 187

Pahnke, W., 82
Palladino, Eusapia, 36, 175
Palmer, J., 151, 155
Panati, Charles, 179
Papez, J. W., 216
Paracelsus, 37, 263, 267
Parapsychiatry, *ix*, 189
Parent-child symbiosis, 14–26, 279; of adults and aged parents, 19–21; of handicapped, 18–19; neurotic acting out and, 17, 88; reproduced in psychoanalytic situation, 51–57; revolt of poltergeist children against, 130–41; schizophrenia and, 113; telepathy in, 22–25, 229
Parks, Susie, 133
Parris, Betty, 144
Parris, Samuel, 144, 147
Paul, G. I., 133, 261
Pauli, W., 196, 213
Paulus, Friedrich, 170

Index